MINISTRY OF DEFENCE

REPORT OF THE INQUIRY INTO

HULL FORMS FOR WARSHIPS

Prepared by: Lloyd's Register of Shipping
71, Fenchurch Street
London EC3M 4BS

London: Her Majesty's Stationery Office

© *Crown copyright 1988*

First published 1988

ISBN 0 11 772600 1

FROM THE CHAIRMAN
H. R. MacLeod

Telephone: 01-709 9166
Telex: 888379
Fax: 01-488 4796 (Gp III)

Dear Secretary of State,

The Terms of Reference

1.   On 13th November 1986 you commissioned Lloyd's Register of Shipping:

> 'to consider the advantages and disadvantages of the S90 hull form for the purposes of meeting the Naval Staff Requirement (NSR 7069) for an anti-submarine frigate (insofar as the current state of the development of the S90 permits), taking account of independent assessments made in 1983 by YARD and by the Marine Technology Board of the Defence Scientific Advisory Council, and of the Hill-Norton Committee Report *Hull Forms for Warships* published in May 1986, and to identify any implications for the design of future destroyers and frigates for the RN.'

The Action Taken

2.   We have completed an assessment of the S90 hull form against the NSR 7069 and the attached report discusses the main issues and states our conclusions.   The terms of reference also required us to identify any implications for the future and these are referred to from paragraph 27 onwards.

3.   Our report lists all the written submissions that we have received, the authorities we have consulted, the evidence that we have heard and the studies that we have undertaken or commissioned.

4.   As well as sending direct invitations for evidence to be given to the Inquiry, we advertised our willingness to receive evidence so that anyone who believed that they could contribute to the Inquiry would come forward. We are not aware of any authoritative source of information that has not been consulted or of anyone who wishes to give evidence who has not been given the opportunity to do so.

5.   All formal oral evidence has been recorded and transcripts are available, subject to the agreement of those who gave evidence. We have been mindful throughout of the need to protect national security and commercial confidentiality. All those who gave evidence were told that a full report would be made to the Secretary of State for Defence and it would be for him to decide what parts of that report should be published. A confidential annex, which accompanies our report, contains the information which has been given to the Inquiry on a confidential basis or which is classified material. All who gave evidence were told that they could stipulate what material given to the Inquiry they wished to be kept in confidence for commercial or other valid reasons.

The S90 Hull Form

6.   The S90 hull form, designed by Thornycroft, Giles & Associates Ltd (TGA), has been developed in accordance with TGA's own Sirius design concept/philosophy. This concept is based on the proposition that hull forms which are successfully used for small working craft can, with advantage, be scaled up in size and used for much larger vessels. For frigates and destroyers, a feature of a hull form based on the Sirius concept is its low length to breadth ratio (L/B) which is around 5 to 6 compared with values of 8 and above usually associated with such vessels. These different L/B ratios have resulted in the terms 'short/fat' and 'long/thin' being coined.

The Nature of the Inquiry's Task

7.   The determination of the optimum specification of a warship to perform a given role is far from being a simple matter. Even if it were possible to confine the task to reconciling a large number of operational requirements, many of which are in direct conflict, with a technical assessment of the most efficient and economical hull form, it would still be a complex study.

The task is made more complicated when there is disagreement between technical men themselves on some important principles of warship design and when there has been a long dispute during which opposing views have been sincerely held and passionately expressed.

Finally, when elements in some designs must be kept confidential because of the requirements of national security, and others must be kept confidential in order to protect the legitimate commercial interests of parties involved in the controversy, it can be difficult to make an open and constructive comparison between different designs or to obtain evidence without reservations.

8. In these circumstances it is not surprising that the dispute about the comparative merits of the long/thin and short/fat hull forms for frigates and destroyers has a long history. Our main task has been to compare the technical, operational and economic merits of the S90 hull form in relation to the NSR 7069 and in comparison with the Type 23 frigate, designed by the MoD to meet this NSR - in the light of all relevant information available to us at the present time, making whatever further studies we think necessary. We have not sought to carry out a post-mortem into the rights and wrongs of past arguments - except when it is necessary to understand the history of a particular issue before a proper judgement can be made in the light of present day knowledge and circumstances.

The Report of the Hill-Norton Committee

9. The Committee

(a) said that they believed that for ships up to destroyer size the short/fat hull form offered enough advantages, compared with the more conventional long/thin design, to merit much more serious consideration than it had received up to the time of the Committee's deliberations,

(b) found that the short/fat hull form may offer a significant increase in top speed over the maximum which can be realised in a long/thin hull of similar size,

(c) pointed to the advantages in terms of an increase in military capability or a reduction in the procurement budget that would ensue if a 25% saving in unit costs could be achieved, as had been suggested to them.

10. The length/breadth ratio of any warship is not normally a predetermined parameter but one that emerges during the design development as part of the process of identifying the most satisfactory and cost-effective solution to the operational requirement. As such, and depending on that operational requirement, it can vary over a wide range of values. The terms long/thin and short/fat are not therefore as precise as might be thought from the public positions taken in support of one or the other in the course of the dispute. Furthermore, it has not been the case that throughout the dispute there have been two worked out designs, with characteristics that were fully understood by all concerned, which enabled a true comparison to be made. Comparisons have been made throughout the dispute between the Sirius design concept/S90 proposal put forward by TGA to the MoD in 1983, the Leander class and the Type 23 frigate which is now being built. However, unless designs are compared which are intended to meet the same

operational requirement and have been developed sufficiently, then comparisons can be very misleading.

The Hill-Norton Committee was fully aware of this difficulty. As the Committee itself made clear, it had no access to classified information and no qualified staff or support, and this limited the extent of the evaluation that it was able to make.

11. The Hill-Norton Committee also fully appreciated the fundamental point that the design of a warship, like any other ship, requires a compromise to be made between a number of operational, technical and economic factors. If this compromise is not worked out in detail there is a real risk that advantages will be claimed for a design without the extent of the corresponding disadvantages being properly assessed. We believe that this is the principal reason that this dispute has gone on so long, especially when it was hoped that such a valuable prize might be won in terms of defence economies or an improvement in the operational capability of the Royal Navy. It should also be noted that design work is expensive and in the case of a warship it requires access to a great deal of classified information.

The Development of a Geosim

12. Having received the main part of the evidence, we concluded that we could best make the assessment required by our terms of reference by developing the S90 hull form into a design that was worked out in sufficient detail to be measured against the NSR 7069 and validly compared with the Type 23 design. This development required exhaustive discussion at both formal and informal meetings with TGA. Our initial findings indicated that the S90 design proposal that had been submitted by TGA to the MoD in 1983 was too small to meet the spatial requirements associated with the NSR 7069. Therefore, a 'geosim' (described in Chapter 5 of our report) was developed which was a scaled up version of the S90 underwater hull form, as shown in the plans given by TGA, and was of the minimum size sufficient to meet the NSR spatial requirements, while still seeking to preserve the features that TGA considered to be inherent in their S90 design proposal. This design is referred to hereafter as the S102, indicating its increase in length compared with the original S90 design proposal.

13. We were anxious that full justice should be done to the Sirius concept and so, besides developing the S102 design ourselves, we agreed that TGA should undertake a design study so that they could take an informed view of the Inquiry's design development and could also ensure that the Inquiry's design incorporated the features that TGA considered to be inherent in their concept. To make this study, TGA were given the version of the NSR 7069 which the Inquiry used to develop the S102. After this work (funded as part of the cost of the Inquiry) had been completed, and after

full discussion of the results, TGA told us that they were satisfied that the S102 provided a reasonable basis (as far as size and general layout were concerned) on which to assess a design using the S90 hull form in relation to the requirements of the NSR 7069, and in comparison with the Type 23 design - although they reserved full approval of the S102 until they could see the results of the calculations of speed, power and stability made for the S102.

The Inquiry's Tentative Conclusions on Geosim Study

14.   Using the S102 design we then made the necessary powering and speed calculations and detailed studies of the military features, seakeeping, manoeuvrability, stability, habitability and construction and through life costs associated with this design.

These studies led us to the tentative conclusion that the Type 23 was both a cheaper and a more effective design in terms of the NSR 7069 than the S102 and therefore that the Sirius concept, as expressed in the S102, did not offer the substantial advantages for frigates/destroyers that had been hoped for in comparison with what has been described as the conventional hull form.   In particular it did not offer the possibility of a substantial increase in overall military capability without an increase in total cost which provided the main thrust to the Report of the Hill-Norton Committee.   In the Inquiry's opinion the contrary was true.

TGA's Comments on Tentative Conclusions

15.   When we had reached initial broad and tentative findings following our assessment of the S102 in relation to the NSR 7069 and in comparison with the Type 23, we discussed these findings with TGA and invited them to comment on them if they wished.   We did so for two reasons.   Firstly, it was possible that we had failed to appreciate some fundamental point or that we had overlooked some important source of information, bearing in mind that TGA have considerable experience in designing this type of vessel. Secondly, we thought it fair to explain to TGA, in the light of their special interest, how we had approached each of the principal points and, in very broad terms, how we had arrived at our tentative findings.   We wished to consider TGA's comments on the main points before we reached firm conclusions and completed our report to you.

16.   (a)   Although TGA accepted the powering and speed calculations based on the S102 dimensions, they believed that by varying the hull form it would be possible to eliminate the S102's speed disadvantage in relation to the NSR 7069, or at least reduce it to acceptable proportions.

(b)   TGA said that they did not believe that the Inquiry had given sufficient credit to what they saw as the much superior seakeeping, manoeuvrability, stability and habitability of a ship of the Sirius family when compared with the Type 23.

(c)   In the light of the costing information supplied to the Hill-Norton Committee by Frederikshavn Vaerft and TGA's own contact with the source of that information, TGA questioned the Inquiry's findings that the hull construction cost of the S102 would be more than the Type 23 if both were built in the same yard.

The Development and Examination of a Further Design Proposal

17.   Paragraph 13 refers to a study that TGA undertook in order to judge the validity of the comparison between the S102, against the NSR 7069, and the Type 23. This study is referred to hereafter as the S110 study. The Inquiry agreed that TGA, funded by the Inquiry, should ascertain whether the requirements of the NSR 7069 could be met by developing a longer version of the S110, the S115. This extended version was said by TGA to be the limit of the Sirius design concept for the purposes of meeting the NSR. The length of the S115 is half way between that of the S90 design proposal and the Type 23 and the length/breadth ratio of the S115 is larger than that of the S90.

18.   The Inquiry has considered carefully every point that TGA made in relation to their S115 proposal and our report describes the areas in which we consider the S115 to be superior to the S102 in relation to the NSR 7069 and in comparison with the Type 23.

The Inquiry calculated that with the same engines proposed for the S102 (which are approximately 35% more powerful than those fitted to the Type 23), the S115 would offer improved speed over the S102 (and over the S110) but would still fall short of the NSR requirement unless a performance prediction factor less than that which the Inquiry would consider realistic, was adopted. Although the noise level of the S115 would be less than the S102, it would still be greater than the Type 23 and, as a result, the S115 would still be unlikely to meet the NSR 7069 requirement at the maximum quiet towed array speed. In all other respects the S115, as it stands, is considered to meet the NSR requirements.

The characteristics of seakeeping, manoeuvrability, stability and habitability will change with the increase in the length/breadth ratio and will move towards the characteristics of the Type 23 as the overall dimensions approach those of the Type 23.

The Cost of Construction

19.   At the suggestion of TGA, the Inquiry checked the basis of the construction cost figures in the Report of the Hill-Norton Committee with the source of this information. After this discussion, the Inquiry saw no reason to change its assessment that the construction cost of the S102 would exceed that of the Type 23. The Inquiry has calculated that the S115 construction cost would be less than that of the S102 but still more than that of the Type 23. The Inquiry calculates that the through life cost would be less for the S115 than the S102 due to the reduced power requirement. However, the through life cost of the S115 would still be more than that of the Type 23 and, as a result, although the overall cost differential with the Type 23 would be reduced for the S115 when compared with the S102, the S115 would still cost more than the Type 23.

There are two important points to be made in connection with the cost comparisons given in the Report of the Hill-Norton Committee. Firstly, a cost comparison is only meaningful when vessels designed to meet the same operational requirement are being compared.

Secondly, it is necessary to have carefully constructed and consistent definitions when comparing cost breakdowns from different sources. The comparison made in the Report of the Hill-Norton Committee, where a breakdown based on a typical percentage breakdown for any conventional frigate is compared with that of a detailed shipyard estimate for a specific ship, illustrates the danger of not comparing like with like. We have accepted, of course, that no better figures were available to the Committee.

Comparisons between building prices between different countries, or even different yards in the same country, can be very misleading because of differences in costs, working practices, pricing policies, government subsidies and so on. The Inquiry concluded that the only way of making a reliable comparison between two developed designs was to judge the differences in cost which would stem from the hull form if both designs were built under similar conditions in the same yard. The Inquiry went carefully into this matter with a number of the British shipyards which have the capability of building warships. The Inquiry took great care to establish an independent and valid basis for this comparison, and we are satisfied that our conclusions are sound.

The Inquiry's Conclusions on Basic Design Factors

20.   The Inquiry's studies lead to the firm conclusion that the basic factors affecting the speed, power, seakeeping, manoeuvrability, stability and habitability of a ship of this type are as already known, and that there is nothing in the Sirius concept which requires them to be substantially

reconsidered - or which offers the possibility of the breakthrough in terms of cost and performance that the Hill-Norton Committee hoped might be achievable. After careful consideration, we have concluded that the development of the S115 does not materially change the findings that the Inquiry drew from the S102 design. Our report sets out our reasons in support of these conclusions, and when drafting our report we have considered carefully each of the points made by the Hill-Norton Committee.

The Case For and Against Further Development

21. TGA suggested that the Inquiry should make an evaluation of the S115 in the same detail as our evaluation of the S102, on the grounds that the S115 would show an improved performance, in particular in respect to achievable speeds, and therefore it should be the S115 rather than the S102 that should be assessed in relation to the NSR 7069 and compared with the Type 23.

The Inquiry carefully considered this suggestion and, as we have said above, we judged that whilst the S115 went further towards meeting the requirements of the NSR 7069 than did the S102, and therefore it provided a better solution than the S102, it would still require more power than the Type 23 to achieve a given speed and it would still cost more both to build and to operate. In addition, all the other performance parameters (e.g. seakeeping and manoeuvrability) had done no more than tend towards the behaviour of the Type 23. Hence both the advantages and disadvantages of the S102 in comparison with the Type 23 were reduced but not to such an extent as to invalidate our previous assessment. The Inquiry therefore considered that a firm and valid comparison could be made between the S102/S115 on the one hand, and the Type 23 on the other, without further development of the S115.

It is not feasible or necessary to make a full study of every possible design iteration. We believe that an evaluation of the S90 design proposal, the S102 design, the S110 and the S115 studies gives us a sound basis on which to make our judgement that no further studies are necessary before we report in accordance with our terms of reference.

The Overall Dimensions

22. The attached sheet of diagrams shows, in general illustrative terms, how the deck and profile of the Type 23 compare with the S90, the S102, the S110 and the S115. It will be clearly seen that the S90 is markedly shorter than the Type 23, but the difference in beam is less pronounced than the public usage of the terms long/thin and short/fat might suggest. In addition, the S90 design proposal is compared with the Leander class frigate, the Hill-Norton Committee having based their comparative study on these two

vessels. It should, however, be understood that the underwater hull forms of the Sirius derivatives and the Leander and Type 23 illustrated in this figure are still markedly different.

Some Comments on the Iterative Process

23. In paragraph 7 we refer to the complexity of the process of warship design - a process that has been fully described by Sir Lindsay Bryson in his paper on warship procurement that he delivered to the Royal Institution of Naval Architects in 1984. In paragraph 10 we express our belief that the dispute about the optimum frigate design for a given requirement would have been much shorter if fully worked out comparisons between the different proposals had been made.

24. It is manifestly very difficult for an independent designer to challenge the effectiveness of the iterative process leading up to the definition of the NSR for a warship - by suggesting that a more cost effective balance of characteristics could be made - when he has not been involved in the iterative process and cannot know all the relevant factors. Furthermore, the development of a warship design to a point when a true comparison can be made between alternative designs to meet a given NSR requires considerable financial resources which an independent designer may not possess or may not wish to hazard.

25. If an independent designer was able to demonstrate, however, the possibility of a significant improvement in performance by a re-evaluation of the technical principles on which past warship designs had been based, his challenge to the accepted principles of warship design and established system of warship procurement would be much more effective.

26. When assessing the Sirius concept we have made a distinction between the suggestion that established principles may need to be reconsidered in the case of a hull form of this kind and the suggestion that there may be a better balance of recognised principles to achieve the NSR 7069 - or indeed to justify a variation in the NSR. Although the Sirius concept includes both suggestions, and both will affect the final result, we believe it is important to consider them separately. If it could be shown that established principles of ship design needed to be reconsidered, that would have a considerable general implication for the design of future naval vessels. However, the judgement of the optimum balance of known factors can be made only against a specific requirement at a specific time and generalisation may be very misleading.

The Suggested Technical Advantages of the Sirius Concept

27. As the Inquiry's terms of reference required Lloyd's Register, after considering the advantages and disadvantages of the S90 hull form in relation to the NSR 7069, to identify any implications for the design of future destroyers and frigates for the Royal Navy, the Inquiry paid a great deal of attention to the possible technical advantages of the Sirius concept that were mentioned in the Report of the Hill-Norton Committee.

    In particular, we discussed each point extensively with all the authorities that we considered would be able to help us, including TGA. Chapter 8 of our report sets out our conclusions. Based on this assessment, along with the detailed comparison of the S90 hull form against the NSR 7069, the Inquiry has concluded that there are no identifiable implications for the design of future destroyers and frigates for the Royal Navy arising from the Sirius design concept, as far as the Inquiry is able to foresee the likely role and operating requirements for future warships of this type.

The Suggested Design Advantages of the Sirius Concept

28. The Inquiry considered the possibility that the Sirius concept embodied a better balance of recognised principles of warship design (as distinct from a reconsideration of the established principles themselves) to achieve the NSR 7069 than does the Type 23. In our judgement this is not the case.

29. Whether or not the balance of recognised principles embodied in the Sirius hull form would have special advantages in designs for warships other than destroyers and frigates is beyond our terms of reference. In some other application the Sirius hull form could provide the most cost-effective solution but no generalisation can usefully be made on this point - in each case a design has to be fully worked out against a defined requirement so that the balance of all the factors can be properly judged. Ships of similar proportions are undoubtedly successful in many commercial and naval applications.

The Questions of Seakeeping and Habitability

30. The Hill-Norton Committee placed particular emphasis on the desirability of better seakeeping and, as a result, improved habitability. The Inquiry endorses the Hill-Norton Committee's view that seakeeping is a very controversial issue. It is an area with a high level of uncertainty attached to it and is one that relies heavily on subjective judgements in offsetting superior performance in one respect against inferior behaviour in another. However, although the Inquiry has identified a number of areas where the seakeeping performance of the S102/S115 is better than the Type 23, for

instance reduced bottom slamming and deck wetness in head seas, in overall terms the Inquiry considers that the seakeeping performance of the Type 23 is superior to that of the S102/S115.

The Inquiry considers that the overall seakeeping performance of the S115 would be better than that of the S102. However, such overall performance would still be worse, we believe, than the Type 23.

31.   The one area where a clear advantage has been identified for the S102/S115 in comparison with the Type 23, is in regard to manoeuvrability. The S102/S115 is considered to have a superior manoeuvring performance. However, although this is considered to be an advantage, manoeuvrability is not regarded as a principal requirement of the NSR 7069 and therefore cannot be 'traded-off' to any great effect against the increased cost and reduced operational performance in other respects, that the S102/S115 has compared with the Type 23.

The Inquiry considers that whilst the S115 would still maintain an advantage in manoeuvrability over the Type 23, the performance would be worse than that of the S102.

The Firm Conclusion of the Inquiry

32.   We have made a very thorough assessment of the advantages and disadvantages of the S90 hull form and the associated Sirius design concept for the purposes of meeting the NSR 7069 for an anti-submarine warfare frigate. Arising from this assessment, the Inquiry can find no reason to disagree with the MoD's preference for the Type 23.

In reaching this overall conclusion, and wishing to avoid any possibility of an unfair penalty accruing to the Sirius hull form due to the unfinished state of the designs considered, we have consistently, throughout our investigations, assigned every reasonable benefit of doubt to the Sirius concept. We have assumed, for example, the optimum trim conditions when calculating the speeds, although this has not been achieved in practice, and if it were to be achieved may still involve some other operational penalty. To counter the large rolling motions, it has been assumed that suitable roll damping devices are fitted, although no account has been taken of the implications of such devices on the speed and noise characteristics of the design. There are other similar instances. Our adverse conclusion with respect to the Sirius design concept as embodied in the S102 and S115 must therefore be considered as the most optimistic view with respect to the suitability of such a design for the current ASW frigate requirement.

The Possible Construction of a Prototype

33.   Although it has been suggested that a prototype based on a Sirius hull form should be built to resolve this dispute, it is the Inquiry's firm opinion that such an exercise is unnecessary as the performance of a Sirius hull form can be adequately evaluated by normal naval architecture assessment procedures.

The Procurement Process

34.   Although we have referred to the significance of the iterative procurement process, we have not seen it as part of our terms of reference to examine this process in detail, or to consider if or how it could be amended, perhaps to enable the possible contribution of an independent designer to be more easily assessed. Such a study would go well beyond technical matters, and it would have to consider how the preservation of commercial rights in a private design could be reconciled with a lengthy iterative process which is affected by a very wide range of factors. Nevertheless, if you would like us to carry out any further work in this direction, we shall be happy to discuss this possibility with you.

Yours sincerely,

Roderick MacLeod

H.R. MacLeod
Chairman

31st March 1988

Pre-Inquiry Situation

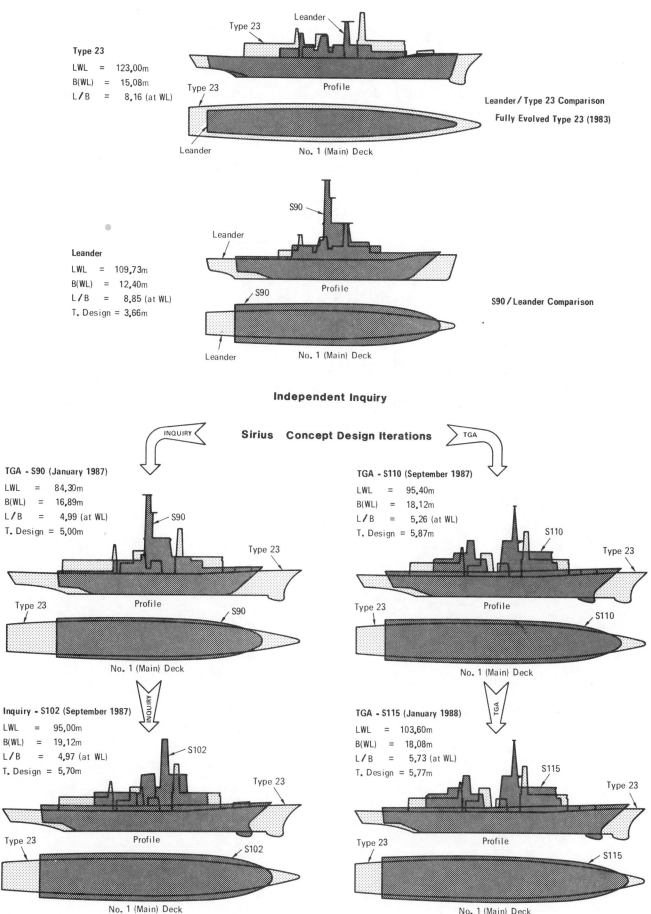

Type 23

LWL = 123,00m
B(WL) = 15,08m
L/B = 8,16 (at WL)

Type 23

Leander

Type 23

Profile

Type 23

Leander

No. 1 (Main) Deck

Leander / Type 23 Comparison

Fully Evolved Type 23 (1983)

Leander

LWL = 109,73m
B(WL) = 12,40m
L/B = 8,85 (at WL)
T. Design = 3,66m

S90

Leander

Profile

S90

Leander

No. 1 (Main) Deck

S90 / Leander Comparison

Independent Inquiry

Sirius   Concept Design Iterations

INQUIRY

TGA

TGA - S90 (January 1987)

LWL = 84,30m
B(WL) = 16,89m
L/B = 4,99 (at WL)
T. Design = 5,00m

S90

Type 23

Type 23

Profile

S90

Type 23

No. 1 (Main) Deck

TGA - S110 (September 1987)

LWL = 95,40m
B(WL) = 18,12m
L/B = 5,26 (at WL)
T. Design = 5,87m

S110

Type 23

Type 23

Profile

S110

No. 1 (Main) Deck

INQUIRY

TGA

Inquiry - S102 (September 1987)

LWL = 95,00m
B(WL) = 19,12m
L/B = 4,97 (at WL)
T. Design = 5,70m

S102

Type 23

Type 23

Profile

S102

No. 1 (Main) Deck

TGA - S115 (January 1988)

LWL = 103,60m
B(WL) = 18,08m
L/B = 5,73 (at WL)
T. Design = 5,77m

S115

Type 23

Type 23

Profile

S115

No. 1 (Main) Deck

CONTENTS

APPENDICES

CHAPTER 1

INTRODUCTION

1. **The Appointment and Terms of Reference of the Inquiry**

In November 1986 the Secretary of State for Defence appointed Lloyd's Register of Shipping, under the Chairmanship of Mr H.R. MacLeod, to conduct an independent Inquiry whose task was:

> 'To consider the advantages and disadvantages of the S90 hull form for the purposes of meeting the Naval Staff Requirement (NSR 7069) for an anti-submarine frigate (insofar as the current state of the development of the S90 permits), taking account of independent assessments made in 1983 by YARD and by the Marine Technology Board of the Defence Scientific Advisory Council, and of the Hill-Norton Committee Report *Hull Forms for Warships* published in May 1986, and to identify any implications for the design of future destroyers and frigates for the RN.'

2. **Summary of the Background to the Appointment of the Inquiry**

In 1979 the Naval Staff began to consider a possible cheap replacement for the Type 22 frigate which had an anti-submarine warfare (ASW) capability. Following consideration of a number of possible alternatives, the Type 23 frigate was conceived as being the most effective solution to the operational capability required by the Naval Staff. This required operational capability is expressed in the Naval Staff Requirement (NSR) 7069. From the initial recognition of the need to replace the Type 22 frigate, containment of costs was a paramount consideration both in terms of the required numbers of ships and in terms of their effective performance.

In 1981, whilst looking for a cheap solution to the Naval Staff's requirement for an ASW frigate, the Under Secretary of State for Defence Procurement had discussed with Thornycroft, Giles & Associates Ltd (TGA), the possibility of them putting forward a cheaper alternative to the Type 23 frigate based on their Sirius design concept.

The Sirius design concept is based on the proposition that hull forms which are commonly used for small successful work boats (e.g. pilot launches) can, with advantage, be scaled up in size and used for much larger vessels. One particular application by TGA of this approach is the 50 metre Osprey class of patrol vessels, the first of which, the 'Havornen', was built by Frederikshavn Vaerft (FHV) A/S of Denmark (now known as Danyard A/S) for the Danish Ministry of Fisheries in 1979.

For frigates and destroyers, a feature of a hull form based on the Sirius concept is its low length to breadth ratio (L/B) which is between 5 and 6 compared with values of 8 and above for the hull forms usually adopted for such vessels. These different L/B ratios have resulted in the terms 'short/fat' and 'long/thin' being used to describe the two hull form variants. It is claimed that the adoption of a 'short/fat' in preference to a 'long/thin' hull form would provide substantial advantages in terms of building and maintenance costs, construction time and simplicity of layout, without incurring any operational penalties. It is further claimed that such vessels would be more stable, with better seakeeping and manoeuvring performance, would have more commodious between-decks space and thus better accommodation and that they would be able to carry a greater weapon fit.

Arising from the discussions between TGA, the Under Secretary and the Ministry of Defence (MoD), TGA decided to put forward a private proposal to the MoD at the end of May 1982. This proposal detailed a programme of work which TGA considered necessary to demonstrate the feasibility of producing an alternative to the Type 23, based on their design concept, which met the version of the NSR 7069 current at that time, but at a substantially lower cost than that of a conventional vessel. It was in this proposal that TGA first put forward the Sirius 90 (S90) as an alternative to the Type 23.

In response to this proposal, the MoD informed TGA that it was for TGA to decide whether or not they wished to proceed with the programme of work which they were proposing for the purposes of validating the S90 as an acceptable alternative to the Type 23. If TGA did decide to proceed, such work would have to be funded by themselves.

Subsequently, TGA with the other members of the then S90 Consortium[1] did decide to proceed with the validation phase. It was agreed that the first phase of this programme would be to validate the seakeeping and powering performance of the S90 and to undertake, in parallel, sufficient design work to ensure that the S90 met the NSR 7069. The consortium were informed that if the results of the validation phase satisfied the NSR 7069, then funding would be provided by the MoD to cover the further work necessary to provide a fully detailed design and consideration would also be given to reimbursing the Consortium for the expenditure they had incurred as a result of the validation phase.

TGA presented their 'Validation Report for the S90 Escort Frigate' to the MoD on the 20th May 1983.

This Validation Report presented the results of model tests of the S90 carried out by the British Hovercraft Corporation (BHC), now known as

---

1.   The S90 Consortium initially comprised TGA, FHV and British Aerospace Dynamics
        Group. It was later joined by NEI/APE Ltd, Crossley Engines, Dowty Fuel Systems Ltd,
        Graseby Dynamics Ltd and Corlett Consultants.

Experimental and Electronic Laboratories (EEL) and the National Maritime Institute (NMI), now part of British Maritime Technology (BMT), to quantify the powering and seakeeping performance of the S90 hull form. It also presented the results of parallel design work undertaken to ensure that the S90 design proposal met the NSR.

Due to the problems of raising sufficient funding, the parallel design work, required to ensure that the S90 design proposal met the NSR, was not fully completed. In addition, the proposed 1:10 scale comparative seakeeping model tests of the S90 and the Leander frigate had not been carried out at the time of the submission of the Validation Report. However, TGA and the S90 Consortium considered that the S90, as presented in the Validation Report, would meet the general requirements of the NSR 7069 as it then stood and that sufficient potential had been demonstrated to warrant the period of detailed design development which would be funded by the MoD.

On receipt of the Validation Report, the MoD Ship Department undertook their own technical assessment of the S90 design proposal. In addition, with TGA's permission, the MoD commissioned YARD to conduct a separate and independent appraisal of the adequacy of the S90 proposal to meet the NSR 7069.

The major conclusions from these two appraisals were that the S90 had insufficient space to accommodate all the crew, weapons, stores and equipment required by the NSR 7069 and, in addition, it required a considerable increase in the proposed installed power to reach the NSR maximum speed. Further areas of non-compliance with the NSR were alleged in respect to noise levels, endurance, damaged stability characteristics and excessively high accelerations due to the ship motions. It was also considered unlikely that the S90 would be cheaper to build and operate than the Type 23.

Independently of the MoD and YARD assessments, the Hull Committee of the Marine Technology Board of the Defence Scientific Advisory Council (DSAC) had assessed the S90 design concept as part of their examination of the methods of reducing the cost of warships. At the invitation of the Hull Committee, Mr D.L. Giles, a director of TGA, presented a private paper to them on 10th March 1983. This paper dealt with the Sirius design concept and also presented preliminary results of the S90 validation programme. Following this meeting, the Hull Committee submitted its review of the S90 design philosophy to the Marine Technology Board on the 16th May 1983. The major conclusion was that the S90 did not have the advantages claimed by TGA in respect to its powering performance and that it was, on the contrary, substantially more 'resistful' hydrodynamically than conventional frigate hull forms. It should be noted that the Hull Committee did not see the S90 Validation Report.

The close unanimity of the conclusions of the three separate studies led the MoD to advise the Under Secretary of State for Defence Procurement that the S90 design proposal, and its underlying philosophy, fell short of meeting the requirements of the NSR as it then stood. As a result, TGA were informed that the MoD would not be justified in supporting the detailed development of the S90 design proposal and a press statement to this effect was issued on 18th November 1983.

However, TGA believed that the powering predictions made by YARD had grossly over-estimated the power required for the S90 since they considered that YARD had substituted their own power predictions, based on computer data derived from conventional hulls, rather than accepting the NMI S90 model test results. TGA also believed that the Hull Committee of the DSAC had rejected the NMI tank test results in favour of the computer predictions made by YARD and had, therefore, ignored the benefit of hydrodynamic lift for the S90 hull form which they considered would reduce the required power below that predicted by methods based on conventional hull forms.

Furthermore, TGA felt that the 1:10 scale S90 and Leander frigate comparative seakeeping model tests carried out in October and December 1983 demonstrated that the S90 had a superior seakeeping performance compared with the Leander which was considered to be a very good 'long/thin' seakeeping vessel.

The resulting controversy surrounding the rejection of the S90 proposal led to the formation of an unofficial committee under the chairmanship of Admiral of the Fleet The Lord Hill-Norton. This Committee reported in April 1986, its major conclusion being that certainly for ships up to destroyer size, the 'short/fat' concept offered enough advantages over the conventional 'long/thin' design to merit more serious consideration than it had been given. The Committee recommended that, as the resolution of the controversy was of the utmost importance for the operational capability of the Royal Navy,

> 'an Official Committee of Enquiry or Investigation should be put
> to work at once to validate or reject our conclusions and the bases
> for them.'

The foregoing events led to Lloyd's Register being requested in November 1986 to conduct this Inquiry.

3.   **The Scope of the Inquiry**

The Inquiry established, at an early stage, that the S90 design proposal put forward by TGA to the MoD in 1983 was too small to accommodate all the requirements of the NSR 7069 as it stood at the time of submission of the Validation Report. However, as the Inquiry's terms of reference required it to assess the S90 hull form, rather than the S90 proposal, against the NSR, the Inquiry decided to develop a design using the same hull form but of a minimum size sufficient to meet the spatial requirements of the NSR while still seeking to preserve the features that TGA considered to be inherent in their S90 design proposal. In this respect, the Inquiry considered that the Sirius design concept should not be rejected on grounds of precise size.

In order to enable a valid comparison to be made with a frigate designed, using the current warship design philosophy, to meet the same operational specification, i.e. the Type 23 frigate, the larger version of the S90 was developed to meet the NSR 7069 dated 14th October 1985. The Type 23 design used as a basis for comparison is that corresponding to this NSR. It should be noted that, throughout this report, it is this version of the NSR that is implied when referenced unless otherwise stated.

The larger version of the S90, designated the S102, is a geosim of the original S90 design proposal since, although the underwater hull form differs in absolute size from that used for the S90 proposal, it has maintained the same geometric proportions. In particular, the waterline length to breadth (L/B) ratio is virtually unchanged. This design has been used by the Inquiry in its assessment of the advantages and disadvantages of the S90 hull form.

The Inquiry, throughout its assessment of the Sirius design concept, as embodied in the S102, has sought to identify those issues which are strongly influenced by the hull form adopted. Although some of the issues raised in the debate leading up to this Inquiry have been vigorously contested by the parties involved, the Inquiry has found that not all of these issues are hull form related. In this respect, the Inquiry has examined the influence of hull form in the following areas:

> Speed, Power and Endurance
> Space, Layout, Structural Design and Weight
> Intact and Damaged Stability
> Seakeeping
> Manoeuvrability
> Military Features
> Construction Costs and Build Time
> Through Life Costs

Where possible, the performance of the S102, in the areas listed above, has been assessed in relation to the requirements of the NSR 7069. However, in order to identify the advantages and disadvantages of the S90 hull form in relation to a current frigate hull form, the Inquiry has compared the S102, where possible, with the Type 23. In some of the areas examined, the NSR has no specific requirements and, in these cases, the assessment has been based principally on a comparison of the S102 with the Type 23.

Upon reaching its initial findings concerning the potential performance of the S102 relative to the NSR 7069 and the Type 23, the Inquiry discussed these findings with TGA, together with the reasoning supporting them. This was done to ensure that no fundamental point or important source of information which TGA were aware of had been overlooked and, in addition, to allow TGA to respond with any relevant comments for further consideration.

TGA's response was to propose a further and quite radical iteration of their Sirius hull form concept which was longer and thinner than the S102. This proposal was designated the S115 in view of its increased length compared with the S102, and was put forward by TGA as being capable of providing a better vessel in relation to the NSR requirements than the S102, particularly in terms of its achievable speed.

Accordingly, the Inquiry's principal conclusions, which are given in Chapter 8, are based both on the detailed assessment of the advantages and disadvantages of the S90 hull form (as manifest in the S102 design) in relation to the NSR 7069 and Type 23 frigate and, in addition, the evaluation undertaken of the S115 proposal.

4.   **Outline of the Report**

Chapter 1 Introduction.

Chapter 2 gives details of the Inquiry's procedural matters including the methods by which written and verbal evidence was collected.

Chapter 3 discusses, in order to assist in an understanding of the underlying principles which are considered in later chapters, the current warship design process, the development and definition of the Type 23 design, the Sirius design concept and the evolution of the S90 hull form.

Chapter 4 covers the assessment of the original S90 design proposal put forward by TGA to the MoD in 1983 and examines the principal hydrodynamic points of disagreement identified during the Inquiry's review of the previous assessments.

Chapter 5 describes the development of the S102 design.

Chapter 6 presents the Inquiry's detailed assessment of the S102 design in relation to the NSR 7069 and in comparison with the Type 23.

Chapter 7 presents and discusses TGA's response to the S102 design, the S115 proposal.

Chapter 8 presents the Inquiry's principal conclusions and recommendations.

Much of the data considered by the Inquiry is either of a classified or commercially confidential nature and cannot, therefore, be reproduced in this report.   Where detailed information cannot be given due to these constraints, a summary of the work undertaken and the general conclusions reached is given, as appropriate.

All work which is of a commercially confidential nature or is subject to national security requirements has been reported separately in a confidential annex which has been sent to the Secretary of State for Defence.

CHAPTER 2

PROCEDURAL MATTERS

1.   **Inquiry Team**

The Inquiry team, along with their respective areas of work, are detailed in Appendix 1.

2.   **National Security and Commercial Confidentiality**

The Inquiry's investigations have involved access to classified and commercially confidential information.

All members of the Inquiry team were given the appropriate security clearance to receive classified material relevant to the Inquiry.

The commercial confidentiality of all information submitted to the Inquiry has been strictly safeguarded.

3.   **Publicity**

Following the publication of the Hill-Norton Committee Report and the Government's announcement that an Inquiry was to be set up to consider the S90 hull form in the role of an anti-submarine warfare frigate, a number of interested parties contacted both the Ministry of Defence and Lloyd's Register to offer their services.

In addition, and in order that the Inquiry could benefit from an input from as wide a spectrum of informed parties as possible, the appointment of the Inquiry, its terms of reference and the issues being examined were advertised in December 1986 and January 1987 in the national and technical press together with a request for interested parties to contact Lloyd's Register stating their areas of expertise. A copy of this advertisement appears in Appendix 2. Parties responding to this advertisement were then advised, where applicable, of the appropriate procedure for making a written submission to the Inquiry.

Responses to the formation of the Inquiry and the subsequent advertisement numbered approximately fifty in all.

4.   **Written Submissions**

The Ministry of Defence and Thornycroft, Giles & Associates Ltd were invited to submit to the Inquiry whatever information they considered pertinent to the Inquiry's terms of reference.

Parties who offered their services or made written submissions to the Inquiry are detailed in Appendix 3.

In addition, the Inquiry addressed written questions to a number of parties who had examined, or been involved with, the S90 design proposal prior to the establishment of the Inquiry. Formal written answers to the Inquiry's questions were submitted by the parties concerned. Details of these parties are given in Appendix 4.

5. Formal Inquiry Meetings

The Inquiry examined all the material submitted to it and, where it considered it necessary, invited the relevant party to attend a formal Inquiry meeting at which the matters under consideration were further discussed. The meetings were held in private and the parties concerned were not represented by Counsel or Solicitors.

Formal meetings were held with the parties detailed in Appendix 5.

All formal meetings were audio taped and a written record of the proceedings was produced. Agreement that the written record was adequate and accurate was obtained from the party concerned. These records have been retained by Lloyd's Register and will not be released unless requested by the Secretary of State for Defence and the release agreed by the party concerned.

6. Informal Inquiry Meetings

The Inquiry held a number of informal meetings with parties external to Lloyd's Register which it considered could provide expert advice on certain aspects of the Inquiry's investigations. The parties concerned are detailed in Appendix 6.

Informal discussions were held with TGA to ensure that the features TGA saw as inherent in the S90 hull form were properly identified. Notes of these informal meetings were made and TGA's agreement that these notes represented an adequate and accurate record of the meetings was subsequently obtained.

Informal discussions were also held with the Type 23 frigate project team at Bath in order to discuss the design of the Type 23 and to obtain their comments on the S102 development undertaken by the Inquiry.

7.   **Inquiry Ship Visits**

In order to obtain an appreciation of current MoD and TGA designs, the Inquiry visited a number of vessels which were either in service or being built. These visits are detailed in Appendix 7.

8.   **Work Undertaken on Behalf of the Inquiry**

The Inquiry approached a number of parties external to Lloyd's Register to commission work or to request information and data relating to various aspects of the Inquiry's work.

Details of these organisations and the work undertaken are given in Appendix 8.

9.   **Glossary and Abbreviations**

A glossary of technical terms used in the report is included in Appendix 9. A list of abbreviations used in the report is contained in Appendix 10.

10.   **Acknowledgements**

Lloyd's Register would like to thank all those who have contributed to the work of the Inquiry.

In particular, Lloyd's Register wish to thank Mr Alan Bond for his kind permission for the Inquiry to use the Southern Cross III and Suisse Outremer for their assistance in arranging the trials, the Danish Ministry of Fisheries for allowing the Inquiry to visit their vessel, the Havornen, Yarrow Shipbuilders Ltd for allowing the Inquiry to visit the Type 23 frigate, HMS Norfolk, during construction and the ship's company of HMS Broadsword for their assistance during the Inquiry's trip to sea aboard this vessel on 8th April 1987.

CHAPTER 3

THE SHIP DESIGN PROCESS

1.   Introduction

TGA consider that a frigate or destroyer based on their Sirius design concept would present substantial advantages both technically and economically when compared with such a vessel designed using the current warship design philosophy.

This chapter seeks to identify the difference between the Sirius design concept and the current warship design philosophy. The current MoD ship design process is summarized in general terms with this process being illustrated by outlining the development of the Type 23 frigate, designed by the MoD to meet the NSR 7069. In particular, the process by which the MoD derived the hull form for this vessel is described.

The Sirius design concept and the development of the S90 hull form put forward by TGA to meet the NSR 7069 are also discussed.

2.   The Current Warship Design Process

2.1   General

The basic requirement for a warship is that it can support a given weapon payload and achieve specified operational criteria (for example, maximum speed).

2.2   Definition of Requirements

The desired weapon payload and operational criteria are usually specified by the 'Customer'. For the Royal Navy, the 'Customer' is the Naval Staff in the Ministry of Defence who act on behalf of the Nation in accordance with the Government's defence policy. The required operational capability of a particular warship is expressed in the Naval Staff Requirement (NSR) for that vessel. The NSR 7069 defines the weapon payload and performance criteria required by the Naval Staff for the Type 23 frigate.

However, before the NSR can be drafted, it is necessary for the Naval Staff to formulate their basic requirements. Although, in the strictest sense, it is the Naval Staff who specify what a vessel is required to do, they are assisted by the technical departments concerned, in particular the Ship Departments at Bath and London, who ensure that the Staff's basic requirements are both feasible and achievable within technical and economic constraints. This they achieve by means of conceptual and preliminary design studies which are undertaken prior to the NSR being formalised.

2.3   Conceptual Design Studies

As the Naval Staff identify and develop their requirements in response to a perceived need, the Ship Department undertakes a number of conceptual studies which examine possible solutions to what the Naval Staff desire. Such solutions may be unconventional. For example, for a given requirement, vessels based on the SWATH, hydrofoil or hovercraft concept may be compared with designs based on the monohull concept. The effects on cost, performance and military capability are assessed enabling the Naval Staff to decide on the best concept to adopt in respect to their requirements. These conceptual studies play a major role in the development of the Naval Staff requirements and the ideas put forward by the ship design team will obviously have a fundamental bearing on the option which is adopted for further development.

2.4   Preliminary Design Studies

Arising from the conceptual design studies, the Naval Staff write a brief statement of the desired weapon payload, equipment, functions and characteristics of the intended vessel, including cost. This statement is called the Naval Staff Target (NST). In parallel, the preferred option to meet this Target is being developed from the conceptual stage. It is during this period that the Ship Department concentrates on the main parameters of the intended vessel and a number of alternative designs, based on the chosen concept, will be developed and compared in order to identify the best of the contending solutions.

2.4.1   The Design Iteration

The following outline description is provided for the benefit of those who are unfamiliar with the process by which a ship is normally designed.

Designing a ship is essentially an iterative process. This process has been described as proceeding along a spiral, the centre of which is reached when all the features making up the design have been balanced. Figure 3.2.1 is an example of such a design spiral for a warship. This iterative process has to develop within technical and economic constraints and, therefore, throughout the development of the design, trade-offs between sometimes conflicting requirements have to be made in order to achieve a balanced design. This trade-off process, and the success of the ultimate design, depends to a large extent on the skill and experience of the ship design team.

In reality, many of the items indicated in Figure 3.2.1 will be developed almost simultaneously. However, the starting point for the design of a warship is usually taken as the required weapon fit since this determines, to a large extent, the space (in this context space refers to the internal volume and deck area) that is required to accommodate the crew, control spaces, etc. Accumulated data from previous designs are used extensively to assess the space requirements of each item to be included in the new design.

In conjunction with estimating the required space, an initial estimate of the principal dimensions is made. The absolute minimum length of a warship, such as a frigate, is generally governed to a large extent by the weapons which have to be accommodated on the upper deck. In addition, the length will also be influenced by the intended speed of the vessel. The beam is largely governed by stability considerations and the draught by seakeeping and the required propeller immersion. The depth of the vessel is governed by freeboard, 'tween deck heights and hull girder strength. Again, considerable use is made of data and coefficients obtained from previous ships. The designer will usually base his initial estimates on recent ships which resemble the intended design. The ease with which a design is subsequently developed depends to a considerable extent on a good choice of preliminary dimensions, hence satisfactory designs of comparable size are a good indicator of the initial dimensions to be selected.

Having estimated the main dimensions, the hull form is developed. The initial choice is normally made on the basis of the required power necessary to achieve the specified speeds, for example the maximum speed and the endurance speed. Certain hull form ratios will be chosen based on past data or data from systematic model tests and a body plan will be produced showing the underwater hull form. In conjunction, an estimate of the power to achieve the required speeds will be made enabling suitable machinery installations to be selected.

Having determined the initial dimensions and hull form, an estimate of the displacement can be made. The displacement corresponding to the design draught and trim must equal the estimated weight of the weapons, equipment and ship. If sufficient displacement is not provided, then the hull form and or dimensions must be altered accordingly.

Space can then be allocated for the machinery and associated fuel tanks to give the endurance range and, based on the planned ship's complement and the spaces required for the weapon control systems, etc, a preliminary general arrangement plan of the vessel is produced.

Based on this arrangement, the main hull structure (i.e. shell envelope plating, stiffeners, framing, etc) of the vessel can be determined. The calculation of the required sizes of the various items will be based on an accepted strength standard.

The vertical and longitudinal positions of the weights are then determined and, based on the hydrostatic data derived from the hull form, the trim and stability of the design can be calculated. If the trim is not desirable, weights (e.g. fuel) are re-distributed along the length of the vessel until a suitable trim is achieved. If the stability does not meet the specified criteria or is considered to be unsuitable because, for instance, the vessel will roll excessively, then either the vertical disposition of weights is altered or, more commonly, the ship's beam is changed. The effect of changing the beam must be reflected in revised powering calculations. The principal dimensions and the hull form may, as a result, be altered accordingly and the design reiterated.

As the hull form and weight distribution are developed, computer predictions of the seakeeping performance are undertaken and alterations to the hull form again might be made to improve the seakeeping performance. In addition, for warships, other factors such as the infra-red, magnetic and noise signatures, the vulnerability of the vessel and the arcs of fire of the weapons, will be assessed by means of feasibility studies and modifications to the design will be incorporated where necessary.

Once the ship structure and general arrangement have been defined, it is possible to estimate the cost of the vessel. Since cost is a principal constraint in warship design, it is necessary, at this stage, to review whether the design is within the budget and can be considered the best value for money. The ship design team and the Naval Staff will jointly debate the advantages and disadvantages of the developing design. If the cost is too high, it may be necessary to reduce the Naval Staff requirements. In addition, the design team may suggest changes which, although increasing the cost of the ship, would greatly improve the design. Trade-offs between the operational capability of the vessel and cost will be made. The NST may be re-drafted and then the process of iteration continues along the next loop of the design spiral.

During the first iteration of a design, it is usual to consider a number of alternative arrangements of dimensions, hull form, machinery configurations, layout, etc, in order to be sure of deriving an optimum arrangement. At the end of this iteration a number of the options can be rejected and only those remaining are carried through to the next stage. As the iterations become more detailed, the optimum arrangement is identified leading to the final solution.

During the later stages of the preliminary design studies, it is normal to conduct model tests with the hull form. These model tests will assess the resistance and propulsion of the hull form and, in addition, may address the seakeeping and manoeuvring characteristics. The results of the experiments may result in further changes being made to the hull form. Based on the model tests, a more accurate prediction of the full scale power requirement is made and the designer is then able to confirm the machinery selected to achieve the desired speeds and to make a better estimate of the fuel required to achieve the endurance range.

It should be noted that the above is a very general description of the ship design iterative process. There is no fixed procedure for designing a ship and there could be many variations in the process described and illustrated in Figure 3.2.1. In particular, many design offices now use computer aided ship design packages which avoid the need to use the traditional 'hand' methods of ship design which are relatively slow due to the number and complexity of the design calculations. The computer system can perform these calculations at great speed.

As the preliminary studies develop, the Naval Staff are able to draft the NSR for the vessel. This is an amplified version of the NST in which the weapon payload and operational criteria are specified in more precise terms. The draft NSR is submitted to a number of committees within the MoD. Once they have endorsed the NSR, it is submitted to Ministers and the Treasury for their approval. With their endorsement, the ship design is further refined to meet the NSR. At this point, the nominated shipbuilder becomes heavily involved with the next stage of the design development, the detailed design phase.

2.5   Detailed Design Phase

During this stage, the design produced by the Ship Department is taken over by the shipbuilder who produces detailed construction plans of the vessel. The drawings show, in detail, the arrangement of each individual compartment and how it fits into the overall ship. Particular attention must be given to ensuring that the necessary ship services can be efficiently routed to the required spaces (e.g. chilled water for cooling of electrical equipment).

Once the shipbuilder has produced sufficient detailed design drawings to be in a position to negotiate a contract to build the vessel, the design is submitted to the Admiralty Board for approval. Once such an endorsement has been made, approval is sought from the Minister and Treasury to negotiate a contract for the first of class ship. When a contract has been agreed, an order for the ship is placed and building commences.

3.   Outline Development and Definition of the Type 23 ASW Frigate

3.1   Definition of Requirements

In 1979, the Naval Staff began to consider a possible cheap replacement for the Type 22 frigate which concentrated on providing an anti-submarine warfare capability.

3.2   Conceptual Design Studies

A number of possible options were assessed in response to the Naval Staff's initial requirements, ranging from a joint study with British Shipbuilders (the Type 24 frigate) to the possibility of using simple towed arrayed corvettes.

It was decided that the best solution would be a vessel based on the monohull concept.

3.3   Preliminary Design Studies

Prior to the first draft of the NST, a number of different ship options with various propulsion arrangements and weapon fits were assessed.

Arising from these studies, the first draft of the NST was made in April 1981. The preliminary design studies indicated that the initial length of the vessel should be set at 100m. Reference 3.1 states that the essential features of the vessel were to be:

> *'a quiet platform to maximise the effectiveness of the current and projected towed array, high endurance at the moderate towing speeds, a flight deck for a medium helicopter (EH101) with the ability to refuel and rearm the aircraft, hull and superstructure configured to minimise radar echoing area (REA) and, perhaps most importantly, the unit production cost (UPC) was fixed at a maximum of £70M at September 1980 prices.'*

By the end of 1981, a number of revisions to the NST had been made and the vessel had increased in length to 107m. As the design developed, the Naval Staff decided to remove one gas turbine and accept a reduction in top speed to reduce the cost of the vessel. However, it was decided that a hangar should be provided for the helicopter and the fitting of a point defence missile system was considered desirable. This resulted in the vessel being increased in length to 115m.

The NSR was drafted in the early part of 1982 and was given ministerial approval in May 1982. The committees endorsing the NSR decided that the second gas turbine should be reinstated together with the corresponding higher top speed, a second Seawolf tracker should be added and that additional area should be provided to enable a Sea King helicopter to land as well as the proposed EH101 helicopter which the Type 23 was to carry. These modifications in the requirements led to a further 3m increase in the length of the vessel.

Although an order to proceed with the detailed design of the Type 23 was placed by the MoD with Yarrow Shipbuilders Ltd in June 1982, the lessons learned from the Falklands War were to have a major impact on the design. The review of the Falklands War was completed towards the end of 1982 and resulted in the length of the vessel being increased to 123m to accommodate the changes that were considered necessary in view of the experience gained from this war. One of the most notable changes was the addition of the 4.5 inch Mk 8 medium calibre gun for shore bombardment. It is interesting to note that the increase in length was constrained by the maximum length of ship that could be accommodated in the frigate complex at Devonport. As a result of the extensive modifications to the design, the NSR was re-submitted to the Minister and was duly approved.

3.4   Detailed Design Phase

With the approval of the NSR by the Minister, the responsibility for the detailed design of the vessel was passed to Yarrow Shipbuilders Ltd who had been selected as the lead shipbuilder. The detailed design was submitted to the Admiralty Board and approved in the middle of 1983 with a contract being placed for the build of the first of class. The first Type 23 frigate, HMS Norfolk, was launched at Yarrow Shipbuilders in July 1986.

3.5   The Type 23 Hull Form

The MoD Ship Department have developed a computer aided ship design system called GODDESS (Government Defence Design System for Ships). This system enables the ship design team to search for the best combination of overall dimensions and hull form to meet the specified requirements, having already decided approximate initial dimensions for the proposed vessel.

In developing the Type 23, the design team sought to provide the minimum length and space to accommodate the required weapon fit. As indicated in Section 3.3, the length of the vessel was increased a number of times from the initial length of 100m before being finally fixed at 123m. These increases were primarily due to changing Naval Staff requirements, in particular the addition of weapon systems. With each increase in length, it was necessary to re-consider the other principal dimensions and the hull form. The preliminary beam of the vessel was selected to provide the required space and to meet the stability criteria.

The GODDESS system relies on a database which primarily comprises data obtained from a wide range of previous ships. In particular, a library of 'basic' warship hull forms is provided. A basis hull form is selected which is then optimised for the new vessel by investigating the implications of changing the principal dimensions on the internal space available, the powering, the endurance, the stability, the seakeeping and all the other integrated aspects of ship design. This approach has the advantage, particularly in the early stages of design, that more options can be investigated in greater detail because the traditional 'hand' methods of ship design are relatively slow due to the number and complexity of the design calculations. The computer system can perform these calculations at great speed and, therefore, can give the designer more scope for investigating new ideas and variations in a proposed design.

This system has been used in the development of the Type 23. The resulting hull form has the following main particulars:

Length on load waterline	=	123.00	m
Greatest moulded breadth	=	16.20	m
Moulded breadth on waterline	=	15.08	m
Load draught	=	4.55	m
L/B ratio	=	8.16	

4.   The Sirius Design Concept

4.1   General

The features that TGA consider would present substantial advantages for a frigate or destroyer based on their Sirius design concept, in contrast to such a ship based on the current warship design philosophy, arise primarily from their choice of hull form.

4.2   The Sirius Hull Form

TGA have indicated that the Sirius hull form is an expansion of a design 'family' of hull forms. This 'family' has its origins in small fast launches such as the 40 foot 'Nelson' pilot launch designed by Commander P. Thornycroft in the early 1960's. Larger variants of this 'family' which are in service are said to include the 'Azteca' class of 34 metre patrol craft and the 50 metre 'Osprey' class of patrol vessels. This latter class has recently been lengthened by the addition of a 5 metre extension in the afterbody of the hull.

TGA provided the Inquiry with the following definition of their Sirius concept in terms of hull form:

> *'The Sirius concept is a range of round bilge hulls incorporating the following features:*
>
> *1.   Fine straight waterlines forward.*
> *2.   Flared bow with knuckle above waterline.*
> *3.   Afterbody incorporating rounded bilge sections with pronounced flare at waterline.*
> *4.   Straight parallel aft buttocks with small steady rise aft.*
> *5.   Afterbody underwater sections with slight deadrise.*
>
> *The Parent hull form is varied within these constraints to a wide range of length/beam ratios, but ideally between 5 and 6. Other features such as rise of buttocks aft, deadrise, angle of entry and LCB position are optimised as required as with any parent hull form.*
>
> *The Sirius concept has been tested with varying L/B ratios and with design features optimised for operating at speeds of up to $V/\sqrt{L} = 4$.'*

Concerning the development of the S90 hull form, the Inquiry was informed by the independent naval architect commissioned by TGA to design this hull form, that he had developed the hull form based on speed/length and beam/displacement ratios along with other coefficients and ratios that he had developed for small craft. He had also used a similar approach in developing the Osprey hull form. In this respect, he stated that the Osprey hull form was not a strict derivative of the Azteca class; it had been produced by him to meet length, displacement and speed range criteria specified by TGA. Furthermore, he stated that the S90 hull form was not formally derived from any other specific hull form and was certainly not derived from the Osprey which is a 'faster' hull form.

As indicated in Section 2.4.1, the approach adopted by the designer of the S90 hull form is common to the naval architectural profession, namely the basing of new designs on coefficients and ratios from previous successful designs. However, the difference between the approach adopted to design the S90 hull form and that adopted to design the Type 23 hull form is that the S90 hull form is based on coefficients derived from small craft, whereas the Type 23 hull form is based on coefficients derived from current frigate and destroyer designs. The fundamental question which is, therefore, posed by TGA's approach to designing a frigate or destroyer is whether or not the use of coefficients and ratios used in the design of small successful craft will produce a more efficient and cost effective frigate or destroyer hull form than using coefficients and ratios derived from similar sized frigates and destroyers.

Apart from the different underwater hull form, the major feature distinguishing the S90 hull form, from that of the Type 23, is that the S90 hull form has a L/B ratio around 5.0, as compared with an L/B ratio of 8.2 for the Type 23.

4.3   Assessing the Sirius Design Concept

TGA claim that the adoption of their Sirius design concept would produce a vessel which would have substantial advantages compared with such a vessel based on current frigate and destroyer design philosophy. Paragraph 2 of the Hill-Norton Committee Report summarizes TGA's claims:

> *'It is claimed that a radical alternative {to a current conventional design}, in the shape of a short/fat hull form, would provide very substantial advantages in building and maintenance costs, in construction time, and in simplicity of layout, with no operational penalties. Indeed, it is further claimed that such vessels would be more stable, with better sea-keeping and manoeuvring performance,*

more commodious between-decks space and thus better accommodation, and that they would be able to carry a greater weapon outfit.'

However, before such claims can be assessed, it is necessary to translate the concept into a design which meets a defined requirement. The design of any ship, as indicated in Section 2.4.1, requires a balance to be achieved between a number of operational, technical and economic factors. These factors are often in direct conflict with each other and, as a result, the success or otherwise of a design is determined primarily by the overall balance that is finally reached between the various parameters which influence it. Therefore, the suitability of a concept cannot be effectively judged until a design, which meets a specific requirement, has been developed to the point at which the overall balance, or compromise, of the various parameters can be assessed. If the overall balance is not established by means of a realistic design, then there is a real risk that advantages will be claimed without the extent of the corresponding disadvantages being properly assessed. Therefore, without a realistic design, meeting a defined requirement, objective assessments of a given design concept cannot be made.

The Inquiry's terms of reference require it to assess the S90 hull form against the NSR 7069 for an ASW frigate. Therefore, the Inquiry has sought to quantify the overall balance achieved by a vessel based on the Sirius design concept by examining the design solution this particular hull form provides to the NSR 7069.

References

3.1　　Bryson, L.: 'The Procurement of a Warship', Trans.RINA, Volume 127, 1985.

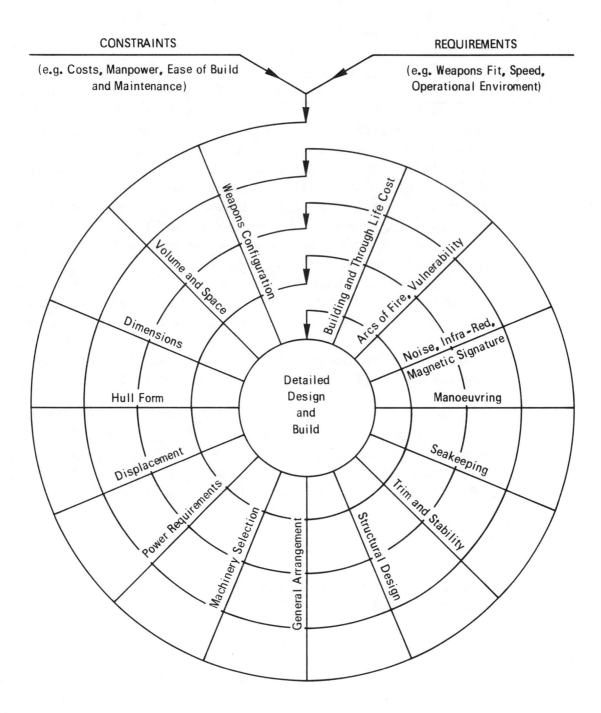

FIGURE 3.2.1   ITERATIVE DESIGN SPIRAL FOR A WARSHIP

CHAPTER 4

ASSESSMENT OF THE ORIGINAL
S90 DESIGN PROPOSAL

1.   Introduction

In order to examine the advantages and disadvantages of the S90 hull form for the purposes of meeting the NSR 7069, the Inquiry undertook, as a first step, a review of the S90 frigate proposal which TGA presented to the MoD on 20th May 1983. Previous assessments of this proposal for compliance with the NSR 7069 carried out by YARD and the MoD Ship Department in June 1983 were also reviewed by the Inquiry.

In addition, the Inquiry considered the assessment of the S90 design philosophy undertaken by the Hull Committee of the Marine Technology Board of the DSAC in 1983 and the subsequent assessment by the Hill-Norton Committee in 1985/86 of using the Sirius concept for vessels up to destroyer size in preference to the current hull forms adopted for such warships.

Following these studies, the Inquiry undertook:

i)   an independent assessment of the S90 design proposal for compliance with the NSR 7069, and

ii)   an examination of the points of disagreement regarding the claimed propulsive performance of the S90 hull form which were identified during the Inquiry's review of the previous assessments.

This chapter summarizes the main results of the above assessments.

2.   The S90 Frigate Proposal Presented by TGA to the MoD

The S90 frigate proposal presented by TGA to the MoD in May 1983 is described in the document entitled 'Validation Report for the S90 Escort Frigate'. This document presents the results of the model tests carried out by BHC and NMI to quantify the powering and seakeeping of the S90 hull form and, in addition, provides an outline specification, general arrangement plan, some intact stability and weight calculations and a construction and through life cost breakdown for the S90.

A number of features were proposed for the S90 which, TGA considered, would provide a vessel which was cheaper both to build and to operate than a more conventional frigate and, in addition, would have the capability of carrying a greater weapon load than that required by the NSR 7069.

In particular, TGA considered that the hull form of the S90 would enable the ship to operate at over twice the displacement (and therefore weight) of conventional warships of her length. TGA chose to use this wider margin of weight for two main purposes:

i)   To allow the structural weight to be increased. This would allow a commercial strength standard to be adopted; such a standard providing heavier scantlings and hence more weight than a naval standard. TGA considered that the advantages of adopting a commercial standard were twofold; firstly, the S90 would be stronger than a conventional frigate because the heavier and shorter structure would result in a less highly stressed hull girder; secondly, the use of a commercial strength standard would allow lower grade, cheaper steel to be used and would also mean that the S90 could be built using commercial shipbuilding techniques which would be less labour intensive than corresponding naval building techniques. This would result in a considerable saving in the construction cost compared with a conventional frigate.

ii)   To allow the installation of heavier diesel engines instead of the gas turbines usually installed in RN frigates and destroyers. Such engines would be more economical than gas turbines and could operate on cheaper, and more widely available, residual fuel oil rather than the 'Dieso' used by the Royal Navy. The ability to operate with residual fuel oil would mean that the S90 would not normally have to refuel at sea from the Royal Fleet Auxiliary (RFA) tankers. This would result in a further reduction in the running costs of the S90 compared with a conventional frigate design.

Other features of the S90 which, it was considered, would enhance the vessel in comparison with a conventional frigate were:

i)   The greater available midship volume in the S90 compared with that in a conventional frigate could be used to provide 'more space per man.' In addition, more fuel could be carried, resulting in increased endurance.

ii)   The large stability margin available with the S90 would permit the radar and communications equipment to be positioned much higher than was possible on a conventional hull form, resulting in improved performance.

iii)   More weapons and ammunition than specified in the NSR could be carried due to the available weight and stability margins provided by the hull form.

With respect to the speed of the S90, TGA concluded that the vessel would achieve the NSR required speeds, at a full load displacement of 2800 tonnes, with four Pielstick PC2 diesel engines. It was also proposed that a fuel transfer system would be fitted to the S90 which would allow the LCG to be moved by the redistribution of fuel, enabling the resistance of the vessel to be minimised at low speeds. It was suggested that the fuel transfer system would also provide a number of other advantages, such as damage control.

With respect to seakeeping, TGA's tentative conclusions, based on the NMI seakeeping tests, were that the S90 would be able to maintain full power in head seas up to and including North Atlantic Sea-state 6. It should be noted that the 1:10 scale S90 and Leander frigate comparative seakeeping model tests had not been carried out at the time the S90 Validation Report was submitted to the MoD. These model tests were performed subsequently in October and December of 1983 and TGA felt that the results of these tests demonstrated that the S90 had a superior seakeeping performance compared with the Leander which was considered to be a very good 'long/thin' seakeeping vessel.

TGA's conclusion was that the outline specification that had been produced for the S90 illustrated, on paper at least, that they had succeeded in suggesting what would be the most heavily armed ship in the Royal Navy (excluding aircraft), with the longest endurance; and available at the lowest possible hull cost per ton of payload, when carrying some 100 tonnes more weapons and ammunition than specified in the NSR 7069. They considered that all the major areas of naval requirement had been examined, as far as cost and time permitted them, and, in their view, the design was not found to be wanting.

3.   **The Inquiry's Assessment of the S90 Design Proposal for Compliance with the NSR 7069**

The general arrangement plan of the S90 design proposal is reproduced in Figure 4.3.1 and the following main particulars were deduced from the lines plan supplied to the Inquiry by TGA:

Length overall	93.30	m
Length on design w.l.	84.30	m
Greatest moulded breadth	19.00	m
Moulded breadth on design w.l.	16.89	m
Moulded depth	10.50	m
Design draught	5.00	m
Deep draught	5.19	m
Extreme displacement	2830.0	tonnes

The Inquiry first undertook an assessment of the adequacy of the S90 design proposal to meet the spatial requirements associated with the NSR 7069. In order to do this, the Inquiry advanced the internal layout and construction aspects of the design to a stage at which its capability to accommodate the required equipment and machinery could be assessed (see the general arrangement plans reproduced in Figures 4.3.2, 4.3.3 and 4.3.4).

The resulting assessment showed that the S90 hull and superstructure was too small to accommodate all the necessary spaces. It should be noted that, in parallel, the Inquiry had assessed the space allocated in the Type 23 design and had concluded that it was the minimum required consistent with the spatial requirements associated with the NSR 7069. Based on a comparison with the areas allocated in the Type 23, the deficiency in the total usable deck area of the S90 compared with the Type 23 was calculated to be approximately 685m^2. A qualitative impression of the relative sizes of the S90 and the Type 23 may be obtained from Figure 4.3.5.

The Inquiry's estimate of the displacement of the S90 exceeded that estimated by TGA by approximately 595 tonnes (using the scantlings proposed in the Validation Report).

As a result of the fundamental deficiencies in area and displacement, the Inquiry concluded that the S90 design proposal submitted by TGA to the MoD could not satisfy the spatial requirements of the NSR 7069.

The Inquiry's conclusions regarding the size and weight deficiencies of the S90 proposal are in agreement with the previous assessments undertaken by YARD and the MoD Ship Department. In addition, the Hull Committee of the DSAC reached a similar conclusion based on the preliminary data which was presented to them by TGA in March 1983.

TGA's agreement was obtained at the end of April 1987 that the S90 design proposal was too small to meet the spatial requirements of the NSR 7069.

In view of the foregoing, the Inquiry concluded that it would not be possible to make objective assessments of the other key issues (speed, powering, seakeeping, etc) in the absence of a design which met the basic space requirements associated with the NSR 7069. The Inquiry decided, therefore, to develop a design using the same S90 hull form but of a minimum size sufficient to accommodate the spatial requirements associated with the NSR 7069. The development of this larger version of the S90 is described fully in Chapter 5 and the resulting assessment of the advantages and disadvantages of the S90 hull form in relation to the NSR 7069 and in comparison with the Type 23 frigate are discussed in detail in Chapter 6.

4.   **Examination of the Hydrodynamic Points of Disagreement Identified during the Inquiry's Review of the Previous Assessments**

The Inquiry has identified that the major points of disagreement related to the claimed hydrodynamic performance of the S90 hull form. In particular, a number of apparently unresolved differences of opinion had arisen concerning the propulsive performance of the S90 hull form. The Inquiry has identified the following five principal areas which were in dispute:

i)   Whether model tests were a suitable basis for determining the resistance and propulsion characteristics of S90 type hull forms or whether 'computer modelling' should be used. This is addressed in Section 4.2.

ii)   What effect hydrodynamic lift would have on the resistance of the S90 type of hull form at the speeds required by the NSR 7069. This is addressed in Section 4.3.

iii)   How predictions based on model experiments compared with the achieved speeds and powers for full scale S90 type hull forms. This is addressed in Section 4.4.

iv)   How the resistance of the S90 type of hull form compared with the resistance of conventional frigate hull forms. This is addressed in Section 4.5.

v)   How the propulsive efficiency of the S90 type of hull form compared with that of conventional frigate hull forms. This is addressed in Section 4.6.

The Inquiry has examined, in detail, the background to these disputes and the technical aspects involved.

4.1   **Power Prediction Methods**

There are two approaches which naval architects use to predict the power required to propel a ship at a given speed. The first approach uses the known resistance and propulsion properties of previous designs that are similar to the design under consideration. Modifications are made to the estimates of speed and power to account for the differences between the previous designs and the design under consideration. This approach is very useful in the early design stages but does not generally give sufficiently accurate results for the final estimates. A formalised approach of this type is given in Reference 4.1.

The second approach is generally used in the latter stages of design when a more accurate estimation of the necessary power is required. This method relies upon conducting tests on a scale model of the ship.

The principle underlying the second method is that a model is tested at a similar Froude number[1] as that for the ship and the results are scaled to full size by using a frictional resistance extrapolation formula. There are a number of these extrapolation formulae in existence; the one used for all the S90 model tests was the 'ITTC(1957) Line'. The use of this procedure enables the resistance of the ship to be predicted. To predict the power required to overcome this resistance, further tests are required running the model largely self-propelled with the model propellers running at scaled speeds. These tests enable the interaction effects between the propeller and the hull to be determined.

It is not possible to determine, directly from model tests, the exact power that would be required by a ship to attain a given speed. The reasons for this are discussed in Section 4.4. However, since there are, at present, no satisfactory theoretical techniques for accurately predicting the powering requirements for a given hull form, model tests are the normal way of obtaining reliable estimates.

4.2   Computer Modelling

TGA have asserted that YARD had rejected the NMI S90 model tank test results and had based their speed and power estimates for the S90 on computer predictions instead. The implication of this assertion is that YARD did not believe that model tests were a suitable means of predicting the performance of S90 type ships.

The Inquiry has established that YARD did use a computer program, called PREDICT, to perform the calculations necessary to obtain powering and speed estimates for the S90. However, the function of this program is to automate the traditional calculations of speed and power that used to be performed by hand. It is fundamental to the operation of the program that basic resistance data (e.g. model test data) are input. The program does not provide theoretical estimates of resistance or powering.

In the case of the S90 assessment, YARD did input the NMI S90 model test results into the program to obtain powering and speed

---

1.   Froude number is a non-dimensional speed to length ratio given by $Fn = V/\sqrt{gL}$, where V = ship speed, g = acceleration due to gravity and L = ship length.

estimates for the S90.   The Inquiry is satisfied that YARD's assessment was based on the model test results submitted by TGA and that at no stage did they reject the model tests.

TGA further asserted that the Hull Committee of the DSAC had also rejected the NMI model tests and had relied instead on YARD's computer predictions in their assessment of the resistance of the S90.

The Inquiry has established that the conclusions reached by the Hull Committee of the DSAC, concerning the powering of the S90, were based upon the earlier BHC S90 model test results presented to them by TGA in March 1983. The Hull Committee did not see the NMI model test results during their assessment of the S90 as they reported before these results were available.

In summary, the dispute over the alleged rejection of the S90 model tests by YARD and their replacement by 'computer predictions' is based on a misunderstanding of the nature of the procedure used by YARD to calculate speed and power. The Hull Committee of the DSAC did not reject the earlier BHC S90 model tests and they did not see the NMI model tests or YARD's assessment.

Both YARD and DSAC confirmed in their evidence that they saw no reason to reject the S90 model tests and that such model tests could be used to predict the performance of the S90. The Inquiry concurs with this view and has used the S90 model test results, submitted by TGA, in assessing the power requirements of the S90 hull form.

4.3   Hydrodynamic Lift

Hydrodynamic lift occurs when a hull lifts partially out of the water due to the hydrodynamic forces generated by the ship's forward speed.   Its causes and effects are relatively well known and many vessels, such as fast patrol craft, are designed specifically to take advantage of it.

A considerable part of the debate over the powering characteristics of the S90 hull form has concerned the claimed benefits that arise from hydrodynamic lift for this hull form. The Inquiry was informed that the S90 would exhibit hydrodynamic lift at speeds much lower than conventionally shaped warships.   It was also claimed that in rejecting the S90 model test results in favour of 'computer predictions', YARD and the Hull Committee of the DSAC had not taken into account this advantage in their assessment of the powering characteristics of the S90. This latter assertion has been discussed in Section 4.2.

All the evidence submitted to the Inquiry on the subject of hydrodynamic lift was in agreement that:

i)   The extent of hydrodynamic lift experienced by the S90 would be fully represented in the model test data.

ii)   The effects of hydrodynamic lift on the resistance of a full size ship are automatically taken into account in the normal prediction procedures based on model tests.

The Inquiry concurs with these views.   A number of contributors claimed, however, that at the speeds required to satisfy the NSR 7069, the S90 would not benefit from significant hydrodynamic lift.

The Inquiry has examined the evidence which, it was suggested, showed that hydrodynamic lift did occur at unusually low speeds for the S90. This evidence consisted of measurements of 'tow point rise' of the model whilst undergoing resistance and propulsion tests.

The measurements showed that at the speeds at which the model was tested (these being appropriate to the NSR required speeds), the tow point did not rise but did, in fact, sink. Indeed, it sank as far as would be expected for a ship of that length, breadth and speed. Thus, there is no evidence of anything unusual in the forces experienced by the S90 hull.

This does not mean, of course, that there is no hydrodynamic lift on the S90 hull at the speeds being considered. It does mean, however, that the benefit of hydrodynamic lift for the S90 is insignificant at these speeds.

The Inquiry concludes that the effect of hydrodynamic lift on the S90 is automatically included in prediction procedures based on appropriate resistance and propulsion model tests. However, at the speeds under consideration, it does not consider that the S90 would gain any appreciable benefit from hydrodynamic lift.

4.4   Correlation Between Model and Full Scale Performance

TGA, in the S90 Validation Report, made the statement that:

> *There is evidence that both the 50 metre Osprey and the 34 metre Azteca self-propulsion tests were some 30-40% pessimistic compared with the full scale trials measured on 25 ships; and this probable error was regarded as being unacceptable for the S90 validation.'*

The Inquiry addressed the following written question to TGA:

'Would TGA explain exactly what resistance and propulsion benefits the use of a shorter hull with larger beam has over a longer hull with narrower beam at the same displacement.'

In reply, TGA stated:

'The major benefit, in terms of "R & P", is in the (1+x) or correlation factor.'

The Inquiry has received oral and written evidence on the nature of correlation factors. Some of the contributors maintained that a number of vessels with hull forms similar to that of the S90 had performed very much better than model tests predicted. It was suggested to the Inquiry that the S90 hull form would benefit from a low correlation factor, relating model test results to full scale, and thus require less power than predicted by conventional techniques.

The Inquiry has, therefore, examined the correlation between model test results and full scale performance for hull forms of similar proportions to the S90.

It was suggested that a possible explanation for low values of (1+x) could be that ships with the proportions of the S90 experience very high form factors. The Inquiry has, therefore, considered these factors for hull forms of similar proportions to the S90.

4.4.1   Correlation Procedure

It is not possible to calculate directly from model tests the exact power that will be required for a ship to attain a given speed. The reasons for this fall into two groups, namely:

i)   Those relating to the accuracy of model tests as a means of predicting ship resistance. These are principally due to the shortcomings in model data extrapolation procedures. For example, there are difficulties in scaling the model appendage resistance and the interaction between hull and propeller. There is also the problem associated with obtaining the proper level of turbulence over the model and propeller. In addition, the geometry of the model testing tank can have an effect.

ii)   Those relating to the difference in conditions under which the model and full scale tests were carried out. For example, the roughness of the hull, the weather and sea conditions, the water depth and the accuracy with which ship performance can be measured.

As a result, a difference exists between the delivered power determined by model tests and the actual delivered power required for a ship to achieve a given speed.

The correlation between model tests and full scale performance has been, and continues to be, the subject of a considerable amount of research. This research has been conducted by the individual towing tanks and through the regular International Towing Tank Conferences (ITTC). As part of this research, two principal methods have been developed for predicting the actual ship performance from the results of model tests. The first is the British Towing Tank Panel (BTTP) 1965 method which involves the use of the following three factors:

i) $(1+x)$ - the ratio between the actual ship delivered power (P_{Da}) and the delivered power derived from the model tests (P_{Dm}).

ii) k_1 - the ratio between the ship quasi-propulsive coefficient (QPC_s) and the model quasi-propulsive coefficient (QPC_m). k_1 is usually taken as unity unless the model propeller is extremely small.

iii) k_2 - the ratio between the actual ship propeller speed (N_a) to deliver P_{Da} and the predicted propeller speed (N_p) to deliver P_{Dm}.

This method has been developed and used by the major British commercial towing tanks. The actual values of the three correlation coefficients are subject to continual update as new information becomes available.

The alternative method, which is used by the major foreign commercial towing tanks, uses a factor C_A or δC_t instead of $(1+x)$. This is a supplementary resistance coefficient (which could be negative) that is added to the predicted ship resistance coefficient.

The evidence relating to the correlation between ship and model for hull forms of similar proportions to the S90 has been presented principally in terms of the BTTP nomenclature. Therefore, the Inquiry has adopted this approach.

The factor $(1+x)$ has three uses in the correlation between ship and model, namely:

i)   As a ship Performance Prediction Factor used to adjust the model test prediction of the power which should be provided in order that a ship, which is yet to be built, can achieve its specified speed.   The adjusted value represents the best estimate of the power which should be provided in order that the ship can achieve its specified speed.

ii)   As a ship Correlation Factor accounting for the difference between carefully conducted ship trials for a particular ship and the corresponding model tests using a geometrically similar (geosim) hull, appendages and propellers and run at the correct equivalent speeds, displacement and draughts.

iii)   As a Load Factor used during the model tests to enable propulsion tests to be undertaken at the correct propeller loading.

The Inquiry is concerned with predicting the power required by the S90 hull form to achieve the speeds defined in the NSR 7069. In this respect, it is necessary to determine a suitable performance prediction factor as the vessel has not been built. The selection of this factor is normally made on the basis of accumulated ship correlation factor data. Therefore, the correlation factors for hull forms of similar proportions to the S90 must be assessed not only to establish whether they are particularly low, but also to assist in the selection of a suitable performance prediction factor.

4.4.2   Examination of Ship Correlation Factors for S90 Type Hull Forms.

TGA submitted data relating to the model and full scale tests for the Azteca and Osprey class vessels along with the reports of correlation studies on two smaller vessels.

TGA also informed the Inquiry of the existence of the Southern Cross III, a 51 metre motor yacht with a similar hull form to the S90. The Inquiry decided that it should carry out trials on this vessel in order to determine a correlation factor. These trials were carried out in September 1987, followed by the associated model tests which were performed by the Netherlands Maritime Research Institute (MARIN).

The Inquiry obtained evidence on the performance of the Peacock class of patrol vessels, built by Hall Russell Ltd for the Royal Navy, as it was suggested during the course of the Inquiry that these vessels provided evidence that hull forms similar to the S90 benefited from low correlation factors.

The Inquiry has also taken evidence from British Maritime Technology (BMT) and the Experimental Electronic Laboratories Ltd (EEL), the latter having performed a large number of model tests for TGA. A number of individuals with experience in this field have also given written and oral evidence to the Inquiry.

4.4.2.1   The Azteca Class

The Azteca class vessels are patrol boats of approximately 34 metres length, 130 tonnes displacement with a length to breadth ratio of 4.6. Twenty-one of these vessels have been built in British shipyards for the Mexican Navy with a further ten being built in Mexican yards. The vessels were designed by Associated British Machine Tool Manufacturers (ABMTM) with the hull lines being provided by Commander P. Thornycroft through TT Boat Designs.

A number of trials results for Azteca class vessels were submitted to the Inquiry by TGA. These results indicated that the trials were probably carried out to prove that the contract speed could be achieved. In order to do this, it was only necessary to run the engines at the design rpm and measure the ship's speed. Unfortunately, this procedure does not provide sufficient information to enable exact correlation factors to be derived with any degree of confidence, particularly as the power being developed by the engines was not measured. The correlation factor is the ratio of actual power to predicted power; if the actual power is not measured, the correlation factor cannot be deduced.

Nevertheless, the Inquiry has examined the trials results and compared them to the model test results which were also submitted by TGA.

Trials results were submitted for nine vessels built at two separate yards. The information for seven of the vessels consisted only of the displacement, engine rpm's and speeds. The Inquiry formed the conclusion that the displacements and engine rpm's were nominal rather than actual and had to reject the data as having too great a level of uncertainty associated with it.

The reports for the other two trials were more detailed. Of these, only one gave sufficient information to be able to deduce the displacement at the time the trials were run. However, this displacement was not the same as that of the model in the resistance and propulsion tests and the engine rpm's reported on trial are believed, again, to be nominal rather than actual.

As the shaft power was not measured on these trials, the values used in the analysis undertaken by the Inquiry are the engine manufacturer's nominal figures of maximum power for the engine speeds quoted in the trials report. It is possible for an engine to develop more or less power than its nominal rating at a particular rpm.

The correlation factors resulting from the limited analysis which the Inquiry has undertaken are 0.92 and 0.96. However, it is the Inquiry's opinion, based on the quality of the data, especially the estimated shaft power, that these figures should not be used for predicting the power of future vessels.

4.4.2.2   The Osprey Class

The original Osprey class vessels are 50 metre patrol boats with a displacement of around 380 tonnes and a length to breadth ratio of 5.6. A number of these vessels have been built by the Danish shipyard Frederikshavn Vaerft A/S, to a hull design by TGA. New vessels in this class have recently been lengthened by 5 metres in the after section of the hull.

As part of the S90 validation programme, TGA commissioned NMI to perform model experiments using a 1:10 scale model of the Osprey class vessel at the draughts corresponding to the Osprey vessel 'Havornen' during its trials. The Inquiry has examined this correlation exercise and has no reason to doubt its accuracy or validity. Doubt was, at one stage, cast on whether the trials and model tests had been conducted at the corresponding displacement. However, this matter has been resolved and the Inquiry accepts that the trials and model tests were conducted properly.

This study produced a correlation factor of between 0.97 and 0.98.

Model tests were also conducted at the Danish Hydrodynamics Laboratory and at British Shipbuilders Hydrodynamics Ltd, St Albans. The results of these model tests were submitted to the Inquiry. However, the Inquiry has not considered the correlation between the trials and the Danish or St Albans model tests because the tests were performed with the models in a different loading condition to that of the trials.

4.4.2.3   The Southern Cross III

In addition to considering the data provided by TGA, the Inquiry carried out measured distance trials aboard the 51 metre motor yacht Southern Cross III in order to determine the speed and power relationship for this vessel. The hull form of the Southern Cross III was designed by TGA and is similar to that of the S90.

The associated model tests were undertaken by the Netherlands Maritime Research Institute (MARIN).

Unfortunately, due to poor visibility caused by haze, it was not possible to observe the shore-based transit markers which is the normal method of determining the distance run by a vessel. Since the vessel's schedule precluded the postponement of the trials, the distance run was determined using the ship's radar sets. This technique cannot be regarded as being of acceptable accuracy for determining correlation factors and, therefore, the Inquiry has only been able to place minimal weight on the value of 0.87 obtained.

4.4.2.4   The Peacock Class

The main particulars of the Peacock class and the S90 are as follows:

		Peacock	S90
Length overall	(m)	62.60	93.30
Length on waterline	(m)	60.00	84.30
Breadth on waterline	(m)	9.37	16.89
Max. load draught	(m)	2.72	5.19
L_{WL}/B_{WL}		6.40	4.99

It should be noted from the above table that the Peacock class has an L/B ratio which is higher than the S90. However, in view of the claims concerning low correlation factors obtained for these vessels, the Inquiry has examined the model tests and trial results of the Peacock class.

Altogether five Peacock class vessels have been built and all conducted speed trials in 1983/84. HMS Peacock, the first of class, ran five sets of trials. A series of model tests was undertaken at British Shipbuilders Hydrodynamics Ltd, St Albans, following the first HMS Peacock trial. Unfortunately, the displacement at which the model was tested and the bilge keel configuration effectively restricts valid comparison to the first trial of HMS Peacock alone.

The validity of this first trial has been questioned as the engines were producing more power than their continuous rating during part of the trials. This does not affect the validity of the correlation exercise since the power was measured.

A correlation factor of 0.90 was obtained.

4.4.2.5   Other Data

BSRA and NMI (now known collectively as BMT) have undertaken, over a number of years, formal carefully controlled correlation trials on a relatively large number of wide beam, fast vessels for the express purpose of comparing model test and full scale results. This data has been submitted to the Inquiry by BMT.

Not all of this data was applicable to the Inquiry's assessment of correlation factors for vessels of similar hull form to the S90 and appropriate weighting was, therefore, given to relevant data.

This data indicated a range of correlation factors from 0.88 to 1.14 with a mean value slightly greater than 1.0.

TGA have also submitted two correlation studies for small vessels. One of these studies was discounted because of doubts concerning its validity. The Inquiry has taken the results of the other study into consideration.

4.4.3   Interpretation of Evidence

The data submitted by TGA does not show that the Azteca and Osprey classes required '30 to 40%' less power than model tests would predict. The data for the Azteca class is of insufficient accuracy for deriving correlation factors. The single reliable value for the Osprey class vessel, the Havornen, indicates that the power required is approximately 2 - 3% less than that given by model tests.

TGA's statement that model test results are 30-40% pessimistic compared with the full scale trials is based, in the case of the Osprey class, on the results of the trials conducted on the 'Havornen' and a set of model tests conducted at the Danish Hydrodynamics Laboratory in a different loading condition to that of the trials.

When the reliable data for the Havornen and HMS Peacock is considered in conjunction with the data from BMT, it is found that, although these two values are lower than average, they are still higher than the lower bound of the BMT correlation data.

In this respect, the Inquiry concludes that there is no reason to assume that the S90 hull form would benefit from a correlation factor substantially lower than has been measured for other vessels of its hull dimensions and speed.

4.4.4 Form Factor

It was suggested to the Inquiry that a possible explanation for low values of correlation factor for vessels of similar proportions to the S90 lay in the model test procedure used by NMI. It was suggested that the two-dimensional extrapolation procedure used by NMI would lead to an over-estimate of the resistance. The explanation for this being that the frictional component of the total resistance was under-estimated by the ITTC(1957) Line at model scale, resulting in an over-large residual component at full size. Three-dimensional methods for dealing with this potential error, which is due to the differences between flow over flat plates (on which frictional resistance formulations are traditionally based) and over curved ship hulls, have been under development since the 1960's.

Some towing tanks do not consider this three-dimensional extrapolation, by itself, to be an improvement upon the older two-dimensional method and have not implemented it as their standard technique. Other tanks either run both methods in parallel or adopt the three-dimensional extrapolation for specific types of ship where it is known to work well. It is not part of the Inquiry's function to decide which method is the better and, therefore, the Inquiry has confined itself to considering whether the two-dimensional extrapolation used by NMI for the S90 model tests can give satisfactory powering predictions.

To do this, the Inquiry examined what the effect of a three-dimensional extrapolation would be on the NMI model test results. The Inquiry also commissioned a series of tests on the model of the Southern Cross III which were analysed using both methods.

The effect of the three-dimensional nature of the flow over the hull of a vessel can be quantified by a form factor, $(1+k)$. If a hull form has a value of $(1+k)$ greater than 1.0 (k greater than 0), then the resistance predicted by two-dimensional extrapolation will be greater than that predicted by three-dimensional extrapolation. The amount that the resistance will be over-predicted depends upon the value of k, the size of the ship and the speed. At high speeds, where the value of the residuary resistance is much greater than that of the frictional resistance, the effect is usually small. In large tankers, for example, the form factor effect is important since k is large, because of the fullness, and the Froude number is low, because of the length and relatively low speed of the ships.

In the case of the Sirius hull forms, the Froude number is so high that a large value of k, if it existed, would have a very small effect on the extrapolated ship performance. If a two-dimensional extrapolation procedure is used, as in the case of the S90, the predicted power can still be relied upon, independent of the form factor effect, as long as a consistent performance prediction factor is used which is based on ships of similar fullness, dimensional ratios and Froude numbers.

As the NMI model tests on the S90 were performed over a wide range of speeds, including very low speeds, the Inquiry has been able to determine the magnitude of form factor present for the S90. Following consideration of this, together with the results of the tests conducted on the Southern Cross III model, the Inquiry concluded that the values of form factor present in the S90 and in the Southern Cross III would not cause a significant difference in predicted power between the two and three-dimensional extrapolation methods. If consistent performance prediction factors are used, then there should be no difference in the final ship powering predictions.

Thus there is no reason to believe that the method used to extrapolate from model to full scale produces pessimistic estimates of the power requirements for the Sirius hull form.

4.4.5 Selection of a Performance Prediction Factor for the S90 Hull Form

As stated in Section 4.4.1, performance prediction factors are normally selected on the basis of accumulated ship correlation factor data. Since a large variability exists, even with properly measured ship correlation factors, it is necessary to consider carefully this variability when selecting a performance prediction factor. It would normally be considered prudent to select a conservative value since most design contracts include financial penalties which are incurred if the design fails to achieve its contractural trials speed.

It should be understood that whatever method is used to predict full scale performance from model scale results, the actual values of $(1+x)$, C_A or δC_t which are used relate only to the particular model extrapolation procedure adopted by the tank performing the model tests. The relevant S90 model tests were performed by NMI; consequently the performance prediction factor chosen must relate to the NMI procedure for model test extrapolation to full scale.

The organisations with the greatest experience in determining performance prediction factors are the towing tanks that carry out the model tests. In the case of the S90, NMI used the value of 0.97 derived from the Havornen correlation exercise, as requested by TGA. NMI indicated that this value was somewhat low in their experience and that a value above 1.00 might have been more appropriate. They subsequently indicated that they would use a performance prediction factor of 1.02 or 1.03 for a ship having the dimensions of the S90. A prudent designer would usually adopt the value of performance prediction factor proposed by the towing tank unless he had sufficient data of his own to take an independent view.

However, for the purposes of the Inquiry, it is considered that rather than select a specific performance prediction factor, a best estimate along with a lower bound should be selected, the lower bound being used to indicate the sensitivity of the required power and resulting costs for a vessel based on the S90 hull form to the value of performance prediction factor chosen.

Based on all the correlation factor data analysed by the Inquiry (described in Section 4.4.2), it has been concluded that a value of 1.0 can be taken as representing the best estimate of the performance prediction factor which would be used, with 0.9 being taken as the lower bound for the purposes of assessing the sensitivity of the required power and resulting costs to the value chosen. These values have been used in the power estimates for the larger version of the S90 referred to in Section 3 of this chapter.

It should be noted that there is evidence to suggest that correlation factors vary to some degree with length and speed. However, over the ranges appropriate to the Inquiry's assessment, the data examined indicate insignificant variation with these parameters.

4.5   Resistance

The Hill-Norton Committee Report, Paragraph 41, states that:

> *'if constructed to the same length as the conventional form a Sirius hull of over 77% greater beam and 77% or even 150% greater displacement would still exhibit similar resistance (in terms of pounds of resistance per ton of displacement at 25 knots) and lesser specific resistance at all higher speeds up to the maximum practical speed of the traditional destroyer.'*

MINISTRY OF DEFENCE

Lloyd's Register WARSHIP HULL DESIGN INQUIRY

ISBN 011 7726001

CORRECTIONS

Page 4-19, Paragraph 2, to be replaced by:

This statement should not be taken to imply that an S90 type frigate would have
the same resistance as a conventional frigate of the same displacement, and
Figure 4.5.1 requires the following careful interpretation if relevant conclusions are
to be drawn.

London Her Majesty's Stationary Office
July 1988

Figure 13 of the Hill-Norton Committee Report, which was originally published as part of the written discussion by Mr D.L. Giles and Commander P. Thornycroft to Reference 4.2, purports to support this statement and has been reproduced as Figure 4.5.1.

The implication of this statement is that an S90 type frigate would have approximately the same resistance as a conventional frigate of the same displacement. This was a point on which many contributors to the Inquiry offered evidence.

From Figure 4.5.1 it can be seen that the vertical axis is *'pounds of resistance per ton of displacement'* and that the horizontal axis is *'ship speed divided by the square root of the vessel's length (V/√L).'* Three curves are shown; two relate to Sirius hull form variants and the third is for the US Navy Perry class frigate (FFG-7).

It would appear from Figure 4.5.1 that the Perry class frigate has a marginally lower specific resistance at low speeds whilst the Sirius variants are better at the higher speeds. It was alleged by some contributors that the data shown in this figure was incorrect. The Inquiry, therefore, obtained the basic resistance data of the Perry class from published literature (Reference 4.3) and has plotted this in Figure 4.5.2. This figure, with the correct Perry class data, appears to show that the Perry has a similar specific resistance to the Sirius, albeit slightly higher at low speeds and slightly lower at high speeds. However, this is an incorrect conclusion to draw as the Perry is a longer ship than the Sirius, and so is operating at a lower $V/\sqrt{L}$ when at the same speed. For example, as shown in Figure 4.5.3, at 28 knots the $V/\sqrt{L}$ of the Perry class is 1.39 whilst that of the Sirius variants is 1.68. Thus, the specific resistance of the Perry is 62 lbs per ton displacement whilst the specific resistance of the best Sirius variant is 119 lbs per ton displacement, i.e. almost double.

This is shown graphically in Figure 4.5.4 where Figure 4.5.3 has been re-drawn with speed as the horizontal axis. The figure also shows that, for example, at 16 knots the specific resistance of the Sirius variants is approximately 40% greater than that of the Perry class frigate.

In addition, the Inquiry obtained from published literature (Reference 4.2) the resistance of a Leander class frigate. This is plotted in Figure 4.5.5. The Leander class frigate, in comparison to the Perry class frigate, operates at a displacement much closer to the design displacement of the S90 and it is also a twin screw vessel whereas the Perry class frigate is a single screw vessel. It can be seen from Figure 4.5.5 that the resistance per ton for the Leander is similar to that of the Perry.

The Inquiry concludes that, based on the data it has examined, the resistance of an S90 type hull is about twice that of a comparable conventional frigate of the same displacement operating over the upper speed range appropriate to the NSR 7069.

4.6   Power

Knowledge of the resistance of a hull form or the effective power, P_E, is not sufficient in itself to determine how much power needs to be installed in a ship to achieve a given speed. It is also necessary to consider the efficiency with which the propulsion system can convert the power available, or shaft power P_S, to useful thrust.

There are three principal components of this efficiency, or Propulsive Coefficient (PC). They are:

i)   The efficiency of the mechanical transmission system between the gearbox output shaft and the propeller, η_S.

ii)   The efficiency of the propeller in converting torque into thrust, η_o.

iii)   The efficiency of the hull form associated with the flow conditions around the propeller. This is the product of the hull efficiency, η_H, and the relative rotative efficiency, η_R.

Components (ii) and (iii) are strongly interrelated.

Thus

$$PC = \frac{P_E}{P_S} = \eta_S \cdot \eta_o \cdot \eta_H \cdot \eta_R$$

Based on a comparison of a derived propulsive coefficient of 0.467 for a Leander frigate and a value of 0.606 for the S90, the Hill-Norton Committee Report states that the '*S90 propulsive coefficient is therefore 30% better than that of the Leander.*' The implication of this is that the S90 hull form requires less power for a given resistance than conventional frigates.

The Inquiry has checked the data used to obtain the values of PC for the Leander and the S90.

The value of PC for the S90 is correct in that the effective power and the shaft power are derived from the NMI model tests and subsequent analysis.

The value of PC for the Leander, however, is incorrect. This is because the wrong value for the shaft power has been used. In calculating the PC it is necessary to use the shaft power actually being developed by the engine at the speed concerned. The PC calculated for the Leander used the total shaft power of 30,000 SHP. However, at 28 knots the corresponding shaft power for the Leander is 23,000 SHP. Thus the PC for the Leander becomes 0.610 rather than 0.467. This value is similar to the S90 at model scale.

Therefore, the Inquiry concludes that the propulsive coefficient for the S90 as tested is similar to that of the Leander at full scale.

4.7   Summary

The Inquiry's findings, as they relate to the points of disagreement concerning the claimed propulsive performance of the S90 hull form, can be summarized as follows:

i)   The dispute over the alleged rejection of the S90 model test results and their replacement by 'computer predictions' was based on a misunderstanding of the function of YARD's computer program PREDICT. The S90 model tests were accepted by YARD. The Hull Committee of the DSAC did not see the NMI model test results but accepted the earlier BHC model test results.

ii)   Model tests are a satisfactory method of predicting the power requirements of full size ships of the S90 type.

iii)   The effects of hydrodynamic lift on a full size ship are automatically taken into account in the normal prediction procedures based on appropriate resistance and propulsion model tests.

iv)   At the operating speeds appropriate to the NSR 7069, the S90 would not benefit from significant hydrodynamic lift.

v)   The correlation factor data submitted to the Inquiry showed that the correlation factors for Sirius type hull forms were not outside the range that would reasonably be expected for vessels of the hull dimensions of a Sirius vessel. Therefore, there is no reason to assume that the S90 hull form would benefit from a correlation factor lower than usual for a vessel of its dimensions and speed.

vi)   The S90 hull form is approximately twice as resistful as a conventional frigate of the same displacement and speed, over the upper operating speed range appropriate to the NSR 7069.

vii)   The Propulsive Coefficient of the S90 as tested is similar to that of a Leander frigate at full scale.

The Inquiry concludes, therefore, that there is nothing unusual or exceptional about the S90 hull form in respect to its powering characteristics and that such performance can be adequately assessed by conventional naval architectural techniques.

References

4.1   Holtrop, J.: 'A Statistical Re-Analysis of Resistance and Propulsion Data', International Shipbuilding Progress, Volume 31, November 1984.

4.2   Bryson, L.: 'The Procurement of a Warship', Trans.RINA, Volume 127, 1985.

4.3   Woo, E.L., Karafiath, G. and Borda, G.: 'Ship-Model Correlation of Powering Performance on USS Oliver Hazard Perry FFG-7 Class', Marine Technology, Volume 20, January 1987.

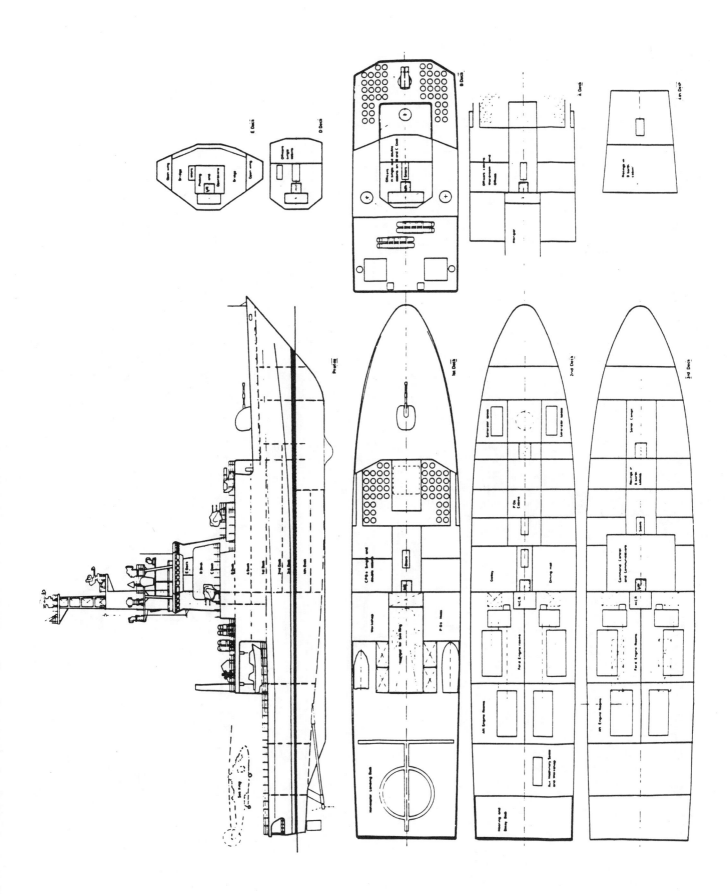

FIGURE 4.3.1   S90 TYPE OCEAN ESCORT VESSEL
              (REPRODUCED FROM S90 VALIDATION REPORT)

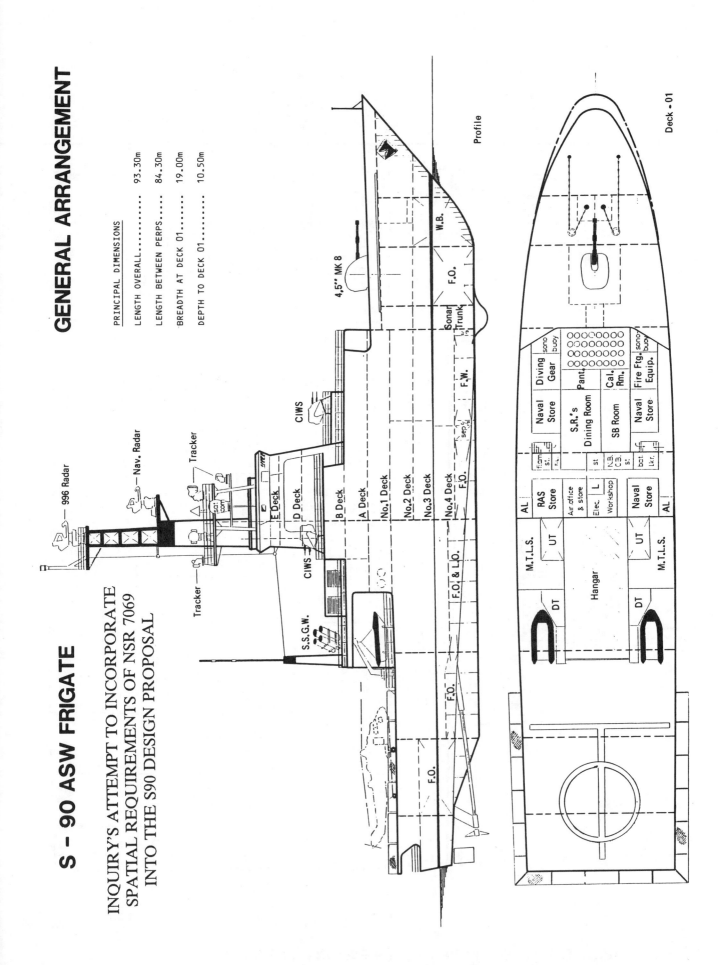

FIGURE 4.3.2   S90 GENERAL ARRANGEMENT

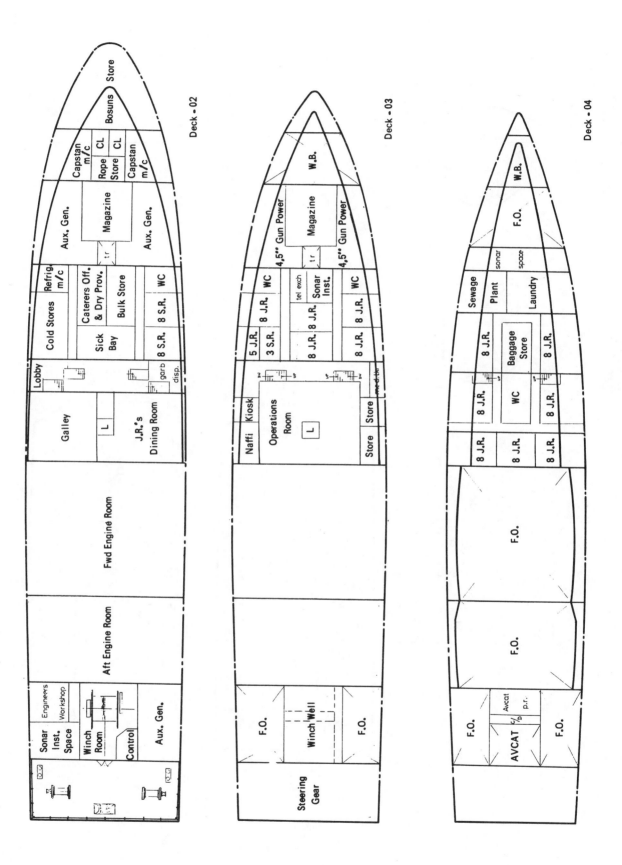

FIGURE 4.3.3   S90 GENERAL ARRANGEMENT

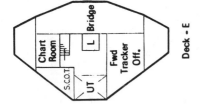

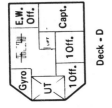

PRINCIPAL DIMENSIONS

LENGTH OVERALL .... 93·30 M

LENGTH W.L. .... 84·30 M

BREADTH .... 19·00 M

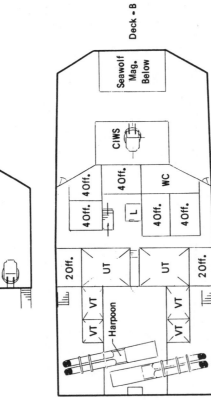

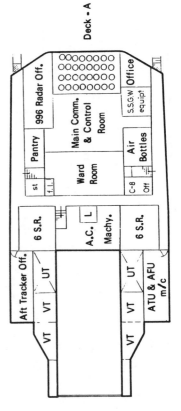

FIGURE 4.3.4   S90 GENERAL ARRANGEMENT

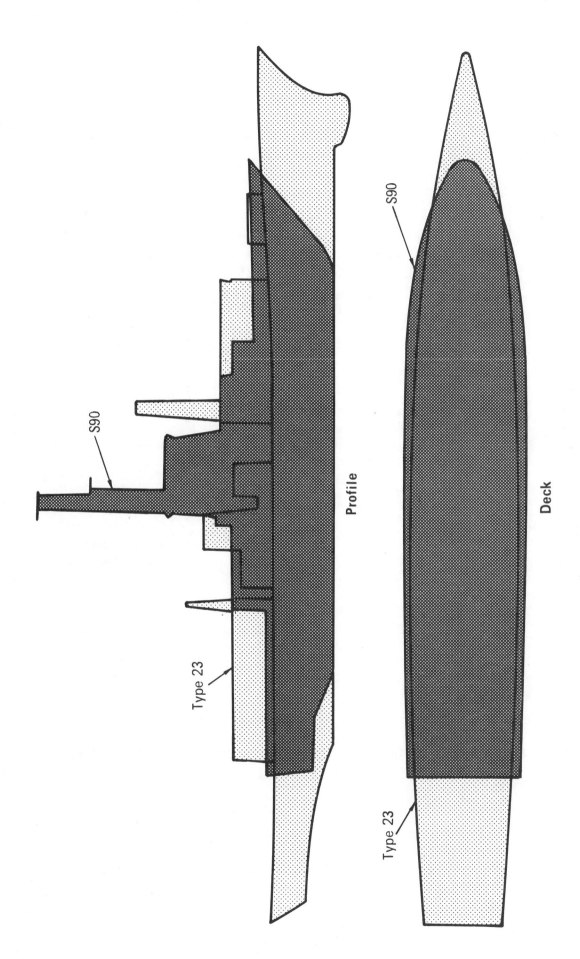

FIGURE 4.3.5   TYPE 23/S90 COMPARISON

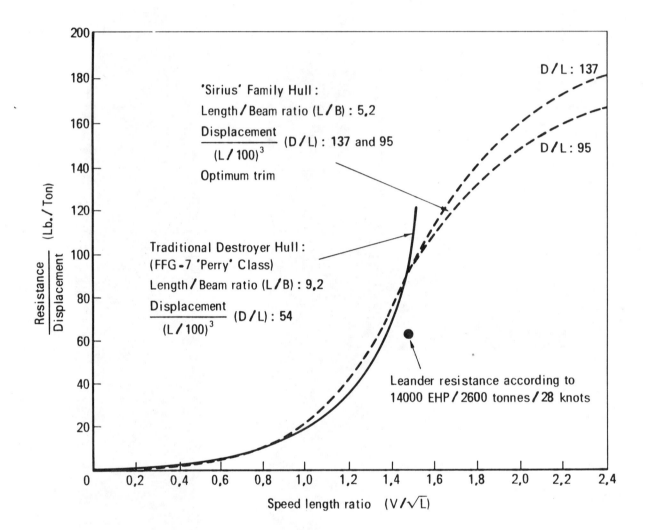

FIGURE 4.5.1   NON-DIMENSIONAL COMPARISON OF HULL RESISTANCE
(REPRODUCED FROM REFERENCE 4.2)

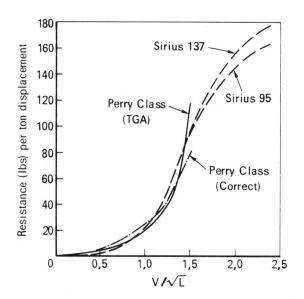

FIGURE 4.5.2

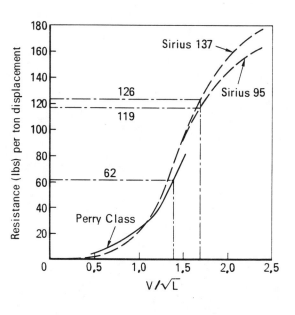

FIGURE 4.5.3

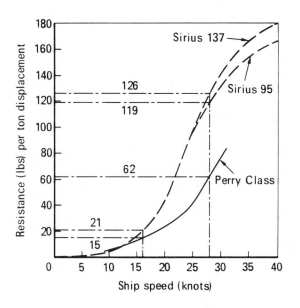

FIGURE 4.5.4

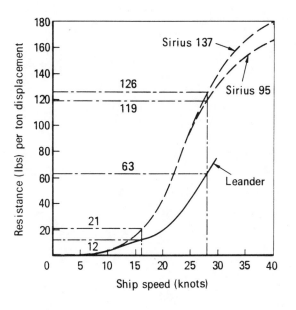

FIGURE 4.5.5

CHAPTER 5

DEVELOPMENT OF AN S90 GEOSIM DESIGN,
THE S102

1.   **Introduction**

As indicated in Chapter 4, Section 3, the S90 design proposal submitted by TGA to the MoD in May 1983 was found to be too small to accommodate all the necessary spaces and equipment associated with the NSR 7069. However, the Inquiry decided to develop a design using the same S90 hull form but of a minimum size sufficient to accommodate the spatial requirements associated with the NSR 7069 while still seeking to preserve the features that TGA considered to be inherent in their S90 design proposal. Such a design, it was considered, would then provide a suitable basis on which to assess the advantages and disadvantages of the S90 hull form in relation to the NSR 7069 and in comparison with the Type 23 design. This chapter outlines the development undertaken by the Inquiry of the S90 hull form.

The developed design, designated the S102, is a geosim of the original S90 design proposal since, although the underwater hull form differs in absolute size from that used for the S90 proposal, it has maintained the same geometric proportions. This enables the model tests carried out to determine the powering requirements for the S90 to be used directly for determining the required power and achievable speeds of the S102. The term '102' has no practical significance and merely approximates to the proportionally increased length of the geosim design from the reference value of '90' used in the S90 terminology.

It was decided that the S102 development would consist of a single design iteration (see Chapter 3, Section 2.4.1 for an explanation of the ship design iterative process) since it was considered that the major advantages and disadvantages of the S90 hull form would be readily identifiable from such an iteration.

The S102 design has been developed to meet the NSR 7069 dated 14th October 1985. Where it has been necessary to refer to design standards in developing or assessing the S102, the appropriate standards have been taken to be the relevant Naval Engineering Standards (NES).

2.   **Design Objectives and Principles**

2.1   **Objectives**

The objectives of the S102 development were as follows:

i)   To obtain the minimum size of vessel, based on the S90 hull form, which provided sufficient space to accommodate all the spaces and equipment relating to the NSR 7069 whilst still preserving the features that TGA considered to be inherent in their S90 design proposal.

ii) To allocate sufficient open deck space to accommodate:-

   a) all the weapons required by the NSR 7069,
   b) helicopter landing area and hangar,
   c) weapon directors and communications,
   d) Replenishment at Sea (RAS) reception areas for bulk stores and fluids,
   e) life saving appliances,
   f) ship handling and mooring equipment.

iii) To arrive at the dispositions and volumes of tanks required to achieve both the endurance range and the trims indicated by the S90 model tests to be the optimum with respect to minimising the resistance of the hull form.

iv) To arrive at a realistic displacement.

The Inquiry considered that a design developed to meet the above objectives would then enable it to make reliable estimates of the powering, stability, seakeeping, manoeuvring and costs for a vessel based on the S90 hull form.

2.2   Design Principles

The Inquiry adopted the following design principles in developing the S102:-

2.2.1   Hull Form

The Inquiry took the S90 lines plan as submitted by TGA and scaled all the dimensions in a geometrically similar fashion, i.e. the underwater hull form of the S102 is geometrically similar (i.e. a geosim) to that of the S90. Although it was intended to maintain a geometrically similar draught to the S90 design draught, this would have meant that the size of the S102 would have been larger than necessary to accommodate all the required spaces. Therefore, it was decided, with TGA's agreement, to increase the draught of the S102, compared with the S90 equivalent draught, rather than increase the size of the vessel.

It should be noted that the S90 lines plan was subsequently modified by the Inquiry in the fore end region to accommodate a bow mounted sonar.

2.2.2   Machinery Arrangement

TGA proposed that a combined diesel-electric and gas turbine (CODLAG) propulsion system similar to that installed in the Type 23 should be fitted to the S102 rather than the diesel engine arrangement that they had proposed for the S90. This was mainly in order that the vessel might meet the noise requirements of the NSR 7069.

The two modes of propulsion which are associated with the CODLAG system are:-

i)   Diesel-electric:
        Propulsion power is provided by a direct drive electric motor mounted on each shaft, power for which is provided by a number of diesel-generator sets. This mode of propulsion, being the most quiet, would be used when the towed array sonar is deployed. In addition, as this mode of propulsion is the most fuel efficient for the proposed machinery installation, it has been used for the evaluation of the NSR endurance requirement.

ii)   Combined diesel-electric and gas turbine (CODLAG):
        Propulsion power in this mode is principally provided by gas turbines which are augmented by the electric motors. This mode of propulsion is used to obtain higher speeds up to the maximum required speed.

TGA subsequently specified that two Spey SM1C gas turbines be fitted in the S102 rather than the Spey SM1A gas turbines installed in the Type 23. Although the Spey SM1C gas turbine is not yet in service, it will provide approximately 40% more power than an SM1A turbine at the maximum continuous rating. The machinery arrangement for the S102 can be summarized as follows:

Machinery	Manufacturers' Continuous Rating
2 × Spey SM1C Gas Turbines	2 × 18 MW
2 × GEC Brush Electric Motors	2 × 1.5 MW
4 × Paxman Diesel-Generators	4 × 1.3 MW

In order to install this machinery arrangement, it was necessary to move the engine room forward from its position in the S90 to approximately amidships in the S102.

2.2.3   Strength Standard

The Inquiry initially adopted the LR 100A1 commercial strength standard in keeping with TGA's proposal to use such a standard for the S90. TGA later requested the Inquiry to modify the scantlings of the S102 obtained from the LR 100A1 standard to give equivalence to the Type 23 scantlings. This was done to reduce the steelweight of the S102 from that which would have been obtained if the LR 100A1 standard was used.   TGA stated that they did consider that a commercial standard was an advantage except when a weight penalty resulted in a design shortcoming such as not being able to achieve a specified speed. In this instance, as the power for the vessel was fixed, they wished to reduce the steelweight.

Given the stage of development of the S102, the process by which the S102 scantlings were modified was necessarily approximate. The scantlings for the S102 obtained using the LR 100A1 standard were either reduced or increased, taking into account the local spacings and spans of stiffening members in both the S102 and Type 23 designs, to obtain the equivalent structural elements of the Type 23 relative to a basis LR 100A1 standard. The resulting midship section for the S102 is shown in Figure 5.2.1.

Since strength standards are independent of hull form, this modification of the S102 scantlings was considered by the Inquiry to be acceptable. In the Inquiry's judgement, compliance with the appropriate naval strength standard, NES 110, would not present major problems and such compliance would not result in a significant change in the steelweight of the S102 above that estimated by the Inquiry for the modified scantlings obtained by the process described above.

The longitudinal framing system, specified for the S90, has been adopted for the S102 and commercial steel sections, materials and structural details have been used throughout.

2.2.4   Layout

In accordance with TGA's design principles, as demonstrated in the S90 design proposal and as conveyed to the Inquiry by TGA during the development of the S102, the following features have been preserved, where possible, by the Inquiry in the development of the S102:

i)   The concentration of the accommodation amidships.
ii)   A two passageway access system within the ship.

iii)   The surveillance and target identification radars mounted as high up as possible.

iv)   The position of the VCG kept as high as possible.

v)   The LCG positions to correspond, as close as possible, to those positions determined by BHC, from the S90 model tests, to be optimum with respect to minimising the resistance of the hull form.

In addition, the 'tweendeck height of 2.8m has been maintained, this being implicit in the S90 design proposal.

3.   The S102 Design

3.1   General Arrangement

The general arrangement of the S102 design is shown in Figures 5.3.1, 5.3.2 and 5.3.3. The resulting main particulars of the S102, compared with the original S90 design proposal, are as follows:

	S90	S102
Length overall	93.30 m	105.00 m
Length on design w.l	84.30 m	95.00 m
Greatest moulded breadth	19.00 m	21.40 m
Moulded breadth on design w.l	16.89 m	19.12 m
Moulded depth	10.50 m	11.40 m
Design draught	5.00 m	5.70 m
Deep draught	5.19 m	5.90 m
Extreme displacement	2830 tonnes	4108 tonnes

Spatial compliance with the NSR 7069 has been achieved as summarized below:

-       Sufficient internal deck area and volume is available in the S102 to accommodate the specified ship's complement, galley and dining spaces, storerooms, offices, workshops and all other necessary spaces to support the ship's company and their functions for the specified mission durations.

-       The specified weapon fit can be accommodated on the free upper deck and superstructure decks and the necessary control spaces can be incorporated in the available under-deck volume given over to such spaces.

- The flight deck and hangar size and disposition are sufficient to provide a suitable operational platform in spatial terms for the EH101 helicopter.

- Hull-mounted and towed array sonar equipment can be satisfactorily housed.

- The preliminary arrangement of masts and aerials in the S102 is considered to be such that after a normal programme of further development, satisfactory communications, navigation and electronic surveillance would be achieved.

- Sufficient space is provided for the CODLAG propulsion machinery specified by TGA. The performance of the S102 with this machinery installation, in terms of achievable speeds, is discussed in Chapter 6, Section 2.

- Nuclear, Biological, Chemical and Damage (NBCD) control arrangements, although not addressed in detail, could be satisfactorily arranged.

- RAS locations, reception areas and stores have been provided which, with subsequent design development, could be arranged to meet the replenishment rate requirements.

- Tankage is such as to provide sufficient volume for the stowage of AVCAT, fuel oil, lub oil and fresh water to meet the NSR mission availability requirements. The fuel oil capacity at the deep displacement provides a margin over and above the minimum range specified.

Figure 5.3.4 shows the outline of the S102 overlaid upon that of the Type 23 to provide a qualitative impression of relative sizes of the two ships. This figure can be compared with Figure 4.3.5 of Chapter 4 which compares the original S90 design proposal with the Type 23. It will be noted that the S102 is considerably larger than the S90 proposed by TGA. Figure 5.3.5 gives a qualitative comparison of the transverse profiles of the S102 and Type 23.

3.2   Lightweight

The lightweight of the S102 design has been calculated to be 3042 tonnes.

This lightweight is made up of the hull, propulsion, electrical, control and communication, auxiliary systems, outfit and furnishing and armament group weights.   With the exception of the hull group weight, a high level of confidence can be given to the derived weights since they have been based on the values supplied for the Type 23 which have been independently verified by the Inquiry.

With reference to the calculated hull weight, this must be regarded as the absolute minimum value since the S102 hull scantlings have been derived on the basis referred to in Section 2.2.3 with no design margin being included.   Experience indicates that the hull weight estimated at the design stage could grow by up to 5% for the ship when it is built and in an actual design and build programme a design margin would normally be included.

Taking account of a 5% design margin in the hull group weight and the steelweight which would be obtained using the LR 100A1 commercial strength standard originally proposed for the S90 by TGA, the possible variations in lightweight together with the corresponding weight growth values for the S102 are summarized below:

Scantling version	Hull Weight (tonnes)	Lightweight (tonnes)	Growth (tonnes)
Normalised, no design margin (Inquiry adopted values)	1402	3042	0
Normalised, with design margin	1472	3112	70
LR 100A1, no design margin	1527	3167	125
LR 100A1 plus design margin	1603	3243	201

3.3   Displacement, Trim and Stability

Using the lightweight value of 3042 tonnes, the deep displacement of the S102 has been calculated to be 4108 tonnes.   A Board Margin[1] of 45 tonnes has been included in this displacement.   The half oil displacement has been calculated to be 3800 tonnes.

Taking account of the possible variations in lightweight referred to in Section 3.2, the deep displacement of the S102 could vary between 4108 and 4309 tonnes depending on the strength standard and design

---

1.   Board Margin - 'This margin is to allow for all additions of weight after the final design caused by approved additions to weapon outfit, equipment, stores, fuel, etc, or any other deliberate design change that affects the weight of the ship.' - Naval Engineering Standard 109.

margin adopted. The half oil displacement would vary by similar amounts.

The initial trim and stability characteristics of the S102 in the deep displacement condition are given in Table 5.3.1.

A fuel load of 576 tonnes has been allocated in order that the S102 might achieve the NSR minimum required endurance range. This fuel load has been calculated assuming that the optimum LCG positions (and hence trim) would be achieved over the full range of displacement conditions.

Table 5.3.2 indicates the optimum LCG positions derived from the BHC S90 model test results for the S102 in the deep and half oil displacement conditions (4108 and 3800 tonnes respectively) at the corresponding NSR required maximum and endurance speeds. It will be noted from this table that these optimum LCG positions have not been achieved for the S102 design at its current stage of development. In particular, with the existing arrangement of tanks in the S102, the most favourable location of the LCG in the half oil condition is 3.9%L_{pp} forward of amidships. Since the location of fuel oil tanks above the design waterline is to be avoided for vulnerability reasons, subsequent iterations of the S102 design would have to move machinery and superstructure to a more forward location to achieve the large bow down trims required. To obtain the optimum LCG location when the speed is changed from the NSR maximum speed to the endurance speed in the half oil condition requires 300 tonnes of fuel oil to be transferred from aft to forward. At the 50%-fuel-used condition only 288 tonnes of fuel remain, and without salt water compensation the necessary trimming moment cannot be achieved when more than 48% of fuel has been used.

Further design iterations would have to achieve a more favourable lightweight LCG otherwise a powering penalty would be incurred which would increase the fuel load above 576 tonnes. However, the trimming moment required to achieve the required envelope of LCG locations is relatively independent of the lightweight LCG location. Therefore, the fuel tank volumes and their location would be unaffected by subsequent design iterations.

4.   **TGA's Involvement with the S102 Development**

In order to ensure that the design features which TGA saw as inherent in their S90 proposal were properly identified and incorporated in the S102 development, a number of informal meetings were held with TGA at which these features were discussed.

In addition, at TGA's request, it was agreed that TGA could undertake a limited design study in order that they could have an informed view of the Inquiry's S102 development. This study was funded by the Inquiry and a copy of the NSR 7069 dated 14th October 1985 was released to TGA to enable them to assess how the Inquiry satisfied the necessary spatial requirements associated with this NSR.

Resulting from this study, TGA produced an alternative outline design which they felt met the spatial requirements of the NSR and demonstrated their design concept. This study has been designated the S110. In developing the S110, TGA had scaled, independently, the length of the original S90 to a similar waterline length to that of the S102. However, the beam of the S90 was scaled by a smaller factor and, therefore, the L/B ratio was increased from about 5.0 for the S90 and S102 to 5.3 for the S110. TGA indicated that they had done this to reduce the power requirements of the S110. A further modification from the original S90 which TGA proposed for their S110 development was to reduce the superstructure height by dividing the tall centralised accommodation block of the original S90 proposal into separate blocks and distributing them in a similar fashion to those on the Type 23, i.e. along the length of the vessel. TGA stated that they had done this in order that the silhouette of their vessel corresponded, as far as possible, to that of the Type 23.

A meeting was held in September 1987, at which TGA's S110 study and the Inquiry's S102 design were discussed. The Inquiry's objective was to ensure that TGA were satisfied that the space allocated by the Inquiry to meet the NSR 7069 and the resulting calculated lightweight and displacements for the S102 were considered consistent with TGA's design concept.

It was established that a number of necessary spaces had not been allocated by TGA in their S110 study since they did not have the access that the Inquiry had to certain data. Hence the S110 was deficient in usable deck area by some 200m^2. However, TGA indicated that they would increase the superstructure height of their design by one tier to provide this extra required area. In addition, as TGA had situated two of the four diesel-generators along side the helicopter hangar, it had been necessary to reduce the width of the hangar. This was considered to be unacceptable and therefore TGA proposed that they would increase the beam to obtain the required hangar width; the beam of the S110 would then be similar to that of the S102. With reference to the deep displacement, the S110 was some 220 tonnes heavier than the S102 design. This was due to TGA using the LR 100A1 strength standard and not having access to accurate group weight data. Therefore, accepting that the S110 displacement could be reduced, it was felt that both designs were of a comparable displacement.

Based on the above assessment of both designs, the Inquiry concluded that the S102, when compared with the TGA S110 outline design, incorporated the design concepts that TGA had proposed, in some instances to a better degree than TGA themselves had achieved in their S110 study. TGA stated that they felt that the Inquiry's design was satisfactory in terms of size and general layout and they considered that their design concepts had been incorporated. In this respect, TGA considered that the S102 provided a reasonable basis (as far as size and general layout was concerned) on which to compare the S90 hull form against the NSR 7069 and, in addition, the Type 23 - although they reserved their full approval of the S102 until they could see the results of the calculations of speed, power and stability.

5.   **MoD's Involvement with the S102 Development**

During the development of the S102 (March to May 1987), at the Inquiry's request, the MoD submitted reference plans for the Type 23 frigate. These were critically appraised by the Inquiry. In addition, the design was discussed with the MoD Ship Department at Bath and the Yarrow Shipbuilders design team involved with the Type 23 frigate.

Further opportunities were taken to obtain a qualitative impression of space utilisation by visiting the Type 23 frigate 'HMS Norfolk' during construction at Yarrow Shipbuilders and the Type 22 frigates 'HMS Cornwall and 'HMS Broadsword' respectively nearing completion at Yarrow Shipbuilders and on exercise off Plymouth.

Though it must be recognised that any ship design is a compromise of a number of sometimes conflicting requirements, the Inquiry concluded that the Type 23 design had been the subject of close control in respect to the allocation of space associated with the NSR 7069. In this respect, the compartmental floor areas of the Type 23 have been taken as the minimum requirement for the S102. As the objective of the S102 design development was to provide the minimum space sufficient to accommodate all the spaces and equipment relating to the NSR, the compartmental floor areas allocated in the Type 23 have also been allocated in the S102. Furthermore, as the group weight data for the Type 23 is at an advanced level of definition, it has been utilised in determining the lightweight of the S102.

On completion of the S102 design, the general arrangement plans were shown to the MoD Type 23 design team at Bath. They raised no major objections to the proposed outline arrangements and weapon layout. In addition, after a normal programme of development, they considered that satisfactory communications, navigation and electronic surveillance would be achieved.

6.   Conclusions

Following the development by the Inquiry of the S102 design, TGA's agreement was obtained that the S102 provided a reasonable basis (as far as size and general layout was concerned) on which to compare the S90 hull form against the NSR 7069 and, in addition, the Type 23 - although they reserved their full approval of the S102 until they could see the results of the calculations of speed, power and stability.

Furthermore, the MoD raised no major objections to the proposed outline arrangements and weapon layout for the S102.

Therefore, although only a single iteration design, the Inquiry considered that the advantages and disadvantages of the S90 hull form for the purposes of meeting the NSR 7069 could be ascertained from an assessment of the S102 design in relation to the NSR 7069 and in comparison with the Type 23 frigate. Although the Type 23 is considerably more advanced than the S102, the Inquiry considers that the major hull form related issues are not dependent on the fully detailed development of either design and, therefore, a valid judgement can be made without further iteration of the S102 design.

With reference to the final displacements of the S102, it should be noted that these displacements have been based on taking the absolute minimum steelweight with no design margin and, in addition, assuming that the vessel could achieve the optimum trims required to avoid an increase in resistance. If a design margin was incorporated, which is normal practice, and the vessel was designed to the LR 100A1 strength standard, as originally proposed for the S90, then the S102 steelweight would increase by about 200 tonnes. At the current stage of iteration, the optimum trims have not been achieved. If further iteration did not produce the required optimum trim, then a powering penalty would be incurred with a resulting increase in the required fuel load and a corresponding increase in the displacement of the S102. In this respect, the Inquiry has given the S102 every benefit in terms of its estimated displacement.

Item	S102
Draught aft (m)	5.02
Draught fwd (m)	6.71
Bow down trim (m)	1.69
VCG (m)	8.40
KM (m)	13.98
GM (solid) (even keel) (m)	5.58
GM (fluid) (trimmed) (m)	4.92

Table 5.3.1   S102 - Trim & Initial Stability Condition at 4108 Tonne Displacement

	NSR Maximum Speed Mode		NSR Endurance Mode	
	Optimum	Actual	Optimum	Actual
Displacement (tonnes)	4108	4108	3800	3800
LCG position (fwd)	2.0%L_{pp}	1.6%L_{pp}	7.1%L_{pp}	3.9%L_{pp}
Bow down trim (m)	1.74	1.69	3.66	2.41
Draught aft (m)	4.91	5.02	4.10	4.65
Draught fwd (m)	6.85	6.71	7.76	7.06

Table 5.3.2   S102 Trim Conditions

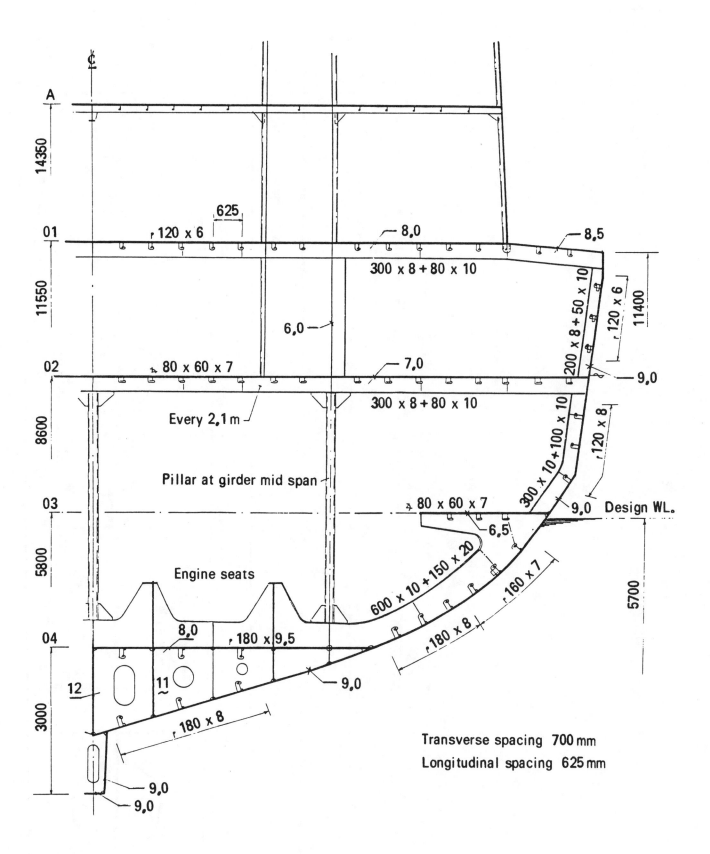

FIGURE 5.2.1   S102 MIDSHIP SECTION (NORMALISED SCANTLINGS)

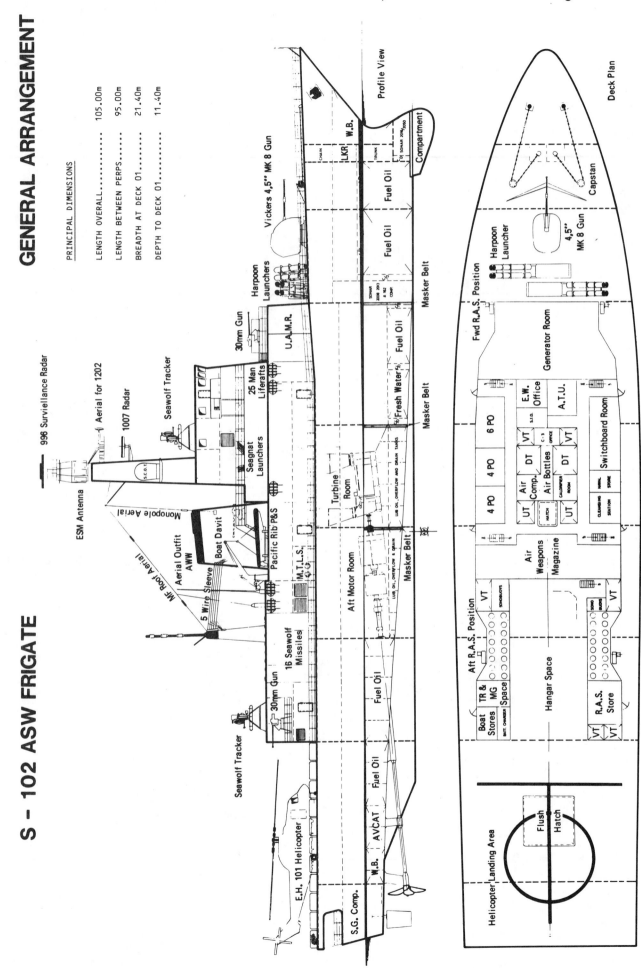

FIGURE 5.3.1   S102 GENERAL ARRANGEMENT

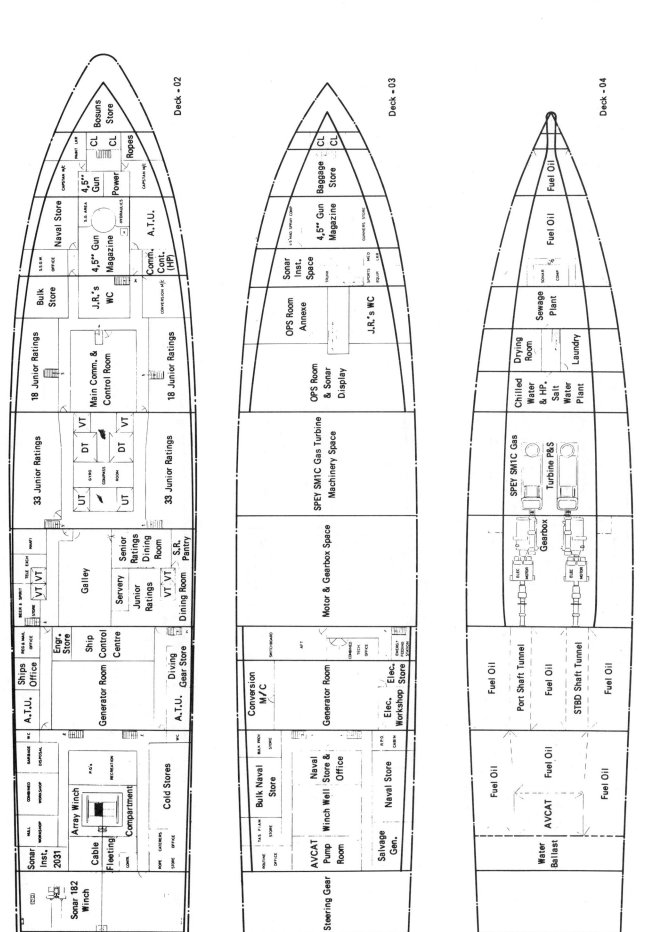

FIGURE 5.3.2   S102 GENERAL ARRANGEMENT

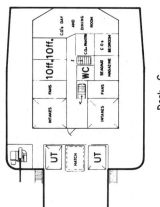

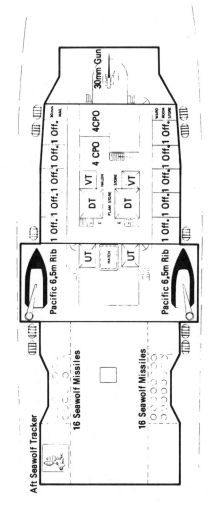

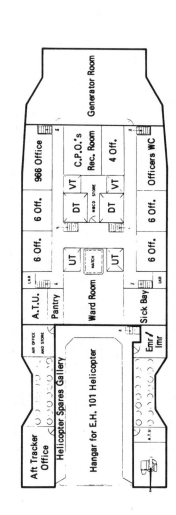

FIGURE 5.3.3   S102 GENERAL ARRANGEMENT

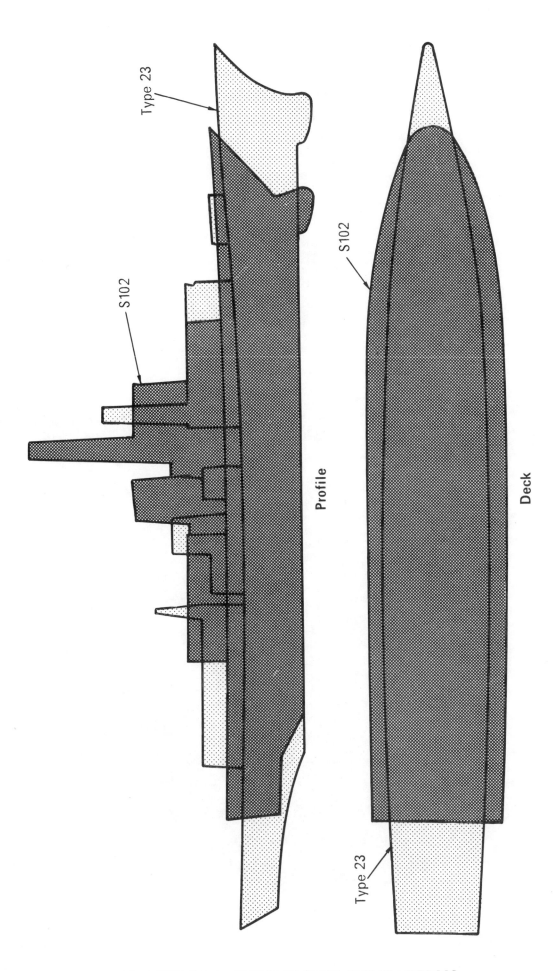

FIGURE 5.3.4   TYPE 23/S102 COMPARISON

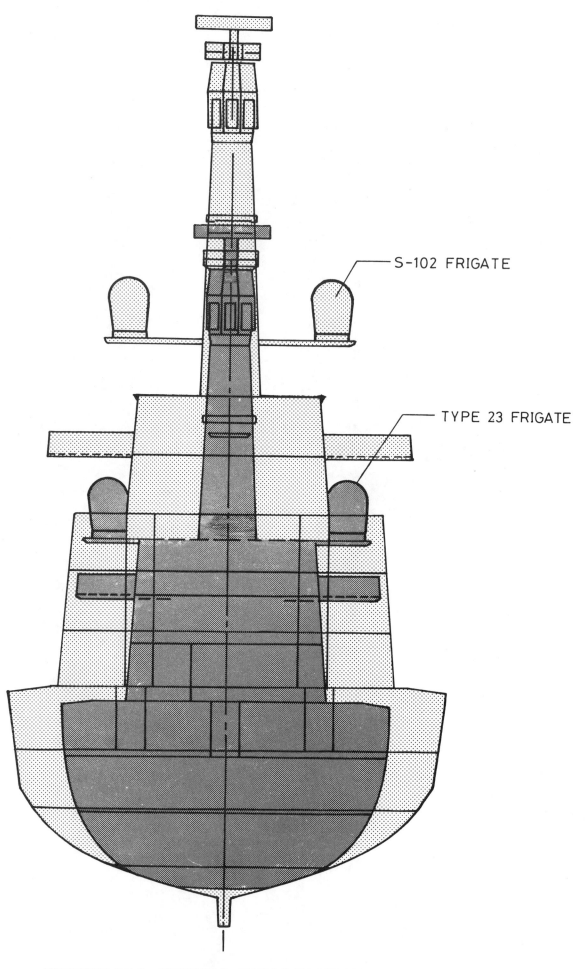

FIGURE 5.3.5   TYPICAL CROSS-SECTION OVERLAY

CHAPTER 6

ASSESSMENT OF THE S102 DESIGN

1.   General

This chapter presents, in detail, the Inquiry's assessment of the Sirius design concept, as embodied in the S102 design based on the S90 hull form. The following key issues are addressed in the respective sections:

Section 2	Speed, Power and Endurance
Section 3	Space, Layout, Structural Design and Weight
Section 4	Intact and Damaged Stability
Section 5	Seakeeping
Section 6	Manoeuvrability
Section 7	Military Features
Section 8	Construction Costs and Build Time
Section 9	Through Life Costs

Where possible, the performance of the S102 design, in the areas listed above, has been assessed in relation to the requirements of the NSR 7069. However, in order to identify the advantages and disadvantages of the S90 hull form in relation to a current frigate hull form, the S102 design has also been compared, where possible, with the Type 23. In some of the areas examined, the NSR has no specific requirements. In such cases, the assessment has been based principally on a comparison of the S102 with the Type 23.

The introduction to each section summarizes the principal claimed advantages made for either the Sirius design concept or the S90 design proposal. The methodology adopted by the Inquiry to assess these claims is also outlined in the introduction. Each section concludes with a summary of the Inquiry's findings along with comments on the respective claims. The reader can therefore obtain an overview of the Inquiry's assessment from a reading of the introduction and conclusion to each section alone.

CHAPTER 6

ASSESSMENT OF THE S102 DESIGN

SECTION 2
Speed, Power and Endurance

2.1   Introduction

The points of disagreement relating to the claimed propulsive performance of the S90 hull form are discussed in Chapter 4, Section 4. This section presents the Inquiry's assessment of the S102's speed, power and endurance capabilities compared with the NSR 7069 requirements.

The Inquiry's assessment of the propulsive performance of the S102 is based on the S90 model tests performed by BHC and NMI in 1982 and 1983 respectively, the results of which were submitted to the Inquiry by TGA. The method adopted by the Inquiry to analyse these model test results and to obtain the resulting power estimates for the S102 has been fully discussed and agreed with TGA.

The propulsive performance of the S102 has also been compared with that of the Type 23 frigate so that a quantitative assessment of the power required for each hull form to achieve given speeds can be made.

In addition, TGA's concept of altering the operating trim of a vessel based on their hull form, in order to minimise its resistance for different speeds, has been assessed.   It should be noted that throughout the Inquiry's assessment of the propulsive performance of the S102, it has been assumed that the trims determined by BHC to be optimum can be achieved. As indicated in Chapter 5, Section 3.3, these trims have not been achieved following the single design iteration. The consequences of not achieving the optimum trims have also been assessed.

2.2   NSR 7069 Speed and Endurance Requirements

The NSR 7069 stipulates three specific speeds which must be achieved by a proposed vessel, namely:

      i)   a maximum quiet speed with the towed array sonar deployed
      ii)   an endurance speed
      iii)   a maximum speed

These speeds are to be achieved with the vessel in the deep displacement condition with a specified allowance made for fouling of the underwater hull.

The NSR specifies a target endurance range along with a stipulated minimum required range. The necessary fuel capacity to achieve these ranges is calculated on the basis of the power required to propel the vessel in the half oil displacement condition at the endurance speed.

2.3   The S102 Powering Estimate

The method of analysis adopted by the Inquiry to determine the power requirements of the S102 is outlined in Figure 6.2.1. The following sub-sections describe how data have been obtained, or derived, for the steps outlined in Figure 6.2.1.

2.3.1   Naked Hull Resistance

The resistance of the S102 has been determined from model tests performed in 1983 by NMI using a 1:20 scale model of the S90. The tests were performed at a displacement which corresponds to neither the deep nor the half oil displacement conditions of the S102. Nevertheless, they are considered by the Inquiry to provide a reliable basis for estimating the resistance of the S102, since the S102 hull form is a geosim of the S90 hull form. Tests performed previously by BHC in 1982 using a 1:43.57 scale model of the S90 at a number of displacements and trims have been used by the Inquiry to factor the NMI test results to the required displacements.

The resistance of the S102 has been calculated using the ITTC(1957) friction line and appropriate procedure to scale from model to full size.

2.3.2   Fouling

The NSR 7069 stipulates that the required speeds must be achieved with the ship in a fouled condition. The MoD have specified the fouling allowances which should be applied, at the design stage, to the frictional component of resistance. The allowances account not only for increased resistance due to fouling, but also for increases in resistance due to roughening and damage to hull coatings, propeller fouling and other effects which, during service, will impair the propulsive performance of the ship. The appropriate allowance to be made depends on whether the ship is coated with conventional paint or erodable anti-fouling (EAF) paint. For the S102, the smaller allowance, associated with EAF paint, has been applied in the powering calculations.

2.3.3   Appendages and Wind Resistance

The contributions of the following appendages to the resistance of the S102 have been considered:

> Stern Gear (shafting, shaft brackets and rudders)
> Noise Reduction Equipment
> Hull Mounted Sonar
> Bilge Keels
> Stabilisers

The effective power absorbed by the shafting and shaft brackets has been determined from the NMI model tests. Rudders were not fitted for the resistance tests, in accordance with the BTTP procedure used by NMI; their effect on resistance is taken into account by the ship performance prediction factor adopted (see Section 2.3.6 of this chapter).

The NSR 7069 requires provision to be made for the fitting of certain external hull mounted equipment to reduce hull radiated noise. The effective power absorbed by such equipment has been taken, in the absence of other data, to be the same as that for the Type 23.

The optimum resistance characteristics of the S102 bow mounted sonar dome would normally be obtained by extensive model testing, performed in conjunction with re-design of the sonar dome and the forward part of the hull. It can reasonably be assumed that the hull and sonar dome could be designed so as to have little effect on the power requirements at maximum speed. TGA have indicated that they would adopt such an approach to designing the sonar dome. The additional resistance which would be incurred at lower speeds has been taken to be, in absolute terms, the same as that for the Type 23.

Bilge keels, although normally fitted to RN frigates, have not been incorporated in the S102 design as TGA have stated that bilge keels are not consistent with their S90 design concept.

TGA have stated that the stabilisers to be fitted should be of the retractable variety and would only be used at low speeds. Therefore, for the purposes of the Inquiry's powering estimate, it has been assumed that the stabilisers are deployed when the ship is operated in the diesel-electric mode (slow speed) and retracted in the CODLAG mode (high speed). In the absence of resistance data being provided to the Inquiry for the stabilisers proposed for the S90, the Inquiry has consulted the available literature and concluded that the appendage resistance due to the stabilisers can be taken to be the same as that for the Type 23.

Wind resistance has been calculated using the method described in Reference 6.2.1.

The effective powers absorbed by the appendages have been taken to be the same in both the deep and the half oil displacement conditions.

2.3.4   Towed Array Sonar

The resistance/speed characteristics of the towed array sonar have been provided to the Inquiry by the MoD.

2.3.5   Propulsive Efficiency

2.3.5.1   Hull Efficiency Elements

The NMI model test report contains curves of thrust deduction t, Taylor wake fraction w_T and relative rotative efficiency η_R for the S90 hull form at 2600 tonnes displacement. As NMI and BHC only performed propulsion tests for the S90 at 2600 tonnes displacement, the Inquiry has consulted the available literature to ascertain the effect a change in displacement has on the values of η_R and the hull efficiency η_H, where

$$\eta_H \quad = \quad \frac{1 - t}{1 - w_T}$$

It has been concluded that, in this instance, the change in displacement has little effect on these values and that the NMI values of t, w_T and η_R can be applied to the S102, at corresponding Froude numbers, in both the deep and half oil displacement conditions.

2.3.5.2   Propeller Efficiency

The model propulsion tests undertaken by NMI were performed using stock propellers selected to meet, as closely as practicable, the specification provided by TGA for the S90. However, the NMI stock propellers cannot be used for the S102 because their cavitation characteristics are unacceptable. Therefore, a propeller design has been developed by the Inquiry specifically for the S102. It should be noted that the maximum open water efficiency, η_o, predicted by NMI for a suitable propeller design for the S90 is close to the maximum value for the propeller design developed by the Inquiry for the S102.

2.3.5.3   Quasi-Propulsive Coefficient

The quasi-propulsive coefficient QPC, which relates effective power to delivered power (i.e. the power delivered to the propellers), is calculated using the expression:

$$QPC \ = \ \eta_H.\eta_R.\eta_o$$

The QPC has been calculated using η_H and η_R determined from the NMI model test results and η_o for the propeller design developed for the S102.

The delivered power determined by the model tests can be obtained from the expression:

$$\text{Delivered power} \quad = \quad \frac{\text{Effective power}}{QPC}$$

2.3.6 Ship Performance Prediction Factor

As indicated in Chapter 4, Section 4.4.1, it is not possible to calculate directly from model tests the exact power that will be required for a full scale ship to attain a given speed. In order to obtain an estimate of the power required for the full scale ship, the delivered power derived from the model tests is multiplied by a performance prediction factor. In accordance with the BTTP procedure which NMI used for the S90 model tests, this factor is commonly referred to as the (1+x) factor. The S102 powering estimates have been determined using (1+x) values of 1.0 and 0.9. The selection of these values is discussed in Chapter 4, Section 4.4.5. Applying these performance prediction factors enables the delivered power required for the full scale ship to attain the necessary speeds to be predicted.

2.4   **Propulsion System**

Given the predicted delivered power required for a ship to achieve certain speeds, the naval architect normally selects a machinery installation which will provide this power taking into account the transmission efficiencies associated with the chosen machinery configuration. However, in the case of the S102, the machinery to be fitted was proposed by TGA (see Chapter 5, Section 2.2.2), as follows:

2 ×	Spey SM1C Gas Turbines	2 ×	18	MW mcr
2 ×	GEC Brush Electric Motors	2 ×	1.5	MW mcr
4 ×	Paxman Diesel-Generators	4 ×	1.3	MW mcr

Two modes of propulsion have been considered:

i)   Diesel-electric:
        Propulsion power is provided by the two direct drive electric motors, one mounted on each shaft, power for which is provided by the four diesel-generator sets. This mode of propulsion, being the most quiet, would be used when the towed array sonar is deployed. In addition, as this mode of propulsion is the most fuel efficient for the proposed machinery installation, it has been used to evaluate the NSR endurance range requirement.

        The maximum achievable quiet towed array speed and the endurance speed have been evaluated using the diesel-electric mode of propulsion.

ii)   Combined diesel-electric and gas turbine ('CODLAG'):
        Propulsion power is provided principally by the two gas turbines which are augmented by the two electric motors.

The maximum service speed of the S102 has been evaluated with the ship propelled simultaneously by the two gas turbines and the two electric motors.

The efficiencies of the elements of the transmission system relating to these two modes of propulsion have been sought from equipment manufacturers. Where such data were unobtainable, appropriate data provided by the MoD for the Type 23 have been used since the Type 23 has a similar CODLAG propulsion system.

Based on these efficiencies, the speeds appropriate to the NSR specified conditions that can be achieved by the S102, given the proposed machinery installation, have been determined.

2.5   S102 Achievable Speeds

2.5.1   Maximum Quiet Speed with the Towed Array Sonar Deployed

The S102 would not meet the NSR maximum required quiet speed with the towed array sonar deployed when propelled by the two 1.5MW electric motors, the short-fall being 1.4 knots (1.1 knots with $(1+x) = 0.9$). An increase in the installed electric motor power of 49% (37% with $(1+x) = 0.9$) would be needed to meet the NSR requirement.

2.5.2   Endurance Speed

The S102 would not meet the NSR required endurance speed when propelled by the two 1.5MW electric motors, the short-fall being 1.6 knots (1.3 knots with $(1+x) = 0.9$). An increase in the installed electric motor power of 53% (37% with $(1+x) = 0.9$) would be needed to meet the NSR requirement.

2.5.3   Maximum Speed

The S102 would not meet the NSR required maximum speed when propelled by the two 1.5MW electric motors and two SM1C gas turbines, the short-fall being 2.5 knots (1.8 knots with $(1+x) = 0.9$). An increase in the installed gas turbine power of 41% (25% with $(1+x) = 0.9$), in addition to the increase in electric motor power identified above, would be needed to meet the NSR requirement.

2.6   Machinery Configurations to Achieve NSR Required Speeds

This section examines possible machinery configurations which could provide sufficient power for the S102 to achieve the NSR required speeds. It should be noted that it is assumed in this section that the proposed configurations could be installed without altering the current size and displacement of the S102 and that optimum trim is achieved. The spatial implications of the proposed machinery installations are discussed in Section 3 of this chapter.

2.6.1   Diesel-Electric Mode

Both the maximum required quiet speed with the towed array sonar deployed and the endurance speed, as indicated in Section 2.4, are to be achieved using the electric motors alone. Of these two requirements, it is the endurance speed which would require the greater power to be provided by the electric motors. To satisfy this requirement would require the maximum continuous rating (mcr) of the electric motors to be increased from 2×1.5MW to a minimum of 2×2.3MW (2×2.1MW with $(1+x) = 0.9$).

Increased diesel-generator capacity would need to be installed in order to meet the increased demand of these larger electric motors. This additional generator capacity could either be provided by more diesel-generators or by replacing the existing generators with larger units. Each solution would have to be carefully evaluated with respect to operational efficiency and noise characteristics. For the purposes of the Inquiry, and since no major penalty would be anticipated, it has been assumed that the additional capacity would be provided by one Paxman 1.3MW generator.

2.6.2   Combined Diesel-Electric and Gas Turbine Mode

To meet the maximum speed requirement of the NSR 7069, a combined machinery installation capable of delivering at least 52MW (46MW with $(1+x) = 0.9$) would be required.

Although the 1.5MW electric motors are de-rated to approximately 60% mcr at the maximum speed, it has been established that the 2.3MW motors could be designed to deliver their full rated power up to this speed, the penalty being an increase in motor size which would have a consequential effect on the space required for the installation.

Assuming that the 2.3MW electric motors deliver their full rated power at the NSR maximum required speed, a gas turbine installation rated at 51MW (45MW with $(1+x) = 0.9$) would be required (assuming appropriate transmission efficiencies).

It has been assumed that a suitable gas turbine configuration to provide this power for the S102 would be selected from the following list of marinised turbine units which are available and in use on Royal Navy ships:

Tyne RM1C	3.98 MW mcr
Spey SM1A	12.75 MW mcr
Spey SM1C (not yet in service)	18.00 MW mcr
Olympus TM3C	21.78 MW mcr

The use of other marine gas turbine options, such as ducted fan engines (e.g. the RB 211 (24.4MW mcr), which is known to be in use on offshore installations) have not been considered as viable alternatives at this time in view of their unproven suitability for naval applications.

Configurations which would provide approximately the required power therefore include:

(a)	4 × Spey SM1A turbines	(51.00 MW mcr)
(b)	3 × Spey SM1C turbines	(54.00 MW mcr)
(c)	2 × Olympus + 1 × Spey SM1A	(56.31 MW mcr)
(d)	2 × Olympus + 2 × Tyne	(51.52 MW mcr)

Of these options only (a) and (d) are considered practical as the other two options would present considerable difficulties either in terms of gearboxes to provide drive from three engines to two shafts or in terms of accommodating a triple screw arrangement.

Whether option (a) or (d) is chosen, suitable gearboxes would be required and unless the available ship beam just above the level of the inner bottom was adequate to accommodate four turbines abreast, a substantial increase in ship length would possibly be required to facilitate a twin in-line turbine arrangement and the associated uptakes/downtakes. The implications of these alternative machinery configurations on space and layout are considered in Section 3 of this chapter.

2.7   Required Endurance Range

As indicated in Section 2.5.2, the S102 will not achieve the NSR required endurance speed with the two 1.5MW electric motors fitted. However, in order to calculate the fuel load to achieve the NSR minimum required endurance range, the calculations have been performed on the assumption that the necessary increase in power is available (i.e. the two 2.3MW electric motors are installed and adequate diesel-generator capacity is provided) and that this increased power could be installed without changing the size and displacement of the vessel.

The endurance calculations have been carried out using the resistance characteristics of the S102 in the half oil displacement condition.

The S102's hotel load has also been taken into account when calculating fuel consumption and hence endurance. The 24 hour mean cruising hotel load has been determined on the basis of the data provided by the MoD for the Type 23.

Having established the total rate of fuel consumption for the S102 at the endurance speed, the usable fuel capacity allocated provides an operational range which meets the minimum requirements of the NSR 7069 (see also Chapter 5, Section 3.3).

2.8   Comparison with the Type 23

The Inquiry has carried out its own estimate of the Type 23 powering performance and has no reason to doubt that the design, as submitted, will achieve the NSR speed requirements.

The Type 23, having been designed to also meet the NSR 7069, enables a comparison to be made between the delivered power required for the S90 hull form to achieve a given speed and the corresponding delivered power required for a current frigate hull form to achieve the same speed.

The S102 requires 59% (42% with $(1+x) = 0.9$) more power to achieve the NSR required endurance speed.

The S102 requires 111% (87% with $(1+x) = 0.9$) more power to achieve the NSR required maximum speed.

In addition, the endurance range of the Type 23 adequately meets the NSR minimum requirement and is considerably in excess of that of the S102.

2.9   Effect of Trim on S102 Powering Estimates

TGA have stated that it is a fundamental part of their concept to be able to trim the vessel in order to reduce transom immersion, and that by moving the LCG forward, up to a 50% reduction in resistance at the deep displacement could be achieved at low speeds. Conversely, an increase in resistance would be incurred if optimum trims are not maintained throughout the speed range.

Tests performed by BHC in 1982 using a scale model of the S90 determined the variation of optimum LCG with speed. Subsequent model tests by BHC and NMI were performed using LCG positions determined by interpolation from the positions which BHC assessed to be optimum. The following observations have been made:

- optimum LCG moves aft with increasing speed;
- optimum LCG varies more with speed at lower displacements.

The Inquiry's assessment of the propulsive performance of the S102 has assumed that the trim, determined by BHC to be optimum for the S90, can be achieved in all conditions by the re-distribution of fuel. However, as indicated in Chapter 5, Section 3.3, the optimum LCG positions have not been achieved after the single design iteration. This would result in an increase in required power at the endurance speed of approximately 8% whilst at the maximum speed, only a small increase in required power would occur.

The TGA statement that up to a 50% reduction in resistance could be achieved at low speeds by moving the LCG forward, requires the optimum LCG positions for high speed operation to be approximately 15%L_{pp} aft of the optimum position for low speed operation. Such a position is outside the anticipated operating envelope for the S102, hence the TGA statement cannot be substantiated.

Furthermore, although the percentage variation in resistance with trim is large at low speeds, the absolute variations in power are small. For example, operating the S102 at 5 knots with the LCG appropriate to the maximum required speed results in an increase in required power of 30%, but in absolute terms this is only about 40kW. In view of this small penalty, the Inquiry considers that the rapid fuel transfer system proposed by TGA to enable the trim of the vessel to be altered quickly is unnecessary. On those occasions when the vessel would require to change trim quickly to maintain optimum trim, i.e. in a 'sprint and drift' mode, the trim could remain at the value appropriate to the sprint speed, the consequential power penalty at the drift speed being small in absolute terms and, therefore, not warranting the additional complication of a rapid fuel transfer system.

However, the necessity of operating the S102 at optimum trims, particularly at the endurance speed, to avoid significant increases in resistance, means that sufficient tankage in appropriate locations must be provided along with the necessary quantity of fuel to achieve the required trims. As indicated in Chapter 5, Section 3.3, the vessel cannot achieve the required trimming moment when more than 48% of fuel has been consumed without resorting to salt water compensation. This is considered by the Inquiry to be an operational disadvantage.

It should be noted that the Type 23 propulsive performance is relatively insensitive to its operational trims.

2.10   Conclusions

The S102 does not meet any of the NSR speed requirements when propelled by the machinery installation proposed by TGA.

The shortfalls in speeds are:

i)   maximum quiet speed with the towed array sonar deployed - 1.4 knots (1.1 knots with $(1+x) = 0.9$)

ii)   endurance speed   -   1.6 knots (1.3 knots with $(1+x) = 0.9$)

iii)   maximum speed   -   2.5 knots (1.8 knots with $(1+x) = 0.9$)

An increase of 53% (37% with $(1+x) = 0.9$) in the electric motor power output is required to achieve those speeds which are to be obtained on electric motors alone. An increase of 41% (25% with $(1+x) = 0.9$) in the gas turbine output is then required to achieve the NSR maximum speed.

Comparison of the delivered power requirements of the S102 with the Type 23 indicates that, at the endurance speed, the S102 requires 59% (42% with $(1+x) = 0.9$) more power than the Type 23, while at the NSR maximum speed the S102 requires 111% (87% with $(1+x) = 0.9$) more power than the Type 23.

The necessity of having to achieve optimum trims to avoid a powering penalty is considered by the Inquiry to be an operational disadvantage for the S102 compared with the Type 23.

References

6.2.1   'Principles of Naval Architecture', ed. COMSTOCK, J.P., Society of Naval Architects and Marine Engineers, 1977.

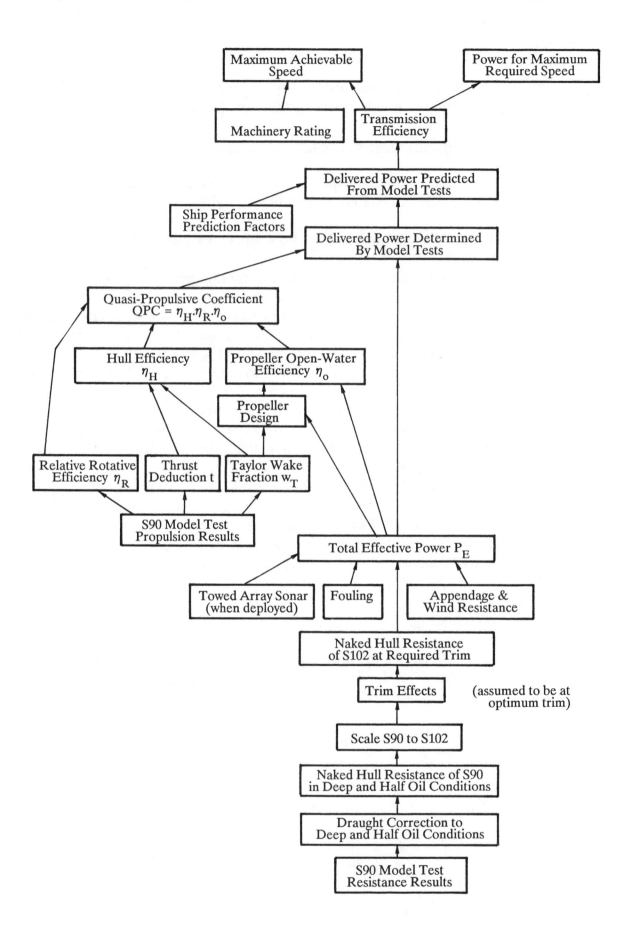

FIGURE 6.2.1   CALCULATION PROCEDURE

CHAPTER 6

ASSESSMENT OF THE S102 DESIGN

SECTION 3
Space, Layout, Structural Design and Weight

3.1   Introduction

The S102 described in Chapter 5 provides a design which is of a sufficient size to meet the spatial requirements associated with the NSR 7069 and, in addition, incorporates the features which TGA considered to be inherent in their S90 design proposal.   This section examines the advantages and disadvantages, in spatial, structural and weight terms, of adopting the S90 hull form in preference to a current hull form for an ASW frigate designed to meet the NSR 7069.   It should be noted that the spatial aspects of weapon layout are dealt with in Section 7 of this chapter.

TGA claim that the S90 hull form would provide an increase in useful internal volume compared with a vessel based on a conventional hull form. This extra internal volume would enable:

i)   More accommodation to be situated in the midship region of the ship where vertical motions are least, thereby reducing crew fatigue.

ii)   Two fore and aft passageways (compared with one in a conventional ship) which give alternative access routes. This would be particularly useful in fire or damaged conditions.

iii)   More available 'elbow room' due to the generally greater size of the compartments compared with those in a conventional ship.   This would provide improved access and enable fitting out to be carried out more easily.

Due to the greater beam in the engine room area, it is claimed that it would be possible to fit a wider variety of machinery configurations than is possible in a conventional frigate.

TGA also claim that, as the vessel is shorter, it would be less likely to suffer from structural failure as a conventional vessel because the longitudinal stresses would be smaller.

TGA have indicated that a major advantage of a vessel designed according to their Sirius concept arises from the ability of the vessel to operate at over twice the displacement of conventional warships of the same length.   The Hill-Norton Committee indicated (paragraph 35 of their report) that, as a result of the increase in beam afforded by the Sirius hull form, it would be possible to sustain a displacement of between two and three times that normally associated with a given length of a traditional long/thin hull.

The Inquiry has assessed all these claims by comparing the S102 with the Type 23 since the NSR 7069 does not contain any specific reference to these matters.

3.2   Comparison of Area, Volume and 'Elbow Room'

3.2.1   Area

The compartmental floor areas in the Type 23, having been closely controlled with respect to the allocation of space associated with the requirements of NSR 7069 (see Chapter 5, Section 5), have been taken as the minimum requirement for the S102.   As the objective of the S102 development was to provide the minimum space sufficient to accommodate all the spaces and equipment relating to the NSR, the compartmental floor areas allocated in the Type 23 have been allocated in the S102.   In this respect, the usable deck area of the individual compartments of the two designs are similar.

The total usable 'tweendeck area provided in the S102 is about 0.4% more than in the Type 23.   As the S102 design is the result of a single design iteration, some rationalisation of space allocation would be expected during subsequent design development.

3.2.2   Volume

Although the usable 'tweendeck areas of the two designs are similar, the total enclosed volume of the hull and superstructure of the S102 exceeds that of the Type 23 by 27%, about half of which is contained in the hull below the upper deck.   This additional volume is distributed as follows:

i)   9.7% is attributable to the difference in the 'tweendeck heights of the S102 and Type 23.   The greater height in the S102 leads to an increase in the volume of every 'tweendeck space.   However, the adoption of a commercial structure in the S102 leads to deeper steel sections being fitted underneath the decks compared with those fitted in the Type 23.   This effectively reduces the available 'tweendeck height from 2.8m to 2.49m which limits the increase of space for the fitting of cables, piping and trunking.

It should be noted that 'tweendeck height is not a function of hull form and increased 'tweendeck height could also be adopted in a conventional frigate hull if the associated penalty of increased displacement and power was considered acceptable.

ii)   3.2% is attributable to the larger fuel tanks. This increase in volume is required mainly to enable the necessary trimming moment to be achieved in order that the envelope of change of LCG position for minimum hull resistance can be obtained in accordance with TGA's design philosophy.   Since the fuel tanks have to be situated at the ends of the ship to achieve the necessary trimming moments, additional cofferdam spaces have had to be introduced to separate fuel tank boundaries from the Mk 8 gun magazine. The cofferdam spaces constitute another 0.7% of the volume.

iii)   5.2% is attributable to the larger main turbine and motor rooms. Although these rooms are similar in length for both designs, the S102 is deeper and considerably beamier than the Type 23, and hence most of the excess engine room volume is located at the ship's sides and deckhead as shown in Figure 6.3.1.

iv)   0.8% is attributable to the larger generator spaces. Extra deck area has been allocated in view of the additional generating capacity which, as indicated in Section 2 of this chapter, would be required in any subsequent design iteration in order to provide sufficient power to drive the larger electric motors necessary for the S102 to achieve the required NSR speeds.

v)   2.6% is attributable to the larger steering gear space. This extra volume is entirely due to the very broad transom which is a feature of the S90 hull form since the length of this space is similar to that in the Type 23.

vi)   0.8% is attributable to the larger turbine uptakes and downtakes which are longer due to the passage through more decks, and are of greater cross-sectional area due to the higher power.

vii)   2.6% is attributable to the twin passageway system compared with the single passageway system in the Type 23.

The residual excess in volume of 1.4% results mainly from the appreciable slope of the body lines compared with those of the Type 23 in way of dry compartments at the ship's sides. A qualitative impression of the distribution of this residual excess volume is given in Figure 6.3.2 (the different lengths of the two vessels should be taken into account when examining this diagram). No deck area is directly associated with this extra volume and its use may, therefore, be restricted to the provision of racks or lockers, or for the mounting of minor machinery and equipment suitable for direct contact with the outer hull.

3.2.3 'Elbow Room'

'Elbow room' has been interpreted to mean the provision of adequate volumetric space around and between structure and equipment in which no linear dimension is so restrictive as to inhibit the ready access of men to work freely. In practice, linear separation in the horizontal plane will tend to be the most important dimension and this is a direct function of the floor area of individual compartments. As indicated in Section 3.2.1, the floor areas and shapes of compartments of the S102 are similar to those of the

Type 23 and, therefore, it is considered that the S102 has no significant extra 'elbow room' compared with the Type 23.

3.3   Layout

A feature of the broader beam of the S90 hull form is that a two access passageway system can be accommodated. This passageway system is considered to be an advantage compared with the single passageway provided in a conventional frigate, since it would ease thoroughfare within the ship for stores, equipment and personnel and would enhance access in routine and operational situations and escape in emergencies.

The concept of concentrating the accommodation amidships, in order to take advantage of the lower vertical accelerations arising from the ship motions in this region, has been preserved, as far as possible. However, the implications of the lateral accelerations, particularly at the bridge height, also need to be considered and both of these aspects are discussed in Section 5 of this chapter.

The concentration of all the accommodation in a single block increases vulnerability to a single missile strike. If the concentration of the accommodation amidships is to be maintained, then there is limited scope for re-arranging the compartment allocation to reduce the vulnerability. However, the greater stability margin would allow armour plating to be fitted, as suggested by TGA. Notwithstanding the possible effectiveness of armour plating, the increase in displacement and further increase in the required power, if such plating were to be fitted, would need to be assessed.

As the hull-mounted sonar must be located at the bow to provide adequate separation from the ship's machinery, there is less below-waterline space available forward in the S102 for the larger fuel oil tanks which would be necessary to achieve the bow down trims required to minimise resistance.

3.4   Propulsion Machinery Arrangement

The apparent advantage of the greater beam of the S102 cannot be fully realised in the region of the machinery spaces. This is a consequence of the S90 hull form which incorporates a deep skeg and a significant rise of floor from the centreline. As indicated in Figure 6.3.1, these features reduce the available height between the bottom shell and the tank top in way of the motor room, particularly outboard of the centreline. This makes it difficult to provide adequate structural supports under the turbines and particularly under the electric motors. To improve this aspect in any subsequent design iteration, it may be necessary to move the machinery spaces and superstructure further forward to permit the double bottom height to be increased. It should be noted that the tank top cannot be raised from its existing position without increasing the shaft rake and incurring a consequential penalty in propeller generated noise (see Section 7 of this chapter for discussion of propeller noise aspects) and a reduction in propeller efficiency.

As indicated in Section 2 of this chapter, the machinery configuration proposed by TGA does not provide sufficient power for the S102 to achieve the NSR required speeds. Section 2.6 discussed possible machinery configurations which could be fitted in order that the S102 might achieve the NSR required speeds; it was concluded that a practical configuration would require a minimum of four turbine units to be installed. At the current stage of development, the S102 has insufficient beam available at the tank top level to accommodate further turbine units abreast of each other. Therefore, a major re-design of the vessel would be required, possibly involving an increase in the length of the ship, to accommodate the extra turbine units. Such a re-design would obviously have major consequences on the other aspects of the design.

An important consideration in the location of main and auxiliary machinery is removal routes for repair or unit replacement. The four diesel-generators fitted in the S102 are located in similar positions to those in the Type 23 design, for vulnerability and noise reduction reasons, i.e. two sets below the main deck and two sets in the superstructure. Removal routes for the diesel-generators and electric propulsion motors are comparable in the two designs. Removal routes for the turbine units will be longer in the S102 by virtue of the passage through four decks compared with three decks in the Type 23.

The noise implications relating to the location of the diesel-generators are discussed in Section 7 of this chapter.

3.5   Structural Design

TGA requested that the Inquiry modify the scantlings of the S102 obtained using the LR 100A1 commercial standard to give equivalence with the Type 23. (This aspect is discussed in Chapter 5, Section 2.2.3). Therefore, the scantlings of the S102 have not been obtained from a specific strength standard. However, since strength standards are independent of hull form and therefore commercial strength standards are as applicable to the Type 23 as they are to the S102, this is not considered relevant to this investigation. In the Inquiry's judgement, compliance with the appropriate naval strength standard, NES 110, would not present major problems and such compliance would not result in a significant change in the steelweight of the S102 above that which the Inquiry has already estimated for the S102 normalised scantlings.

The differences in structural response resulting from the differences in the hull proportions of the S102 and Type 23 have been assessed by the Inquiry.

If both ships were designed to the same standard of hull girder and local strength, their service performance in terms of encounter with extreme sea-states and in terms of fatigue would be similar. However, if local strength criteria dictated the scantlings of the shorter design whilst hull girder strength criteria dictated the scantlings of the longer design, then the cyclic stresses which arise from global loads in the shorter design would be lower than in the longer design. In such circumstances there would be a greater margin against fatigue damage in the shorter ship. However, since the provision of adequate margins against fatigue is implicit in any relevant strength standard together with good associated design detail, it is considered that no significant advantage can be taken of this additional margin.

The Inquiry has considered the effect of shock loading on the two hull forms due to underwater explosion. It has been concluded that the structural arrangements of both vessels are sufficiently similar such that the transmission of shock through either ship, and thus the effect of shock on machinery and equipment, would not be markedly different in either design. It should also be noted that there is no specific NSR 7069 requirement for the structure to be designed to resist shock loading and no special account has, therefore, been taken of shock loading in determining the scantlings of the S102.

One feature of the shorter length of the S102 is that the superstructure is continuous over about 50% of the length of the ship. As a consequence, hull girder bending stresses will be induced into the superstructure. Proper account would therefore have to be taken of the interaction between the hull and superstructure in assessing the topside scantlings. This is not seen to be a major problem for the S102. However, the separated blocks of the Type 23 design avoid significant hull girder bending stresses being induced into the superstructure blocks.

3.6   Displacement

The lightweight and full load displacement of the S102 (see Chapter 5, Section 3.3) and Type 23 designs are very similar.

3.7   Conclusions

The Inquiry has assessed the claimed spatial, layout, structural and weight advantages of the S102, a vessel based on the S90 hull form, by comparing these aspects with the Type 23, a vessel based on a current frigate hull form and designed to meet the same NSR.

The Inquiry's findings are as follows:

i)   The S102 has more internal volume than the Type 23. However, most of this additional volume is taken up as a direct consequence of the S90 design philosophy. For example, the required ability to change trim results in larger fuel tanks; the commercial structure reduces usable 'tweendeck volume; the twin passageway system requires more volume. The remainder of the excess volume is very small and most of this volume has no deck area directly associated with it and is, therefore, of limited use.

ii)   As the compartmental floor areas are similar in each design, there is no significant increase in 'elbow room' in the S102 compared with the Type 23.

iii)   The two passageway system in the S102 is considered to be an advantage arising from the increased beam of the vessel.

iv)   The concentration of all the accommodation into one block could increase vulnerability to a single missile strike. The claimed ship motion benefits arising from the concentration of accommodation in the midship region are discussed in Section 5 of this chapter.

v)   The greater beam of the S102 cannot be fully utilised in the region of the machinery spaces due to the shape of the hull.

        Insufficient beam is available to accommodate further turbine units abreast of each other at the current stage of development of the S102. A major re-design of the vessel, possibly involving an increase in the length of the ship, would be required in order to accommodate the extra turbine units necessary to achieve the NSR speeds.

vi)   Strength standards are independent of hull form. Assuming that the S102 and Type 23 are built to the same strength standard, then the shorter vessel may, depending on the applicable strength criteria and local design detail, have a greater margin against fatigue damage. However, since the provision of adequate margins against fatigue is implicit in any relevant strength standard together with good associated design detail, it is considered that no significant advantage can be taken of any additional margin.

vii)   With reference to TGA's claim that a vessel designed according to their Sirius design concept would be able to operate at over twice the displacement of conventional warships of the same length, and with reference to the Hill-Norton Committee's comments (paragraph 35 of their report), the Inquiry concludes, on the evidence of a vessel designed according to TGA's Sirius concept and a vessel designed according to current warship design philosophy, that there is very little difference in displacement when both are designed to meet the same specification.

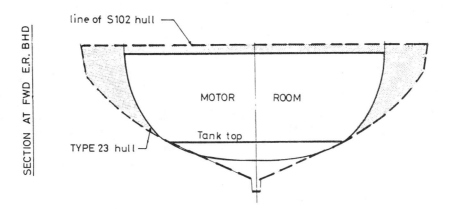

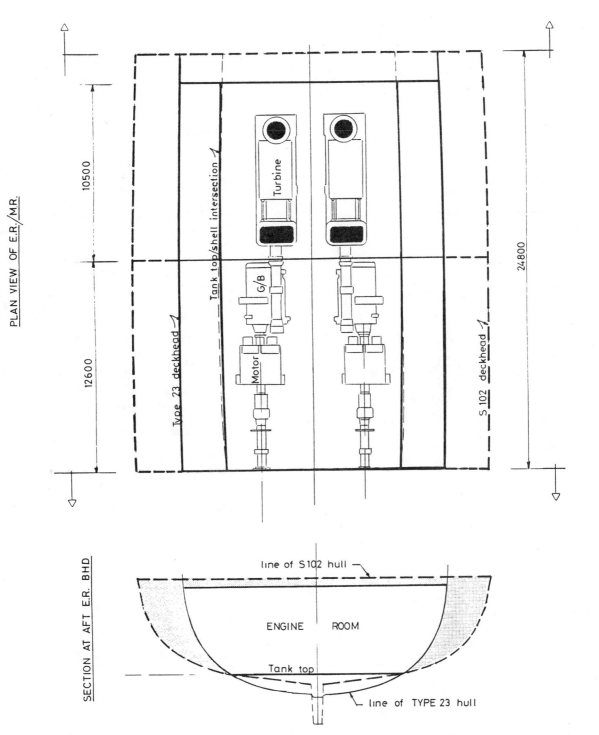

FIGURE 6.3.1   ENGINE ROOM SIZE COMPARISON S102/TYPE 23

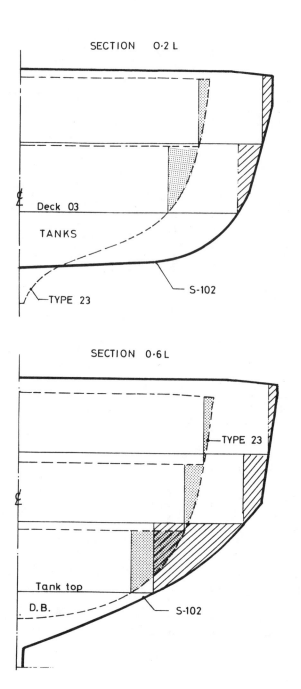

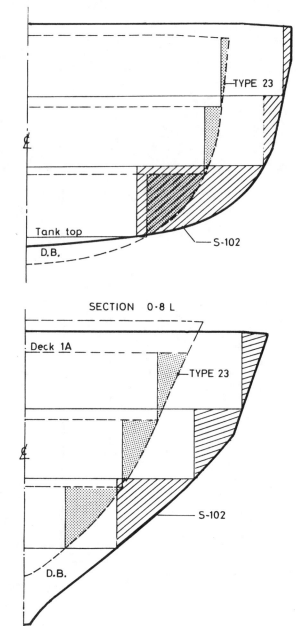

 OR   Denotes hull volume without associated deck area.

FIGURE 6.3.2   SECTION SHAPE COMPARISON S102 AND TYPE 23

CHAPTER 6

ASSESSMENT OF THE S102 DESIGN

SECTION 4
Intact and Damaged Stability

4.1   Introduction

TGA claim that a vessel designed according to their Sirius concept would have a large reserve of intact stability, giving rise to certain advantages when compared with a vessel of more conventional proportions.   These advantages may be summarized as follows:

i)   Flexibility for increasing top weight or positioning equipment and sensors at a greater height.   Allied to this is a greater scope to accommodate subsequent design modifications which increase top weight and vertical centre of gravity.

ii)   Reduced heel when turning at high speed.

iii)   A more stable weapon platform.

TGA have made no claims in relation to the damaged stability capability of a vessel built according to their design concept, but they do not anticipate any difficulty in complying with RN requirements.

Previous assessments of the S90 design proposal, whilst generally accepting the greater intact stability inherent in the S90 hull form, considered that any relevant advantages could be achieved to a sufficient degree by a modest increase in the beam of a conventional vessel. However, some concern was expressed over the ability of such a design to satisfy the damaged stability requirements applied to warships, the main concern being that the wide beam, which gives such a large reserve of intact stability, quickly becomes a disadvantage when the vessel is damaged and flooding occurs. On the one hand, very wide compartments would give rise to large free surface effects which would greatly diminish the vessel's reserve of stability whilst, on the other hand, reducing the width of compartments by longitudinal bulkheads, to combat the effect of free surface, would result in large asymmetrical moments being induced leading to high angles of heel compared with a conventional ship.

The Hill-Norton Committee concluded, on the basis of calculations performed by Frederikshavn Vaerft (FHV), that the S90 satisfied the NSR requirements with regard to damaged stability and that the greater inherent intact stability gave the vessel a definite advantage over a conventional design. The Committee did question the effect that the high profile of the S90 would have on its stability at speed in a cross wind, but observed that the BHC 1:10 scale comparative seakeeping model tests showed that the S90 heeled much less than the Leander at 25 knots in a cross wind of 63 knots.

In order to assess the static stability of a vessel designed according to the Sirius concept, the Inquiry has carried out an appraisal of the intact and damaged stability characteristics of the S102. Since the NSR 7069 does not contain requirements for static stability, the Inquiry has assessed the S102 against the requirements of the MoD Naval Engineering Standard 109 (NES 109) as all intended RN surface warships have to comply with this standard.

In order to assess how the available static stability of the S102 would compare with that of a conventional design, the Inquiry has compared the results of the assessment of the S102 with the results of an intact and damaged stability assessment supplied by the MoD for the Type 23. The Inquiry accepted the Type 23 assessment as valid, noting that the procedures adopted were the same for both designs.

4.2   Analytical Approach

The approach adopted by the Inquiry is outlined in Figure 6.4.1. A description of each stage in this approach is given below:

4.2.1   Hull Form

A computer model definition of the S102 hull was generated using offsets measured from its body plan. This definition only included the extreme volume of the basis hull up to the uppermost continuous deck. No appendages were included.

4.2.2   Floodable Compartments and Exposed Openings

The internal compartments of the hull form were defined, each being assigned a volumetric permeability value as required by the NES 109. In addition, all openings in the exposed hull and superstructure which could, if immersed, lead to the progressive flooding or downflooding of intact spaces were identified and defined in the computer model.

4.2.3   Wind Profile

The wind profile of the S102 was defined in order to enable an assessment to be made of the ship's ability to provide adequate righting energy to resist the heeling moments induced by a beam wind combined with rolling.

4.2.4   Loading Conditions

Twelve loading conditions were compiled for analysis which consisted of three 'basic' conditions and nine others representing variations in the 'basic' conditions due to in-service weight growth and or ice. All the loading conditions included a board margin. The principal properties of the loading conditions are summarized in Table 6.4.1.

The light loading conditions were compiled to represent the lightest conditions envisaged in service and assumed the ship to be structurally complete, fitted out, fully equipped with weapons, ammunition, aircraft, boats, total crew with effects but with almost no fuel or fresh water. The light condition is anticipated by the NES 109 to be the worst in respect of stability. The deep loading conditions represent the ship complete in all respects, fully complemented, ammunitioned, fuelled, stored and provisioned. In such conditions, the fuel oil is distributed either fore and aft or entirely aft in order to represent the possible range of trims.

Having defined the basis model and appropriate loading conditions, it was then possible to perform a series of computer-based intact and damaged stability calculations.

4.2.5   Damage Incidents

Two types of damage incident, i.e. those resulting from weapon attack and collision, are envisaged by the NES 109 which specifies the longitudinal, transverse and vertical extent of damage to be assumed in each incident. Application of the longitudinal extent of weapon damage to the S102 design results in the possibility of damage occurring across three main transverse watertight bulkheads in the foremost portion of the hull and two main transverse watertight bulkheads in the remaining portion. The former results in the flooding of four adjacent compartments whilst the latter results in three. The flooding due to weapon attack damage is considerably in excess of that envisaged by collision damage which, in general, would result in the possibility of flooding only two adjacent main compartments. It was anticipated, therefore, that weapon damage would produce the most onerous results in respect of damaged stability and, for this reason, collision damage was not investigated.

A wide range of major and lesser incidents of weapon damage were examined. Major incidents reflected the maximum amount of flooding possible due to the prescribed extent of damage referred to in the NES 109 whilst lesser incidents reflected the maximum amount of flooding possible due to the prescribed extent, excluding flooding of the double bottom spaces.

All damage incidents have been examined over a range of flooding stages between weapon impact and final equilibrium in order to simulate the worst anticipated floodwater distribution and determine the possibility of transient non-compliance or capsize. The possibility of the progressive flooding of intact spaces, as a result of exposed openings becoming immersed, was carefully monitored. All incidents were analysed over a total of nine stages of flooding, i.e. eight intermediate stages and one final stage.

4.2.6   Intact Stability Calculations

To comply with the NES 109, all the loading conditions were assessed against 25 intact stability criteria which included basic residual stability criteria governing the configuration of the righting lever curve, with and without ice, heeling in wind, high speed turn and crowding of personnel on the upper deck.

4.2.7   Damaged Stability Calculations

The damaged stability analysis was limited to loading conditions 2, 6 & 10, i.e. the 'basic' conditions plus weight growth which is consistent with MoD practice.   The criteria applied reflected survivability after flooding due to weapon damage plus wind induced loading in the flooded state.

4.3   Discussion of Results

4.3.1   Intact Stability

The S102 complied easily with the intact stability criteria of the NES 109. A comparison of the righting lever curve properties for the least and most onerous loading condition is given in Figure 6.4.2 along with the righting lever curve for the most onerous condition.

All the loading conditions examined indicated a high value of transverse metacentric height (GM) even after correction for the effect of liquid free surface (GM (fluid)), the values varying between 4.06m and 5.02m. The effect of this high value on the vessel's seakeeping response is discussed in Section 5 of this chapter.

A comparison with the Type 23 intact stability characteristics indicated that the lightest condition envisaged by the NES 109 (i.e. with little fuel or fresh water onboard) was the most onerous condition for both designs.   In this loading condition, the S102 design possesses significantly more initial stiffness, i.e. a greater transverse metacentric height, and righting energy than the Type 23 design and thereby has an increased margin of compliance with the intact stability criteria of the NES 109. The higher initial stiffness of the S102 design also contributes to a greater resistance to steady beam wind induced loading and consequently a smaller angle of heel in such wind, this being achieved despite the significantly greater applied wind moment.

In the foregoing the S102 is assumed to be at rest, i.e. at zero speed, and although the Inquiry did not specifically assess stability at speed in a steady beam or cross wind, results of the static calculations indicate that the S102 would heel less than the Type 23 with the same strength of beam wind applied. However, the degree of heel was, in general, small for both vessels and the differences were not significant for the normal operating conditions. The Inquiry agrees with the observation made by the Hill-Norton Committee concerning the large degree of heel experienced by the Leander in a beam wind when compared with the S90 during the 1:10 scale model tests; however, it should be noted that the Leander has a much smaller beam and hence lower metacentric height (GM) than the Type 23 and would, therefore, be expected to heel more under such conditions.

The comparison of the S102 and the Type 23 stability results indicated that the S102 would heel less in a high speed turn than the Type 23.

4.3.2   Damaged Stability

The S102 complied with the relevant damaged stability criteria of the NES 109. Figure 6.4.3 indicates the most onerous damage incident for the S102 and the associated damaged residual righting lever curve.

Comparison with the Type 23 revealed that, for the same longitudinal extent of flooding in the critical zone of damage, the S102 design displayed superior residual stability characteristics and thereby a greater ability to comply with the damaged stability criteria of the NES 109.

The concern expressed in previous assessments regarding the heel of the S90 hull form after flooding is supported by the damaged stability results. For the critical zone of damage, the heel induced in the S102 was considerably larger than that in the Type 23. This is a consequence of the combined effect of a considerably greater asymmetric heeling moment due to the flooding of side tanks and the additional liquid free surface effect of the final waterplanes provided by the greater beam. Whilst this may impair operations aboard the S102 more than the Type 23 after such damage, in all other respects the S102 displays significantly better residual stability after flooding than the Type 23, hence providing greater resistance to sustain other moments and forces which could be applied during such a damage incident, e.g. ship's personnel or equipment movement and wind. Furthermore, the results of the damaged stability analysis are heavily dependent on the final arrangement of watertight subdivision. Subsequent design development could lead to a reduction in the heel induced by asymmetric flooding.

Some marginal bow immersion was observed in incidents of flooding in the foremost part of the S102. Therefore, should it be necessary to increase the operational bow down trim in subsequent design iterations to achieve minimum resistance, the tendency for bow immersion would be aggravated. This aspect would require to be carefully assessed in order to avoid the possibility of plunging.

4.4   Conclusions

The S102 design possesses an inherent level of static stability which more than satisfies the intact and damaged stability criteria of the NES 109 in the most onerous loading condition ('basic' light loading with weight growth). In the case of intact stability, compliance with the NES 109 is generally achieved with substantial excess.

In the most onerous loading condition envisaged, the residual intact and damaged stability characteristics of the S102 design are generally significantly greater than those of the Type 23 design and hence it is able to comply with the NES 109 with a larger excess.

The heel induced by flooding in the critical zone of damage is greater in the S102 design than in the Type 23. However, the S102 also has a significant reserve of stability after flooding which enables it to sustain the moments and forces which could be applied following a damage incident better than the Type 23. Subsequent design development could lead to a reduction in the heel induced by asymmetric flooding.

With reference to TGA's claims concerning the advantages relating to the intact stability of a vessel based on their Sirius design concept, the Inquiry concludes:

i)   The flexibility for increasing top weight or positioning equipment and sensors at a greater height is substantiated. Further implications of this are discussed in Section 7 of this chapter.

ii)   The reduced heel when turning at high speed is substantiated.

iii)   The provision of a more stable weapon platform appears valid in the static sense. However, this matter is also related to the vessel's dynamic response in a seaway and this is dealt with in Section 5 of this chapter.

No.	Description	Displ. (tonnes)	Mean Draught (m)	Trim (m)	GM (fluid) (m)
1	Light (Basic)	3416	5.461	0.649F	4.909
2	Light with WG	3621	5.604	0.778F	4.557
3	Light with ice	3694	5.648	0.729F	4.367
4	Light with WG & ice	3899	5.789	0.852F	4.060
5	Deep 1 (Basic)	4108	5.955	1.467F	4.919
6	Deep 1 with WG	4313	6.090	1.580F	4.631
7	Deep 1 with ice	4386	6.131	1.507F	4.468
8	Deep 1 with WG & ice	4591	6.265	1.640F	4.192
9	Deep 2 (Basic)	4108	5.836	0.616A	5.024
10	Deep 2 with WG	4313	5.973	0.558A	4.679
11	Deep 2 with ice	4386	6.023	0.516A	4.503
12	Deep 2 with WG & ice	4591	6.154	0.467A	4.220

Table 6.4.1   S102 Loading Conditions - Principal Properties

Notes:

1.   All loading conditions include a board margin.

2.   Fuel oil is distributed forward and aft in loading conditions 5 to 8.

3.   All fuel oil is located aft in loading conditions 9 to 12.

4.   WG - Weight Growth.

5.   GM (fluid) - transverse metacentric height (GM) corrected for the effect of liquid free surface.

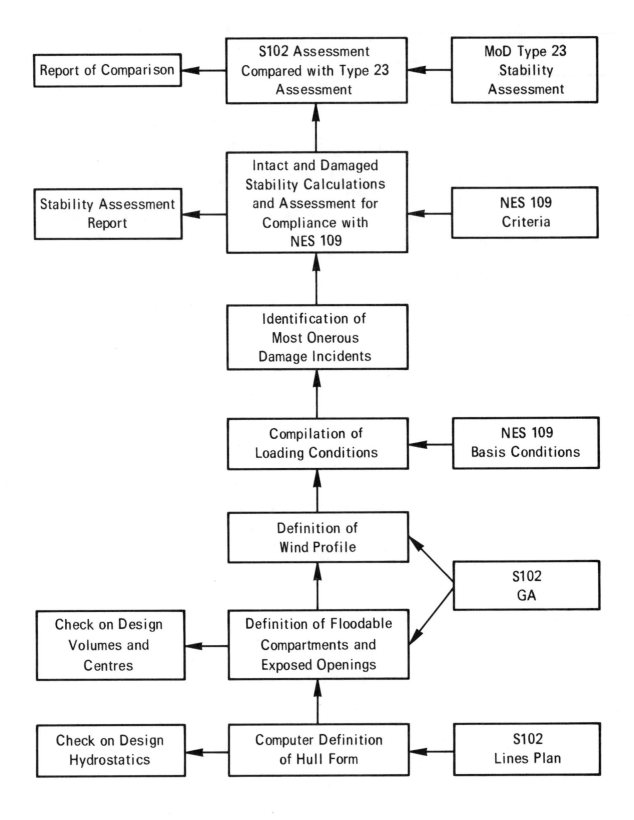

FIGURE 6.4.1   S102 INTACT AND DAMAGED STABILITY
ANALYTICAL APPROACH

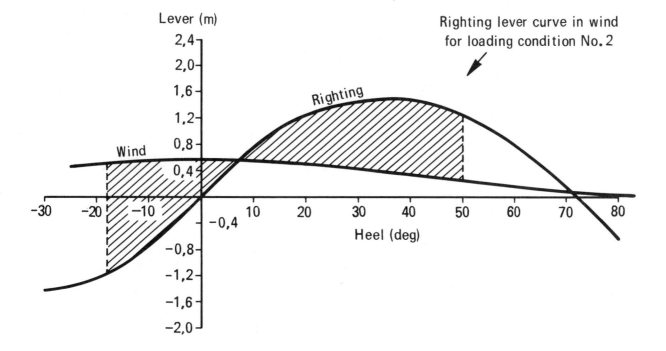

**Comparison of righting lever curve properties for least
and most onerous loading conditions
(No.9 and No.2 respectively)**

Loading condition No.	Slope at Origin GM (fluid) (m)	Range to Vanishing Angle (deg)	Angle of Maximum GZ (deg)	Maximum GZ (m)	Residual Area to 50° (m.rad)
2	4.557	72.0	36.90	1.49	0.622
9	5.024	82.5	39.00	2.12	1.025

FIGURE 6.4.2   RIGHTING LEVER CURVES

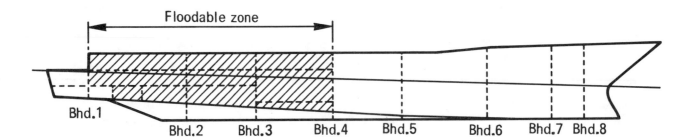

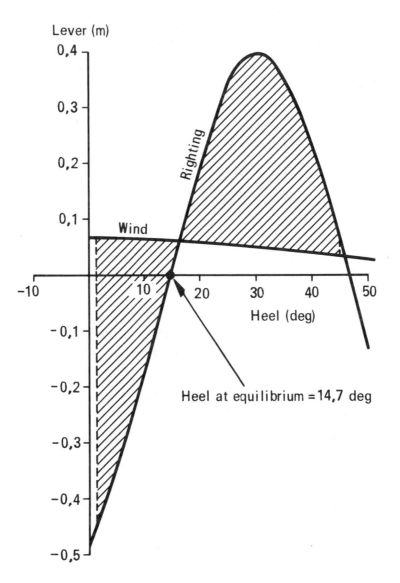

Heel at equilibrium = 14,7 deg

FIGURE 6.4.3   DAMAGED RESIDUAL RIGHTING LEVER CURVE IN
WIND FOR LOADING CONDITION NUMBER 2

CHAPTER 6

ASSESSMENT OF THE S102 DESIGN

SECTION 5
Seakeeping

5.1   Introduction

TGA stated in their S90 Validation Report that they considered, based on advice they had received and from evidence of comparisons between full scale measurements and theoretical predictions, that existing theories could not adequately predict the motions of the S90. As a result, they undertook model tests to demonstrate the seakeeping capability of the S90.   These consisted of tank tests of a 1:20 scale model of the S90 in irregular head seas and 1:10 scale comparative model tests of the S90 and a Leander class frigate in the Solent. The Hill-Norton Committee also indicated that they would place greater confidence in the model test prediction of the seakeeping performance of a Sirius hull form, based on the available data, rather than in theoretical computer predictions.

Arising from these model experiments, TGA claimed that the major advantages with respect to the seakeeping of the S90 compared with a conventional frigate were:

i)   The S90 should be able to maintain a higher speed in more severe sea-states due to reduced vertical responses.

ii)   The S90 would have a lower incidence of deck wetness.

The major reservation expressed in the previous assessments of the S90 proposal related to the high initial stability which, it was said, would cause large lateral accelerations due to the short roll period, particularly on the bridge in view of its high position relative to the centre of roll.

The Inquiry has been concerned with evaluating the seakeeping performance of the S102. In this respect, there are three main methods available for the evaluation of the seakeeping characteristics of a new design such as the S102:

i)   Model experiments in a testing tank where the wave conditions can be fully controlled.

ii)   Model experiments in an open water environment where wave conditions cannot be freely selected but can, to some extent, be measured.

iii)   Theoretical analysis.

Although the Inquiry considers that model tests are the most reliable method of predicting the absolute performance of a new design, a programme covering sufficient model tests to address all the relevant seaways, speeds and loading conditions would be prohibitively expensive and time consuming.   In the case of a theoretical approach, a comprehensive assessment is more feasible; however, there is always some uncertainty with a new design like the S102, concerning the ability of the theoretical method to predict the motions satisfactorily. A more practical approach would be to carry out a limited number of controlled model tests in regular and irregular waves, the results being used to correlate and, if necessary, calibrate the theoretical procedures. The theoretical analysis can then be confidently extended to augment the basic model test results.

As TGA have carried out model tests for the S90, the Inquiry has been able to investigate the correlation of these model tests with an existing theoretical approach. Arising from this investigation, the Inquiry has established that a theoretical approach can be used, albeit with caution and in conjunction with the experimental data, to assess the seakeeping behaviour of the S102 without recourse to further model tests.

This section describes the Inquiry's assessment of the seakeeping performance of the S102 in relation to the seakeeping requirements of the NSR 7069. In addition, the performance of the S102 has been compared with that predicted for the Type 23.

5.2   Seakeeping Responses and Assessment Criteria

Although such expressions as 'good seakeeping' and 'poor seakeeping' are in common usage and, in a qualitative sense, are reasonably well understood, they have no precise meaning unless they are related to the effects of seakeeping behaviour on the overall operational performance of the ship and its company.

In the case of an ASW frigate designed to meet the NSR 7069, the three main operational aspects that may be adversely affected by the seakeeping behaviour are:

i)   The effective deployment of the ship's weapon systems.
ii)   The ability to maintain high speed in rough weather.
iii)   Habitability, i.e. the operational effectiveness of the ship's company.

In order to assess the influence of the seakeeping behaviour of a proposed ASW frigate on these three aspects, a number of parameters relating to the vessel's behaviour in waves require to be quantified and compared with, where applicable, specified criteria which have to be satisfied in order that the vessel can perform its function satisfactorily. Such parameters are:

i)   Ship motions. These are usually referred to as symmetric (surge, heave and pitch) or anti-symmetric (sway, roll and yaw). Figure 6.5.1 illustrates these motions.
ii)   Vertical and horizontal velocities and accelerations associated with the symmetric and anti-symmetric motions respectively.
iii)   Bottom slamming.
iv)   Deck wetness.

v)   Bow flare impact.
vi)   Propeller emergence.
vii)   Added resistance in waves.

With regard to the deployment of weapon systems, the only explicit requirement specified in the NSR 7069 relates to the ship's ability to deploy its helicopter up to a specified sea-state. Motion, velocity and acceleration criteria are given for this in supporting documents to the NSR. Criteria for the other weapon systems are, however, generally implicit in their design specification and, where required, these have been submitted to the Inquiry. These are, again, generally expressed in terms of limiting motions, velocities or accelerations.

Since, in general, only a small part of a frigate's total sea time will be spent in calm water, the ability to maintain speed in a seaway, although not specified in the NSR, is considered by the Inquiry to be, in operational terms, at least as important as the ability to achieve a specified calm water speed. Admiral Sir Lindsay Bryson (the then Controller of the Navy) in his paper 'The Procurement of a Warship' (Reference 6.5.1) stated that *'There has been a major shift in emphasis since the Second World War from requiring high calm water speed to the ability to maintain high speed in rough weather.'* The Inquiry has assessed the overall speed loss in waves of the S102 in comparison with that of the Type 23.

The variability of human sensitivity to ship motions makes it difficult to define meaningful acceptance criteria relevant to crew efficiency. However, one useful parameter, in this respect, is the averaged subjective motion magnitude (SMM) which represents a weighted mean value of the ship's centre-plane vertical response. The MoD have adopted this parameter to assist in the assessment of crew efficiency and they have supplied a limiting SMM value to the Inquiry. The motions environment experienced by the ship's company is also influenced, particularly in a wider ship, by the off-centreline vertical response associated with roll behaviour and by the overall horizontal response. The Inquiry has, therefore, taken account of these factors as well as the SMM in assessing the relative performance of the S102 and Type 23 designs with respect to crew efficiency.

Further criteria concerning the acceptable frequencies of fore end slamming and deck wetness were supplied by the MoD at the Inquiry's request. These criteria had been used during the development of the Type 23 frigate.

5.3   Model and Full Scale Test Data for Sirius Hull Forms

Prior to investigating the correlation between theoretical and experimental results for the S90 hull form, the Inquiry undertook an assessment of the available S90 model test data along with model and full scale data for an Osprey class vessel.

5.3.1   1:20 Scale Model Tests

Model tests were performed in April 1983 by NMI. A 1:20 scale model of the S90 was run at different forward speeds in irregular head waves. Measurements of the model's response were made and a video recording of the tests was produced.

The results from these tests were compared with the full scale measurements taken from the Leander and Tribal class frigates, Reference 6.5.2.

5.3.2   1:10 Scale Model Tests

Model tests were performed in October and December 1983 by BHC off Bembridge, Isle of Wight, in natural, wind-generated, short-crested waves. Two self-propelled 1:10 scale models were used, one a model of the S90 and the other a model of a Leander class frigate.

Both models were ballasted to give the appropriate metacentric height and natural roll period as specified by TGA for the S90 and the Admiralty Research Establishment for the Leander.

Measurements were taken at three different speeds and five different predominant wave headings. Three different sea-states were recorded during the trials. In addition, video recordings of all these tests were made and an abridged version for demonstration purposes was subsequently produced.

5.3.3   Osprey Model and Full Scale Tests

Model and full scale data from tests carried out on the Osprey class vessel 'Indaw' were made available to the Inquiry.

In 1978, 1:10 scale model tests were performed in natural wind-generated seas off Bembridge, Isle of Wight. Full scale trials were performed off the Danish coast in 1980. The loading condition and sea-states were completely different between the model tests and trials and it was not possible, therefore, to make meaningful comparisons.

In order that useful comparisons could be made, further 1:10 scale model tests were performed at exactly the same loading condition as the full scale trials. Once again, these tests were performed off the Isle of Wight.

Although attempts were made to correlate the results obtained from these tests with those obtained from the full scale measurements, the sea-states were not similar enough to enable meaningful comparisons to be made. Although the Inquiry considers that model tests do scale correctly to full scale, it has been unable to place much weight on the results of this correlation study. However, the data obtained have been considered in the Inquiry's assessment of theoretical predictions compared with experimental results.

5.3.4   General Observations on the S90 Model Tests

The 1:20 and 1:10 scale model tests of the S90 have been compared with the model and full scale seakeeping performance of a Leander class frigate. This comparison has indicated the following general trends for the sea-states, loading conditions, headings and speeds considered:

i)   For high speeds, the S90 would have, in general, lower vertical responses than the Leander whereas at low speeds the opposite would be true. In general, for both high and low speeds, the difference would not be significant.

ii)   The horizontal responses measured during the 1:10 scale model tests showed that although the roll amplitude response was similar, the horizontal acceleration on the bridge of the S90 was substantially higher than the Leander's at the lower speeds. At the highest speed the responses were similar.

iii)   The S90 would have a lower incidence of bow emergence and hence a lower probability of bottom slamming. The Inquiry considers that this is due to the deeper draught and reduced vessel motions at the fore end.

iv)   The S90 would be a much drier ship than the Leander. The Inquiry considers that this is due to the reduced vessel motions at the fore end, fuller form and significant flare of the S90 which means that water is directed away from the deck.

v)   The yaw and rudder angles measured in the 1:10 scale model tests were much higher on the Leander than on the S90. It should be noted that although the tuning of the autopilots was the same for both vessels, this could have benefited one vessel more than the other.

With reference to the video recordings of the model tests, these provided useful information concerning the amount of spray and water on deck since such phenomena cannot be measured adequately. With respect to the vessel's motions, however, the Inquiry considers that reference should be made to the actual measurement results rather than the video recordings since, unfortunately, a video recording can give a misleading impression of a vessel's motions.

A problem encountered with the examination of the 1:10 scale comparative model tests was that a number of results were inconsistent with the overall trends discussed above. The Inquiry considers that this was due to the problems associated with determining the input wave conditions, in particular the uncertainty over the predominant wave direction and spread of wave energy.

In addition, it was observed that for the full scale trials of the Leander, the seaway was abating throughout whereas the seaway used in the 1:20 scale S90 model tests was held constant. Consequently, if the Leander had been subjected, throughout its trials, to the same sea-state used in the model tests, then the responses of the Leander would have been higher for the higher speed cases reported.

These problems illustrate the difficulties in obtaining reliable quantitative data from open water model or full scale tests. Furthermore, although the Inquiry considers that the S90 model tests are useful, they have only covered a limited number of sea-states, speeds and headings and, therefore, do not enable a comprehensive assessment of the seakeeping capability of the S90 hull form to be undertaken.

5.4   Comparison of Theoretical and Experimental Results

It is generally accepted that two-dimensional strip theory is capable of predicting, with reasonable accuracy, the motions of conventional 'long/thin' warship designs. This is supported by the results given in Reference 6.5.2 where it can be seen that the comparison between theory and full scale measurements for the Leander was extremely good.

In order to assess whether it was possible to evaluate the seakeeping performance of the S90 hull form using a theoretical analysis, the Inquiry examined the suitability of using a two-dimensional strip theory (based on work given in Reference 6.5.3) to predict the motions of the S90. In this respect, it should be understood that the usefulness of a theoretical analysis is not altogether determined by its ability to achieve quantitatively accurate results since considerable value can also be derived from reliable qualitative predictions.

For completeness, it was necessary to confirm that the adopted strip theory gave a similar level of confidence when used to predict the response of a conventional warship hull form. Therefore, the Inquiry has used the theory to predict the performance of the Leander corresponding to both the model and full scale tests described in Section 5.3, in addition to assessing the S90.

Arising from these theoretical analyses, a comprehensive correlation study was carried out leading to the following principal conclusions:

i)   For the Leander, the correlation between full scale measurements and theory was very good, despite the difficulties associated with the accurate measurement of the full scale sea-state referred to in Section 5.3.4.   This is thought to be due to the strong uni-directionality of the seaway which was reported during the trials.

ii)   For the 1:20 scale S90 model tests, the theory did not predict the pitch response particularly well in a quantitative sense, although the heave response correlation was reasonable.   In both cases, the responses were under-predicted by the theory.   The trend with the accelerations was not so obvious.   Whereas the vertical acceleration at the bridge was extremely well predicted, the correlation for the fore and aft accelerations was not as good with the theory, in general, over-predicting the accelerations.   The averaged subjective motion magnitude predictions were reasonable.   The theory also gave reasonable agreement with the measured incidence of deck wetness and bottom slamming, although in both cases the theory once again under-predicted.   In all the cases, the correct trend was predicted by the theory when compared with the model tests.

iii) For the 1:10 scale comparative S90 and Leander model tests, the agreement between theory and experiment was not very good for either vessel.   The Inquiry considers that this is largely a consequence of the uncertainties associated with the measurement of the input wave spectrum, predominant wave direction and energy spreading for open water conditions.   In general, the theory under-predicted the motions of both the S90 and the Leander, in some cases quite significantly.

It should be noted, in this respect, that it is only in model tank experiments that the input wave energy spectrum can be controlled to sufficient accuracy for reliable correlation or calibration purposes.   The value of results from open water experiments for correlation purposes is limited by the accuracy of full scale sea-state measurements and, in particular, the difficulty of determining the directional wave energy spreading.

In spite of the problems associated with full scale measurements outlined above, the MoD achieved reasonable agreement for the Osprey full scale tests using a similar strip theory program to that used by the Inquiry.

However, the theory again, in general, under-predicted the full scale response.

Notwithstanding this general under-prediction of the responses of the S90 by the theoretical analysis, the predicted trends in all cases were identical to those observed in the model tests. Therefore, bearing in mind the general uncertainties associated with the measured data, particularly that obtained from the open water tests, the correlation obtained between the theoretical and experimental results was considered by the Inquiry to be adequate to enable a theoretical analysis to be used, albeit with caution and in conjunction with the experimental data, in the assessment and comparative evaluation of the seakeeping response of the S102.

5.5   Seakeeping Analysis of the S102 and Type 23

Using the two-dimensional theory referred to in Section 5.4, the Inquiry has assessed the compliance of the S102 with the seakeeping criteria associated with the NSR 7069 and, in addition, has carried out a comparative assessment of the S102 with the Type 23. The results of these assessments are given in Section 5.6.

The deep and half oil displacement loading conditions of the S102 were selected for assessment as these were considered to encompass the normal operational envelope of an ASW frigate. As it is necessary to alter the operational trim of the S102 with displacement and speed to minimise resistance, the Inquiry has assessed these two loading conditions using the even keel and maximum optimum bow down trims as upper and lower bounds for the analysis. For the symmetric responses (surge, heave and pitch), three different forward speeds have been analysed, namely the maximum speed achievable by the S102 with the machinery configuration proposed by TGA (see Chapter 5, Section 2.2.2), the endurance speed and a typical low speed representative of towed array operations. These speeds have also been used for the analysis of the anti-symmetric responses (sway, roll and yaw) along with an additional low speed case because of the sensitivity of roll response to speed and the importance of the low speed towed array operating mode.

The seakeeping analysis indicated that the motions determined for the two displacements were similar. Therefore, it was decided to analyse only the deep displacement condition. The respective S102 parameters used in the seakeeping analysis are given in Table 6.5.1. The Type 23 deep displacement condition has been analysed for the same speeds.

The Inquiry has used the sea-states specified by the MoD as these were considered to be of a sufficient range of severity to be a good test of the seakeeping capabilities of both ships. However, for the roll responses, it was considered necessary to use two additional sea-states which were chosen to excite the S102 and Type 23 at their respective natural roll periods since these periods are different for the two ships, the S102 roll period being approximately two seconds shorter than that of the Type 23.

The Inquiry has considered all wave headings for these sea-states.

5.6   Discussion of Results of Seakeeping Analysis

For simplicity, the results for the S102 are presented in terms of the even keel condition and reference is only made to the trimmed condition if the responses were significantly different.

5.6.1   Heave Response

The calculated differences in heave response between the S102 and the Type 23 were not significant for any speed, heading or sea-state.

In head and following seas, the Type 23 heave response was predicted to be less than that of the S102 at the two lower speeds. At the highest speed, the heave response of both vessels was almost identical, except for the following seas case where the S102 was predicted to have a larger response. For the other headings the responses were similar.

5.6.2   Pitch Response

In head seas, the Type 23 pitch response was predicted to be less than that for the S102 at the lowest speed. However, as the speed increased so the Type 23 pitch response in head seas increased, whereas the opposite was true for the S102. At the highest speed, the pitch response was less for the S102 than the Type 23. In all cases the difference was not significant. This was in agreement with the trend observed in the model tests (see Section 5.3.4).

In following and stern quartering seas, a larger pitch response was predicted for the S102 compared with the Type 23 at all speeds. At the highest speed, a considerable increase in pitch response for the S102 was predicted in the following seas case.

The reason for this is unclear. The results of the optimum bow down trim condition indicate a lower pitch response compared with the level trim condition which suggests that the large pitch response could be a function of the large transom stern.

Only the 1:10 scale model tests addressed the following seas case. Unfortunately, of the four high speed runs in stern quartering and following seas, only two were reported. Of these two runs, the S90 pitch response was considerably higher than the Leander's response in one case and similar in the other.

5.6.3   Surge Response

The surge response of the two vessels has not been calculated as surge is considered to be of secondary importance.

5.6.4   Roll Response

Roll response is difficult to predict accurately for any ship because of the complex effect of viscosity on the roll damping. Further complications also arise from the inclusion of underwater appendages on the ship. The S102 has a large skeg and active fin stabilisers have been proposed. From initial results, it was evident that the S102 would roll significantly at low speeds and that the effect of the skeg, in this case, would not be sufficient to reduce the roll response to an acceptable level. TGA have maintained that they would not fit bilge keels but would consider anti-rolling tanks to try and reduce the rolling at low speeds. The implications of such anti-rolling devices on displacement, powering and radiated noise would require to be fully evaluated in any future design development. In particular, the radiated noise arising from the use of anti-rolling tanks would require to be carefully assessed.

Although TGA have indicated that the proposed fin stabilisers would be retracted at high speed, the roll analysis indicated that the roll amplitude would be unacceptably high if this was the case. The Inquiry has, therefore, assumed that the stabilisers are deployed at all speeds.

With appropriate roll damping devices, it would be possible to obtain similar roll angles for the S102 to those calculated for the Type 23. The Inquiry has assumed that such devices are fitted in assessing the roll response of the S102 and the associated horizontal and vertical velocities and accelerations. However, it should be noted that although the roll angles may be similar, the roll period of the S102 is significantly shorter than the Type 23 (by about two seconds).

The predicted roll amplitude response for the S102 would satisfy the criteria for helicopter operation provided that the appropriate roll damping devices referred to above are fitted and deployed.

5.6.5   Sway and Yaw Response

In following and stern quartering seas, the analysis predicted large sway and yaw responses for the S102 at maximum speed. Similar, although less severe, increases in sway and yaw responses were predicted for the Type 23 in these conditions. However, the theoretical approach has not been well tested under following sea conditions, and consequently a greater level of uncertainty is associated with the corresponding predictions.

A large yaw response in following seas was reported by the crew of the Osprey class vessel 'Havornen' during the Inquiry's visit to the vessel. The crew stated that in some severe stern seas, the yaw was too great for the autopilot to handle. Notwithstanding this, the crew also said that in moderately severe seas the most comfortable heading was with the seas coming from astern, but with the ship's speed reduced on this heading in order to avoid high yaw angles and the danger of broaching.

5.6.6   Vertical Velocity and Acceleration

At all speeds, the vertical velocity and acceleration on the ship's centreline have been calculated to be less for the S102 at the bridge and helipad positions than for the Type 23. This is due to the bridge and helipad being closer to the point of rotation in pitch on the S102 than on the Type 23. At low speeds, the difference was small. As the forward speed increased, the centre-plane vertical velocity and acceleration reduced on the S102 relative to the Type 23. At the highest speed, the theory predicts a 25% reduction for the S102 over the Type 23 for the vertical acceleration at the bridge centreline position.

Away from the centreline of the ship, additional roll-induced vertical velocities and accelerations would be experienced which, due to the shorter roll period of the S102 coupled with its wider beam, would be larger on the S102 in comparison with those at similar positions on the Type 23.

The predicted vertical velocity at the helipad for the S102 satisfied the criteria for helicopter operation.

5.6.7   Horizontal Velocity and Acceleration

The total horizontal velocity or acceleration, at any position, includes contributions from all the anti-symmetric motions, i.e. sway, roll and yaw. The magnitudes of the roll and yaw components are influenced not only by the angular response amplitudes but also by the distances of the point from the appropriate centres of rotation.

At the helipad position, although the S102 was predicted to experience larger roll-induced components, the total horizontal velocity and acceleration were calculated to be slightly lower than on the Type 23. This is chiefly due to a higher contribution from yaw on the Type 23 associated with the greater longitudinal separation of the helipad from the longitudinal centre of gravity.

At the mast radar position, considerably higher horizontal velocities and accelerations were predicted for the S102. This was also the case for another important position on the ship, the bridge. In both these positions, the horizontal accelerations on the S102 were of the order of 1.5-2 times those on the Type 23. The reasons for this are partly due to the shorter roll period of the S102 and partly due to the increased height of the bridge and mast positions above the roll centre. These predicted responses were in agreement with those observed in the model tests.

The predicted horizontal velocity at the helipad for the S102 satisfied the criteria for helicopter operation.

5.6.8   Bottom Slamming

A bottom slam is defined to have occurred if, at a specified position along the length of the vessel, two criteria are satisfied:

i)   Keel emergence has occurred.
ii)   The relative velocity between keel and wave, on re-entry, has exceeded a certain threshold value.

The calculated probability of bottom slamming at the fore end was significantly lower for the S102, for both loading conditions, than for the Type 23.

The S102 was predicted to satisfy the fore end slamming criteria specified by the MoD.

The probability of aft end emergence of the S102, in the even keel condition, was predicted to be lower than for the Type 23. For the optimum trim condition of the S102, the probability was higher than for the Type 23. However, in all cases, the calculated probability of an aft end slam was extremely low for both vessels.

5.6.9   Deck Wetness

The expected incidence of deck wetness, based on the number of times per hour that the wave crest rises above deck level, was predicted to be much lower on the S102 than on the Type 23 for both even keel and optimum trim conditions at high speeds. At lower speeds the difference between the two vessels was less but the S102 was still predicted to be the drier ship. This improvement in deck wetness for the S102 is due to the reduced relative motion at the fore end, the fuller form and the significant bow flare compared with that of the Type 23.

The S102 was predicted to satisfy the criteria for the incidence of deck wetness specified by the MoD.

5.6.10 Bow Flare Loads

The fuller form and significant bow flare of the S102, although helping to reduce the incidence of deck wetness, would, in association with the ship motions, introduce additional dynamic loading on the ship. From the evidence of full scale operations of fast dry cargo vessels, for example Reference 6.5.4, the problems associated with a high degree of bow flare can be significant and can cause both local and global damage. These loads are principally dependent upon the angle the bow flare makes with the horizontal and the relative velocity at the fore end. The MoD have not specified criteria for an acceptable frequency of occurrence for bow flare impact. In general, this type of load is of secondary importance for a conventional frigate bow form which does not have large flare. Although the relative velocity at the fore end has been predicted to be lower on the S102 than the Type 23, it is considered that the S102 would have significantly higher bow flare loads and a corresponding increased incidence of bow flare impact than the Type 23. It should be noted that the larger bow flare is accentuated on the S102 by the high degree of curvature just below the knuckle line.

5.6.11 Subjective Motion Magnitude

The averaged subjective motion magnitude (SMM) parameter, as defined in Reference 6.5.5, has been calculated for both ships. The S102 has a lower SMM value, as averaged over the working spaces of the vessel, than the Type 23 for all the speeds and sea-states considered. At the two lower speeds, an improvement of approximately 10% was predicted whilst at the highest speed the improvement was approximately 20%.

The S102 was predicted to satisfy the specified MoD criteria for the averaged subjective motion magnitude parameter.

5.6.12 Propeller Emergence

The criteria for propeller emergence adopted by the Inquiry is given in Reference 6.5.5, i.e. a quarter of the propeller diameter emerging from the water. The results indicate that for the S102 there would be a low probability of propeller emergence for both displacement conditions and at all speeds and associated optimum trims. A low probability of propeller emergence was also predicted for the Type 23 frigate in similar displacement conditions.

5.6.13 Speed Loss in Waves

The maximum speed that a ship can be expected to maintain in a seaway is less than her maximum calm water speed. This reduction in speed, or speed loss as it is usually termed, arises from two separate sources, one involuntary and the other voluntary. The involuntary speed loss is caused by added resistance in waves and is a function of hull form, sea-state and ship motions together with the installed power characteristics. Voluntary speed loss is the reduction in speed made, as a matter of good seamanship, to avoid undue risk of heavy weather damage and is influenced principally by the vessel's bottom slamming, bow flare impact and deck wetness behaviour.

The involuntary speed loss for both the S102 and Type 23 designs has been investigated using a theoretical method based on the radiated energy approach of Reference 6.5.6 for head to beam waves, and the integrated pressure method given in Reference 6.5.7 for beam to following waves. It was confirmed that the head seas case gave the largest added resistance for both vessels. Under these conditions, the increase in resistance for the S102 was greater, in absolute terms, than that for the Type 23. Consequently, with the proposed machinery configuration, there would be a larger reduction in the top speed of the S102 than in the top speed of the Type 23. In wave heights consistent with Sea-state 6, the maximum speed deficits, relative to the NSR 7069 calm water speed requirement, were calculated to be 3.8 knots for the S102 compared with 0.8 knots for the Type 23. For wave heights consistent with Sea-state 7, the corresponding speed deficits were 4.9 knots for the S102 compared with 2.1 knots for the Type 23. If sufficient power were installed in the S102 to enable the vessel to meet the NSR 7069 speed requirement in calm water (see Section 2 of this chapter), then the corresponding speed deficits would be reduced but would still be larger than those for the Type 23. In this case, the deficits for the S102 were predicted to be 1.3 knots in Sea-state 6 and 2.5 knots in Sea-state 7.

The involuntary speed loss was also estimated using a simple empirical formula derived by the MoD, which expresses speed loss as a function of maximum calm water speed, significant wave height and ship length, and a semi-analytical method based on the work described in Reference 6.5.8. Both methods predicted a larger speed deficit for the S102 than for the Type 23, the values being, in all cases, slightly larger than those given above.

The voluntary speed loss is more difficult to quantify since it results from a subjective evaluation, by the ship's commanding officer, of the risk of heavy weather damage. The Inquiry has investigated this aspect by considering the frequencies of occurrence of bottom slamming, bow flare impact and deck wetness as functions of sea-state and ship speed. With respect to bottom slamming, neither the S102 nor the Type 23 is anticipated to require any voluntary speed reduction below their respective maximum achievable rough water speeds for seaways up to Sea-state 7. The inferior deck wetness performance of the Type 23, compared with the S102, is, however, expected to give rise to some voluntary speed reduction whereas none is anticipated for the S102. Conversely, it is considered that the increased incidence of bow flare impact on the S102 would result in a greater voluntary speed reduction than for the Type 23. On balance, it is considered that the S102 would be able to maintain a higher voluntary speed in head seas than the Type 23. This conclusion stems principally from the inferior deck wetness characteristics of the Type 23. However, it should be stated that the deck wetness of the Type 23 could, if required, be significantly improved by introducing more flare to the above waterline hull form.

5.7   Conclusions

The Hill-Norton Committee considered that the prediction of the seakeeping performance of a vessel based on a Sirius hull form, because of the widely differing technical opinions held on this matter, was the most controversial matter they had examined.

The Inquiry would endorse the Hill-Norton Committee's view that seakeeping represents one of the most controversial issues. It is an area with a high level of uncertainty attached to it and is one that relies heavily on subjective judgements in offsetting superior performance in one respect against inferior behaviour in another.

The Inquiry considers that carefully controlled model tests, assuming that they are sufficiently comprehensive, would provide a more reliable basis than a theoretical analysis of the seakeeping performance of a Sirius design. However, the Inquiry concluded that the extent of the available experimental evidence for the S90 hull form was, on its own, insufficient to provide the basis of an adequate assessment of the S90 hull form. It was considered, nevertheless, that sufficient reliable experimental data was available to correlate and validate a suitable theoretical approach with the conclusion that such a theoretical analysis could be used, albeit with caution and in conjunction with the experimental data, for the assessment and comparative evaluation of the seakeeping behaviour of the S102 in relation to the requirements of the NSR 7069 and in comparison with the Type 23 frigate.

The general trends identified from the comparison of the S90 model test results with model and full scale results for a Leander class frigate have been confirmed by the theoretical analysis, in the context of the S102 and Type 23 designs, over a much wider range of sea-states, speeds and headings. In addition, the theoretical analysis has been able to estimate the relative magnitudes of both the symmetric and the anti-symmetric responses at critical positions on the two designs, for example, the helipad, bridge and mast head.

Arising from its assessment, the Inquiry concludes that with respect to the seakeeping criteria associated with the NSR, or provided by the MoD and or weapon manufacturers, the predicted performance of the S102 will satisfy all the necessary criteria.

With reference to the comparative evaluation of the seakeeping performance of the S102 and the Type 23, the Inquiry concludes that:

i)   The S102 and Type 23 would have similar responses in heave.

ii)   The S102 and Type 23 would have similar pitch responses except for stern quartering and following seas. Under such conditions, the S102 is predicted to have much larger pitch angles, particularly at maximum speed. Although the theoretical approach has not been well tested under following sea conditions, and consequently a greater level of uncertainty is associated with the corresponding predictions, the available model test data also suggests that large pitch responses could be experienced at high speeds in such conditions. Therefore, this aspect would need to be carefully assessed by means of model tests before such behaviour could be confirmed.

iii)   The vertical velocity and acceleration on the ship's centreline at the bridge and helipad would be similar at low speeds. As speed increases, the responses for the S102 would be lower than those for the Type 23. At the highest speed, a 25% reduction was predicted for the S102 compared with the Type 23 for the vertical acceleration at the bridge position.

iv)   The probability of fore end slamming would be significantly lower for the S102.

v)   The incidence of deck wetness at high speed would be significantly lower for the S102, for both the even keel and optimum bow down trim conditions, than that for the Type 23. The improvement would be less at lower speeds but the S102 would still be the drier ship.

vi)   The S102 would have larger bow flare loads than the Type 23 and a higher frequency of occurrence of bow flare impacts.

vii)   The averaged subjective motion magnitude parameter would be lower for the S102. The difference between the two vessels would be small at low speeds but was predicted to increase to a maximum of 20% at top speed.

viii)   Although the roll angles may be similar for both designs, the roll period for the S102 would be significantly shorter than that for the Type 23.

ix)   The horizontal velocities and accelerations at the helipad position would be slightly lower for the S102 than for the Type 23. However, for the bridge and mast positions, the differences would be significant with the S102 having horizontal accelerations between 50%-100% greater than those on the Type 23.

x) The shorter roll period of the S102, coupled with its wider beam, would result in larger roll-induced vertical velocities and accelerations away from the centre-plane on the S102 in comparison with those on the Type 23.

xi) The increased added resistance in waves would result in an increased involuntary speed loss and greater speed deficit for the S102, relative to the NSR 7069 maximum calm water speed requirement, than for the Type 23.

xii) From considerations of the frequencies of occurrence of bottom slamming, bow flare impact and deck wetness, it is considered that the S102 would have a smaller voluntary speed reduction than that for the Type 23.

The implications of the above findings on the comparative overall operational performance of the S102 and Type 23 frigate designs can be summarized as follows:-

The total motions environment, i.e. combined horizontal, vertical and angular motions, velocities and accelerations, would be, in general, more onerous on the S102 than on the Type 23, particularly at the lower speeds associated with towed array operations. However, it is considered that the S102 environment would, provided that suitable anti-rolling devices could be satisfactorily fitted, be accommodated within the operational specification of the weapon systems and other ship's equipment. No consequent appreciable loss in performance or increased maintenance cost or need for any significant re-design effort is anticipated. Therefore, with respect to the effective deployment of the weapon systems and equipment no significant advantage is identified with regard to either the S102 or Type 23.

In terms of the speed which could be achieved in rough weather, the S102 would have an advantage over the Type 23 in terms of speed limitation arising from a voluntary reduction by the ship's commanding officer, due primarily to the reduced incidence of deck wetness. However, the maximum achievable speed in rough weather is limited by the involuntary speed loss in waves and, in this respect, the Type 23 would be able to achieve a higher absolute speed in rough weather than the S102 should this be necessary. This remains the case even when the increased power, necessary for the S102 to meet the NSR maximum calm water speed requirement, is provided. It should also be noted that the deck wetness on the Type 23 could be reduced by increasing the amount of bow flare.

Despite the lower value of the averaged subjective motion magnitude predicted for the S102, the total motions environment is considered to be more onerous, in general, but particularly at the lower speeds where a towed array ASW frigate will spend significant proportions of its sea time. This is considered to represent a significant disadvantage for the S102 with respect to habitability and crew efficiency in comparison with the Type 23.

In view of the above, the Inquiry concludes that, with respect to the overall seakeeping characteristics of the two designs, there is a material advantage in favour of the Type 23 frigate. Should it not be possible to identify suitable anti-roll devices for the S102 of equivalent effectiveness to bilge keels, then the advantage in favour of the Type 23 would be further increased to a significant degree.

References

6.5.1   Bryson, L.: 'The Procurement of a Warship', Trans.RINA, Volume 127, 1985.

6.5.2   Andrew, R.N. and Lloyd, A.R.J.M.: 'Full-Scale Comparative Measurements of the Behaviour of Two Frigates in Severe Head Seas', Trans.RINA, Volume 123, 1981.

6.5.3   Salvesen, N., Tuck, E.O. and Faltinsen, O.: 'Ship Motions and Sea Loads', Trans.SNAME, Volume 78, 1970.

6.5.4   McCallum, J.: 'The Strength of Fast Cargo Ships', Trans.RINA, Volume 117, 1974.

6.5.5   Lloyd, A.R.J.M. and Andrew, R.N.: 'Criteria for Ship Speed in Rough Weather', Proc. 18th American Towing Tank Conference, Annapolis, 1977.

6.5.6   Gerritsma, J. and Beukelman, W.: 'Analysis of the Resistance Increase in Waves of a Fast Cargo Ship', International Shipbuilding Progress, Volume 18, No.217, 1972.

6.5.7   Boese, P.: 'Eine Einfache Method zur Berechnung der Widerstanderhöhung enes Schiffes im Seegang', Instituüt für Schiffbau der Universität Hamburg, Bericht 258, 1970.

6.5.8   Faltinsen, O., Minsaas, K.J., Liapsis, N. and Skjordal, S.: 'Prediction of Resistance and Propulsion of a Ship in a Seaway', ONR Tokyo, 1980.

General Particulars

Length on design waterline	95.00 m
Breadth on design waterline	19.12 m
Deep draught	5.90 m
Displacement	4108 tonne
Vertical Centre of Gravity	8.40 m
Transverse Metacentric Height (GM_T)	5.58 m
GM loss due free liquid surfaces (ΔGM_T)	0.66 m
Radius of Gyration in Roll (K_x)	7.49 m
Radius of Gyration in Pitch (K_y)	21.40 m

Even Keel Condition

Draught Aft	5.90 m
Draught Forward	5.90 m
Longitudinal Centre of Gravity	-2.44 m

Optimum Trim Condition

Draught Aft	4.16 m
Draught Forward	8.12 m
Longitudinal Centre of Gravity	6.75 m

Table 6.5.1   S102 Seakeeping Parameters

Notes:

1. The reference point for the draught is the moulded baseline.

2. The position of the longitudinal centre of gravity is measured from amidships (positive forward, negative aft of amidships).

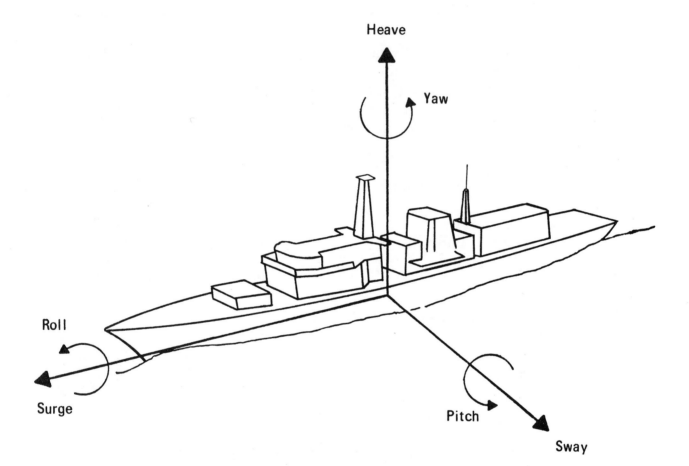

FIGURE 6.5.1   SYMMETRIC AND ANTI-SYMMETRIC SHIP MOTIONS

CHAPTER 6

ASSESSMENT OF THE S102 DESIGN

SECTION 6
Manoeuvrability

6.1   Introduction

The manoeuvring capability of the S90 hull form has not featured prominently in either the S90 design proposal put forward by TGA to the MoD in 1983, or in the subsequent assessments of that proposal. Nevertheless, the Inquiry considers that manoeuvrability is an important feature of frigate performance and has, therefore, assessed this aspect in relation to the S90 hull form.

The manoeuvring capability of the S90 design proposal was stated, in TGA's S90 Validation Report, to be such that the vessel would have a tactical diameter of less than two ship lengths from full speed and that its stopping performance would be better than that of a Leander class frigate.

Neither of these claims was disputed or fully examined in the subsequent assessments of the S90 proposal.

No manoeuvring full scale trial or model test data of sufficient detail were submitted to the Inquiry for any Sirius type hull forms. Therefore, the Inquiry took the opportunity to conduct full scale manoeuvring trials on the Southern Cross III. This vessel has a similar hull form to the S90, the lines also having been developed by TGA. The data obtained from these trials have been used as a basis for establishing the manoeuvring characteristics of the S102.

The Inquiry has assessed the manoeuvring capability of the S102 against the requirements of the NSR 7069 and, in addition, against a number of other manoeuvring characteristics which, although not explicitly stated in the NSR, are considered desirable by the MoD. The Inquiry has also compared the performance of the S102 with trials data provided by the MoD for the Type 22 and Leander class frigates. Such a comparison enables an assessment of the manoeuvrability of the S90 hull form to be made against that of a more conventional hull form. It should be noted that there are no model or full scale manoeuvring data available for the Type 23 design. However, the Inquiry considers that this vessel will exhibit similar manoeuvring characteristics to the Type 22 and Leander class frigates.

6.2   NSR 7069 Manoeuvring Requirements and Additional Desired Characteristics

The NSR 7069 stipulates two specific manoeuvring requirements which must be satisfied:

i)   The ship must have a tactical diameter of less than a given multiple of its length.

ii)   The stopping distance must be similar to, or better than, that of a Leander class frigate.

In addition to these specific requirements, the MoD informed the Inquiry that any proposed frigate should embody a number of other desirable manoeuvring characteristics. These include the ability to:

-    execute steady turning manoeuvres with a small tactical diameter, advance and transfer and with minimal loss of speed. The terms and parameters used in turning manoeuvres are defined in Figure 6.6.1.

-    change course rapidly with minimum use of sea room.

-    maintain course in all conditions with small heading or course error and minimal rudder activity.

-    manoeuvre in harbour, ahead and astern at slow speeds, stationary and starting from rest in any wind strength and heading.

-    retain control whilst accelerating, decelerating, going ahead, stopped or going astern.

The performance of the S102 has been considered in relation to the two criteria specifically mentioned in the NSR 7069, together with the additional desired attributes identified above.

6.3   **Assessment of the Manoeuvring Performance of the S102**

6.3.1 Turning Ability

A series of turning circle trials and Kempf[1] manoeuvres were carried out on the Southern Cross III. The trials results were analysed to determine the relevant manoeuvring performance parameters for incorporation into Lloyd's Register's computer based ship manoeuvring simulator. In order to assess the adequacy of this simulator to predict the turning performance of this type of hull form, theoretical predictions of the turning performance of the Southern Cross III were carried out and compared with the trials results. The measure of agreement achieved between prediction and trial for a typical Southern Cross III turning circle is illustrated in Figure 6.6.2. This validation procedure gave the Inquiry confidence that the ship manoeuvring simulator could be used to predict the manoeuvring performance of the S102.

----

1.   A Kempf manoeuvre is a zig-zag manoeuvre performed to evaluate the ability of the vessel's rudder to initiate and check changes in the ship's heading.

The turning circle performance for the S102 was simulated at two different approach speeds corresponding approximately to the S102 maximum speed and 75% of maximum speed. The results obtained indicated that the S102 design would easily satisfy the NSR 7069 tactical diameter requirement over the full speed range. It should be noted, however, that the tactical diameter predicted for the S102 when expressed in terms of ship length was considerably larger than that claimed for the S90 (i.e. greater than two ship lengths).

A comparison of the predicted turning performance of the S102 with that of the Type 22 and Leander class frigates indicated that the S102 would be considerably better than either of these two vessels over the full speed range. The average percentage improvements in the absolute values of the parameters indicated in Figure 6.6.1, for the S102 compared with the Leander, are given below:-

Tactical diameter	8% better than Leander
Transfer	15% better than Leander
Advance	21% better than Leander
Steady rate of turn	14% better than Leander

The percentage loss of speed during turning could not be determined for the S102 from the results of the Southern Cross III trials using the simulator without modelling the complex characteristics of the two different main propulsion plants. However, based on the speed loss measured on the Southern Cross III trials, the Inquiry has concluded, after giving due consideration to the different propulsion machinery systems, that, for equal rates of turn, the speed loss during a turn for the S102, over its upper operating speed range, would be comparable with that of a conventional frigate.

The results obtained are only applicable, in the strictest sense, to the S102 when operating at the equivalent draught and trim conditions to those pertaining to the Southern Cross III during the manoeuvring trials. Under these conditions, the S102 would have a small stern down trim (instead of the bow down trim required to minimise resistance) and a slightly deeper than design draught. The influence of these changes has been investigated by the Inquiry and it is concluded that, with respect to both these parameters, the turning performance of the S102 would be enhanced at the design operating condition.

6.3.2   Stopping Performance

The stopping distance of a vessel when going from full ahead to full astern depends upon the vessel's resistance, displacement, engine power and mode of astern thrust operation and the four quadrant propeller thrust and torque characteristics.

As both the Type 23 and S102 designs have similar CODLAG machinery configurations and since this machinery would be operated in the same manner, it is possible to compare the stopping performance of the two vessels on the relative merits of their hull, displacement, astern power and propeller characteristics without having to use the manoeuvring simulator. In this context the following is noted:

-       The resistance of the S102 is considerably greater than that of the Type 23.

-       The displacements of the S102 and Type 23 designs are similar.

-       The astern power would normally be provided by the electric motors. As similar electric motors to those installed in the Type 23 have been proposed for the S102, both vessels would have the same astern power.

-       The differences in the four quadrant propeller characteristics for the S102 and Type 23 are assumed to have a negligible effect on the stopping distance.

From a consideration of these points, the Inquiry considers that the stopping distance of the S102 would be considerably less than that of the Type 23. In addition, if the larger electric motors necessary for the S102 to achieve the required quiet towed array and endurance speeds (see Section 2 of this chapter) were to be fitted, then the S102's stopping distance would be further reduced in comparison with that of the Type 23.

Although the stopping distance requirement in the NSR 7069 is expressed in terms of that achieved by the Leander, the Inquiry considers that comparison with the Type 23 would be equally valid and the MoD have confirmed this. As the S102 would have a superior stopping performance to that of the Type 23, it would therefore have no difficulty in satisfying the NSR 7069 requirement.

6.3.3   Directional Stability

A ship is considered to be directionally stable if it continues in a straight line after it has been forced off course, by a wave for example. A directionally unstable ship would continue to turn if the ship was not actively steered back onto course. Directional instability leads to quicker turning response but requires a greater use of rudder to maintain a straight course. If a ship is extremely directionally unstable it can go out of control, especially when manoeuvring in restricted waters, such as harbours, and close to other ships, such as in RAS operations.

The S102's control characteristics have been determined by analysing the results of the Kempf manoeuvres carried out on the Southern Cross III during the full scale trials. These characteristics have been assessed against similar data available for the Type 22 and Leander class frigates.

This analysis indicated that the S102 (with a stern down trim equivalent to that of the Southern Cross III on trials) would have superior course stability to that of the Type 22 and Leander class frigates. However, it must be noted that a main feature of the Sirius concept is the minimisation of resistance by operating with a bow down trim. The effect of this would be to reduce the directional stability.

The influence of trim on the non-dimensional hydrodynamic coefficients governing the directional stability characteristics of the S102 have been investigated using empirical methods and the consequential effect on its directional stability have been evaluated.

The results show that the S102, in the deep displacement condition, would be expected to remain directionally stable in the level and maximum achievable bow down trim condition (see Chapter 5, Section 3.3). However, at the optimum bow down trim appropriate to the endurance speed in the deep displacement condition, the analysis indicates that, in the absence of modifications to the skeg size, the vessel could experience directional instability. It should be noted that it has not been possible to achieve this optimum trim following the single design iteration. However, if subsequent iteration led to large bow down trims then the directional stability of the vessel in such conditions would require careful evaluation.

6.3.4   Additional Characteristics

The Inquiry has considered the performance of the S90 hull form in relation to the other attributes that the MoD have indicated are desirable (see Section 6.2). The Inquiry could find no evidence to suggest that the S102's manoeuvring capability, compared with a conventional hull form, would be reduced whilst accelerating, decelerating, going ahead, stopped or going astern, manoeuvring in a confined environment or whilst operating in strong winds or currents.

6.4   Conclusions

The manoeuvring characteristics of the S102 have been ascertained using the results from the full scale manoeuvring trials carried out on the Southern Cross III.

The predicted performance has been assessed against the requirements of the NSR 7069 and compared with the known performance of the Type 22 and Leander class frigates, or the estimated performance of the Type 23, as appropriate.

With reference to the NSR requirements, the S102 more than adequately satisfies the tactical turning diameter and, based on a comparison with the Type 23, is considered to satisfy with ease the stopping distance requirement.

The S102 is predicted to be capable of turning with a smaller tactical diameter than either the Type 22 or Leander at identical speeds. Similarly, the transfer and advance at 90 degrees is less and the steady state rate of turn is larger.

The speed loss experienced by the S102 during turning is expected to be comparable to that of the Type 22 or Leander for the same rates of turn.

The S102 is predicted to remain directionally stable at level trim and the current maximum achievable bow down trim, in the deep displacement condition. However, the vessel could experience directional instability if the optimum bow down trim, required for minimum resistance at the endurance speed in the deep condition, was achieved in a subsequent design iteration, this optimum trim being larger than that achieved at the current stage of development of the S102.

In overall terms, the Inquiry concludes that the S102 possesses a superior manoeuvring performance to that of a conventional frigate. However, a similar manoeuvring performance to the S102 could be achieved by the Type 23, if required, by suitable design modifications such as increasing the size of the rudders.

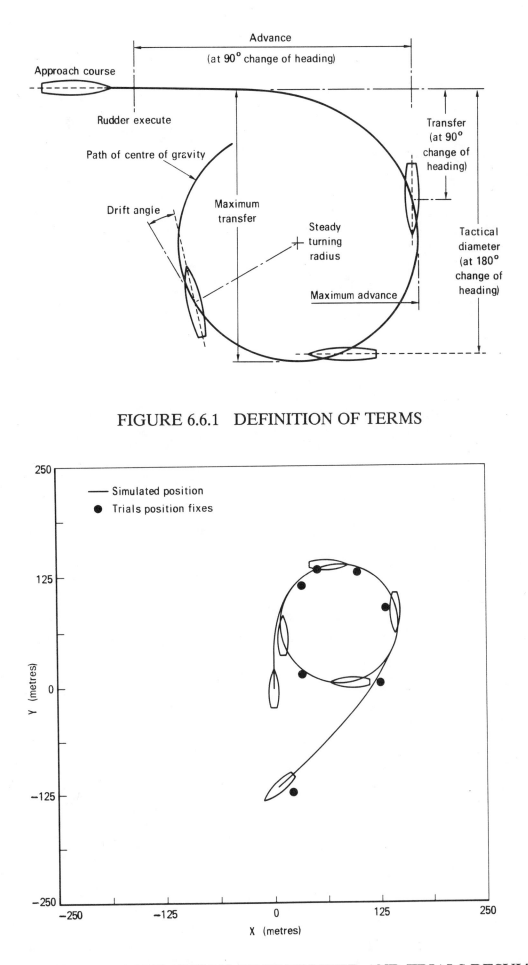

FIGURE 6.6.1   DEFINITION OF TERMS

FIGURE 6.6.2   COMPARISON OF PREDICTED AND TRIALS RESULTS

CHAPTER 6

ASSESSMENT OF THE S102 DESIGN

SECTION 7
Military Features

7.1 Introduction

The overall military effectiveness of a fighting ship depends on a complex interaction of many factors such as speed, endurance, manoeuvrability, seakeeping, stability, internal design, detection systems and weapon fit. This section of the report is concerned with 'military features' and, within the scope of this term, the Inquiry has considered the subjects of weapon systems, radar sensors and detection systems, infra-red emissions, magnetic signature and radiated noise. The more general assessment of military effectiveness is implicit in the overall conclusions of the report.

The radiated noise and self-noise characteristics are important features of any warship but to an anti-submarine warfare (ASW) vessel they are crucial. Radiated noise is the principal means of detection of a submarine by a surface ship and vice versa. The noise generated by an ASW vessel, however, not only gives away her own presence but also down-grades her ability to detect the presence of a submarine by causing interference with her own noise detection systems. In general, the noise that interferes with the ship's own systems is termed 'self-noise' and that by which her presence is detected by other vessels is termed 'radiated noise'. In the case of an ASW ship operating in the towed array mode - that is with an array of sensitive listening sensors (hydrophones) streamed at large distances behind the ship to eliminate self-noise problems - the radiated noise characteristics are also critical with respect to the effectiveness of the towed array. It is this aspect that will generally govern the acceptable levels of radiated noise in an ASW towed array ship.

TGA have claimed few direct advantages for their S90 hull form specific to the above interpretation of 'military features', the principal benefits being ascribed to an increased defensive (and offensive) horizon resulting from a higher location of sensors and the ability to fit a greater weapon payload due to greater reserves of stability. Although they do not contest the theoretical superiority of long/thin ships with respect to wider arcs of fire, TGA suggest that the Sirius concept provides greater scope for concentrating increased fire power around the main target area of the ship and, by implication, sufficient space to accommodate a superior combat suite to that required by the NSR such as was proposed for the S90 design proposal. It is also suggested that the S90 hull and superstructure profile results from an attempt to create the least detectable radar signature consistent with the ship's ability to defend herself. No claims have been identified with respect to infra-red, magnetic or radiated noise signature or with regard to self-noise characteristics.

The principal conclusions of the Hill-Norton Committee Report with respect to the 'military features' of the S90 hull form, can be summarized as follows:

- With respect to efficient weapon fit and layout, the critical dimension was stated to be deck area rather than ship length and it was concluded that a short/fat design would provide greater area at the centre of the ship where weapon systems are most conveniently positioned.

- With regard to weapon systems performance, the Committee considered this to be greatly improved by the ability to mount the radar and other sensors much higher in the Sirius hull than in a conventional design thus giving increased detection ranges. Although no attempt was made to assess them, the potentially disadvantageous implications of extra superstructure height on radar signature were acknowledged.

- In the context of hull radiated noise, the Committee could find no evidence to suggest that the S90 proposal would be at any disadvantage in comparison with conventional hull forms, except at speeds near the onset of cavitation, which they estimated would occur between 12 to 15 knots. Since for most of the time they anticipated towed array speeds around 6 knots, the differences in 'dynamic noise' were considered negligible. In one particular respect, the Sirius hull form was considered to offer a distinct advantage in that the greater stability would make it possible to carry more equipment, generators, systems, etc, higher in the structure, thus further isolating the associated noise source from the waterline.

- The anticipated superior seakeeping characteristics, with regard to bow emergence and bottom slamming, were considered to represent an improvement in self-noise levels and consequently to give rise to more efficient operation of the bow mounted sonar.

- Finally, it was suggested that the BHC analysis of quiescent periods - that is, the periods when the deck motion is within the operating 'window' for helicopter take-off and landing - experienced during the 1:10 scale open water model tests of the S90 and Leander hull forms, clearly indicated that the S90 would provide a more stable platform for helicopter operations.

The majority of criticisms and counter-claims levelled at the S90 proposal were associated with features specific to the S90. In particular, much emphasis was placed on perceived non-compliances relating to the inability of the proposed diesel machinery configurations to meet the stringent NSR noise targets and to deficiencies in usable volume and deck area with respect to weapon layout. In the latter respect, the MoD specifically acknowledged that many of the perceived shortfalls in military capability could be reduced or even eliminated by an increase in size of ship and a re-arrangement of upper deck layout.

In developing the S102 to meet the spatial requirements of the NSR 7069, in particular ensuring that sufficient space was allocated to accommodate all the required weapons, along with TGA's proposal to replace the diesel engine propulsion system proposed for the S90 with a CODLAG propulsion system, these specific criticisms have been addressed. The Inquiry has, therefore, assessed the military features aspects arising from the adoption of the Sirius concept by comparing the S102 against the NSR 7069 and the Type 23 frigate.

7.2   Noise Signature

The radiated noise signature will, in general, comprise contributions from the hull, the machinery installation and the propellers. For conventional general purpose frigates, these noise sources may be ranked in the order given, in terms of increasing magnitude, over all but the lowest part of the operational speed range. Propeller generated noise will, in general, dominate the radiated noise signature. However, for propellers operating well below cavitation inception speeds, machinery generated noise can become of equal or greater importance. For ASW ships, particularly those intended to operate with towed arrays, considerable attention is, therefore, given to designing propellers with high cavitation inception speeds and to sophisticated machinery noise isolation and insulation systems. These noise reduction measures are a function of design detail beyond the extent of that appropriate to the S102 at its current stage of development and for this reason a quantitative assessment of the noise characteristics in relation to the NSR 7069 is not considered feasible.

In order to proceed with this aspect of the investigation, the Inquiry has carried out a qualitative assessment of noise implications inherent in the S102 design in comparison with the Type 23 frigate. The design details of the Type 23 have been subjected to extensive noise evaluation studies and the Inquiry is satisfied that the Type 23 should be able to comply with the NSR 7069 noise targets, but with little or no margin to spare. The Type 23 frigate may, therefore, be regarded as a useful benchmark against which the acceptability or otherwise of the S102 may be qualitatively judged.

7.2.1 Hull Generated Noise

The hull contributes to the radiated and self-noise characteristics in two independent ways. In the first, noise is generated by the hydrodynamic interaction of the hull structure with its fluid environment and in the second, noise generated by the propeller and machinery items is transmitted to the hull, amplified or attenuated according to its own acoustic characteristics, and then re-broadcast.

With regard to the first contribution, no evidence has been submitted to suggest in any sense that the hydrodynamic noise associated with the turbulent boundary layer created by the passage of the hull through the water should be markedly different between the S90 and Type 23 hull forms. The Inquiry can also find no evidence to substantiate any differences in this respect between the two hull forms. Hydrodynamic noise, however, is also generated by the wave making and wave breaking behaviour of the hull form and by ship motion phenomena such as, for example, bottom slamming and bow flare impact. In this respect it is considered that the increased self-noise at the bow sonar resulting from a higher incidence of bow flare impact loading and greater bow splash, associated with the higher waterplane entrance angle on the S90 hull form, must be offset against decreased self-noise associated with its better bottom slamming and bow emergence characteristics as anticipated by the Hill-Norton Committee. The comparative seakeeping behaviour, with respect to these ship motion characteristics, has been discussed in Section 5 of this chapter.

In the case of the second form of noise radiation from the hull, that is when it acts as a sound box by picking up and then re-radiating sound originating from all noise generation sources including the propeller and machinery, it is clear that the geometric form of the hull surface, together with the global and local mass-elastic characteristics of the internal structure, will have some effect. This aspect has, again, not been identified by any of the proponents as representing either a significant advantage or disadvantage with regard to the S90 hull form. The Inquiry, after consideration of these issues, both independently and in consultation with various noise experts, has concluded that the generally greater global hull stiffness of the S102 hull form would be favourable with respect to the low frequency reverberation characteristics. This advantage will be counterbalanced to a greater or lesser extent by the S102's greater capacity to absorb both noise energy generated by the propeller due to the wider, flatter after body lines and to radiate machinery noise due to its greater wetted surface area in the vicinity of the machinery spaces. Properly validated methods for assessing the comparative effect of these two counteracting influences are beyond the current state of the art.

The seakeeping analysis described in Section 5 of this chapter concluded that it would be necessary to fit roll damping devices to the S102 in order to maintain roll responses within acceptable levels, particularly at low speeds. TGA have stated that they would not fit bilge keels to their Sirius hulls but would consider installing anti-rolling tanks to limit the roll amplitude at low speeds. It is considered that the hydrodynamic noise generated by these devices could, in itself, make a significant contribution to the overall radiated noise signature in addition to the indirect implications of such tanks on increased displacement and resistance and hence on the powering requirements. The use of these measures to control roll response during towed array operations would, therefore, need careful evaluation in relation to the specific arrangement proposed.

7.2.2   Machinery Generated Noise

One of the major claimed non-compliances of the original S90 proposal related to perceived difficulties in meeting the stringent noise targets specified in the NSR 7069 which were considered to be insurmountable with any of the proposed diesel engine machinery configurations. In recognition of these requirements, TGA have proposed a CODLAG propulsion system for the S102 which is similar to that fitted in the Type 23 (see Chapter 5, Section 2.2.2). It was considered that, at the current state of proven technology, a CODLAG arrangement represented the best probability of achieving a practical solution to the stringent NSR 7069 noise targets. If alternative practical solutions could be developed, then the Inquiry team could find no reason why they should not be equally applicable to both conventional and Sirius hull forms. The choice of propulsion system was, therefore, considered to be a neutral issue independent of hull form design in the context of radiated and self-noise issues.

The main differences in machinery noise generation characteristics between the Type 23 and S102 designs thus arise from the different powering requirements at a given ship speed. These differences would be further modified by the different noise transmission paths, between machinery items and hull surfaces, associated with differences in machinery location and structural design. Under the critical quiet operating conditions, i.e. when using only the electric motors, the differences in machinery generated radiated noise would be dominated by the load dependent noise characteristics of the generator sets and appropriate transmission paths.

Calculation procedures for quantitative noise transmission assessment are not appropriate at a first iteration stage. However, the Inquiry considers that the differences between the structural arrangements of the S102 and Type 23 would be unlikely to give rise to any significant advantage or disadvantage for the S102.

The locations of the diesel-generator rooms in the S102 are similar to those on the Type 23 and again no significant differences are anticipated in this respect, with regard to radiated noise. It has been suggested by both TGA and the Hill-Norton Committee that the greater reserve stability of the Sirius concept would allow all the diesel-generator sets to be mounted higher in the structure with consequent benefit to the radiated noise characteristics. Whilst the validity of this argument is not disputed, the Inquiry recognises that other considerations, such as vulnerability to a single mode of attack, may take precedence over the noise benefit obtained. The Inquiry is also of the opinion that, should such a benefit be judged worthwhile, then a similar generator siting philosophy could be applied to the conventional hull form, any consequent loss of stability being counterbalanced by a very modest increase in beam.

In the light of the above discussions, and accepting the virtually silent operation of the electric motors, it is the opinion of the Inquiry that, in the quiet operating modes, the only significant differences between the Type 23 and the S102, with respect to radiated noise arising from the machinery, are those due to the different diesel-electric power generation requirements for a given speed. There are, however, many alternative ways of providing the required additional power generation capacity and each alternative would require detailed evaluation. It is anticipated that a solution could be found that would not materially affect the noise radiation levels.

Although the distances between the bow mounted sonar and the relevant machinery items in the S102 design satisfy minimum specified requirements, the corresponding self-noise levels are likely to be marginally greater than those on the Type 23, at all speeds, due to the increased power requirements and the more compact arrangement.

7.2.3 Propeller Generated Noise

With respect to propeller radiated noise, the transition from non-cavitating to cavitating conditions is associated with a significant increase in radiated noise levels. It is considered that, under cavitating conditions, there is no practical possibility of any ASW frigate complying with the stringent noise limits required by the NSR 7069 for towed array operations. It is, therefore, of prime importance that the propulsive system is designed such that cavitation inception occurs at the highest possible speed. Optimum performance of the towed array requires cavitation free conditions over the entire towed array operational speed range.

The ability to design a propeller for cavitation free operation up to a given speed is limited by such factors as the non-uniformity of the effective wake, including axial and transverse components, constraints on propeller diameter and depth of immersion, the rpm and the required thrust.

Under cavitation free conditions, the radiated noise levels, in the frequency range of concern, are principally dependent on the harmonic strengths of the radiated pressure field associated with the pressure difference across the propeller blades. The main governing factors are the wake non-uniformity and the propeller loading.

Following consideration of all relevant factors affecting the above parameters, including analysis of the thrust requirements, the available wake data for the Type 23 frigate and Southern Cross III (no wake data being available for the S90), and taking into account the influences of shaft rake, bow down trim and seakeeping behaviour on the depth of propeller blade immersion, propeller emergence and cross-flow components in the wake, the Inquiry has concluded that the S102 would be at a material disadvantage in comparison to the Type 23 frigate with respect to propeller radiated noise signature.   This conclusion stems chiefly from the higher power requirements of the S102 at any given speed, which would lead to higher propeller rotational speeds, increased propeller loading and, in turn, to a significantly lower cavitation inception speed.   In addition, even below cavitation inception, the higher thrust loading and propeller tip speeds would lead, speed for speed, to higher radiated noise levels on the S102 than is the case for the Type 23 frigate. Alternatively, to achieve the same radiated noise levels as the Type 23, the S102 would have to reduce speed below that of the Type 23 frigate over the whole speed range.

At speeds around 6 knots, suggested by the Hill-Norton Committee to be the most common regime for towed array operations, the differences in radiated sound pressure, from the S102 and Type 23 designs, would be small. However, the Inquiry does not consider them to be negligible. Such speeds would be adopted when very quiet operating conditions were required and under these circumstances small increases in radiated sound pressure could significantly impair the sensitivity of the towed array hydrophones. Similar levels of radiated noise could only be achieved by reducing the speed of the S102, which would adversely affect the operational profile. For example, in the sprint and drift mode the balance of time spent in the sprint phase would be increased at the expense of that spent in the drift phase. The ASW vessel is only able to 'listen' effectively in the drift phase.

The decrease in cavitation inception speed is considered to be the dominating factor in the comparative assessment of the overall radiated noise signatures of the S102 and Type 23 designs.   Furthermore, it is understood that, for the Type 23 frigate, the achievement of a satisfactory cavitation inception speed, relative to the maximum towed array speed requirement, presented considerable design difficulties.   The Inquiry, therefore, concludes that the S102, with a similar 'state of the art' propeller design, would be most unlikely to be able to satisfy the NSR 7069 noise target over the upper speed range for quiet towed array operations.

In addition to the radiated noise signature, the self-noise characteristics of the S102 would also be adversely affected by the increased propeller generated noise. This would be further aggravated by the closer proximity of the propeller to the bow mounted sonar than is the case for the longer Type 23 frigate.

7.3 Weapon Layout and Efficiency

The development of the S102 took as one of its fundamental aims the achievement of an acceptable weapon fit incorporating all the armaments required by the NSR 7069. The resulting weapon layout was submitted to the MoD for comment and, after due study, received their endorsement as a workable first iteration basis. No major impediment against subsequent refinement into an acceptable combat suite was identified.

In view of the above, an S90 hull form of appropriate size can be stated to present no significant problems with respect to compliance with the NSR 7069 combat suite requirements. However, in order to establish whether the Sirius concept could provide any advantage over the conventional frigate hull form, the Inquiry made a comparison between the S102 and Type 23 designs in terms of weapon effectiveness.

The helicopter landing area and hangar space provided in the S102 design was derived on the basis of providing the same distance between the aft end of the flight deck and forward bulkhead of the hangar as in the Type 23 design. This has the effect of producing a flight deck on the S102 which is greater in area than the Type 23 due to the increased beam of the S102. Other differences that could occur between the two designs with respect to helicopter operations are those arising from airflow considerations about the hull and superstructure. These factors could only be quantified by model tests in a wind tunnel. However, no significant overall advantage is anticipated for either design with respect to hangar and flight deck arrangement.

Seakeeping characteristics are discussed in Section 5 of this chapter. In general, it is predicted that the S102 would experience small improvements in both vertical and lateral responses at the flight deck relative to the Type 23 frigate. However, the claim, based on the BHC quiescent period analysis, that the S90 hull form would provide a more stable platform for helicopter operations, is considered to be far from conclusively demonstrated. Examination of the results of the BHC analysis indicated that, even for the limited number of conditions reported (three speeds, four headings and one sea-state), the conclusion that the mean time between quiescent periods (MTBQP) was shorter for the S90 than for the Leander was by no means clear cut. In addition, the definition of the operating window omitted some important parameters, such as the vertical and horizontal responses, and the relevance of the minimum length of a quiescent period assumed for the analysis is, in itself, open to question. Finally, the comparison was made with the Leander, a frigate whose seakeeping characteristics are by no means identical to the Type 23. Notwithstanding the foregoing uncertainties, a shorter MTBQP for the S102 in comparison with the Type 23, in an overall averaged sense, would not be inconsistent with the differences identified in the seakeeping characteristics.

However, a shorter MTBQP would normally be experienced in association with a shorter mean length of the quiescent periods. The comparison of platform stability for helicopter take-off and landing must, therefore, be a trade-off between the advantages of more frequent short operating windows and fewer but longer ones.

In the case of the Type 23 frigate, the vertical launch Sea Wolf missiles are located forward in a single silo. For the S102, the shorter ship length meant that a similar position could not be adopted. Therefore, the Sea Wolf weapon system was split into two silos located port and starboard just aft of amidships. The location of these silos took due account of the clearance cone around each missile necessary to prevent interference with other shipboard systems. Total missile capacity is the same for both designs and, whilst it is unlikely that the differences in location of the silos would have any material effect on weapon system efficiency due to the missiles' vertical launch capability, it could be argued that the separation of this weapon system, in the case of the S102, into two separate silo locations does reduce the vulnerability of the system to attack. However, a split silo location philosophy is also a practical possibility on conventional hull forms and was proposed as an alternative configuration for the Type 23 frigate. The combined coverage provided by the Sea Wolf tracker systems is broadly equivalent in both designs, with the forward tracker on the S102 having a more restricted angle of view than its counterpart on the Type 23, whereas the reverse situation is the case for the aft tracker. Since the relative advantages and disadvantages of the two trackers are broadly equivalent, it is concluded that neither vessel offers a distinct advantage to the Sea Wolf system.

The Vickers 4.5 inch Mk 8 gun is situated in similar locations on each design. The arcs of fire on the Type 23 are superior by about 11%; however, this could well be nullified in subsequent design iterations of the S102. With respect to the remaining gunnery defence systems specified in the NSR 7069, there is judged to be a slight advantage in favour of the Type 23, with respect to arcs of fire, for the current arrangement. However, provision has been made in the NSR for the fitting of additional gun defence systems and this could result in the situation being reversed.

All other weapon systems are located at broadly equivalent positions on the two designs and it is judged that their disposition would provide similar constraints on their performance.

The seakeeping characteristics of the S102, identified in Section 5 of this chapter, indicate a similar roll amplitude response behaviour to that of the Type 23 frigate. However, due to a combination of the S102's shorter roll period and the higher location of most weapons, trackers and sensors, these components would, in general, experience greater angular accelerations and lateral responses than their counterparts on the Type 23. It has been suggested that this more onerous motions environment could result in a degradation of weapon performance or, on the other hand, a need for significant design modification to adapt the weapon stabilisation systems, etc. The Inquiry has consulted with the relevant weapon systems and sensor manufacturers on this issue and has concluded that, although weapon performance could be marginally influenced, it would still remain within specification, any small effects being, in general, amenable to minimisation by system tuning. In addition, the Inquiry has found no evidence to suggest that maintenance requirements would be materially altered.

The shorter length of the S102 leads to a more compact weapon layout. However, no significant advantages relating to the increased concentration of fire power about the main target area of the ship, as claimed by TGA, or locating weapons where they are more conveniently positioned, as suggested by the Hill-Norton Committee, have been identified. The more compact configuration would, on the contrary, be more likely to exacerbate design problems with regard to providing the minimum spatial separations necessary to meet electromagnetic interference (EMI) and radiation hazard (RADHAZ) standards, and also to increase the vulnerability to a single strike attack.

In summary, it is considered that, with respect to weapon layout efficiency, there is little overall advantage associated with either the Sirius or the conventional hull forms for the combat suite specified in the NSR 7069. The greater reserve stability of the S90 hull form would, however, give greater flexibility for subsequent armament refit with little constraint on additional top weight of either weapon systems or ammunition. However, space is likely to be the limiting factor for both design concepts and, in the Inquiry's view, development trends are likely to lead to lighter rather than heavier weapon systems.

7.4   Radar, Infra-red and Magnetic Signature

Radar, infra-red and magnetic signatures are important characteristics of any warship and, together with noise signature, represent the principal factors influencing the ship's detectability or targetability to guided or heat seeking missiles, torpedoes, mines, etc. The minimisation of these signatures is, therefore, considered by the MoD to be of extreme importance.

In considering the evidence submitted on radar signature, the Inquiry has been conscious of the very strong dependence of the effective radar cross-section on the design detail and local shaping of external features of the above water hull and superstructure. While the basic principles relevant to the minimisation of radar cross-section have been borne in mind during the development of the S102, the Inquiry considers that the design would need to be progressed to considerably greater levels of detail before a realistic assessment of radar signature could be made in comparison to a conventional frigate at such an advanced stage of design as the Type 23. Nevertheless, a qualitative assessment, based on examination of the relevant characteristics of the two designs, leads the Inquiry to the conclusion that the S102 would be at an inherent disadvantage with respect to radar signature in comparison with the Type 23 frigate. This conclusion stems principally from considerations of both the increased cross-sectional area of the above water profile of the S102 at any direction other than dead abeam and the increased height distribution of the S102 cross-section leading to a greater detection horizon. The dead abeam profile has a slightly smaller projected area than the Type 23; the front elevation projected area is, however, considerably larger. Both the cross-sectional and height characteristics are illustrated in Figures 5.3.4 and 5.3.5 of Chapter 5.

The increased height of radar and other electronic surveillance sensors on which TGA and the Hill-Norton Committee base their assertions of increased offensive and defensive horizons is also illustrated by Figures 5.3.4 and 5.3.5 of Chapter 5. In general, a sensor's horizon is proportional to the square root of its height above sea level and it is clear that the S102 would have an advantage in this respect. In particular, the main surveillance radar horizon would be greater by some 20% in comparison with the Type 23 frigate. The S102 would, therefore, benefit from increased reaction and target acquisition timescales particularly with respect to sea skimming missiles. At the current stage of development of such weapons, this would represent a marginal benefit for the S102 by increasing the 'wait' time, i.e. the time between target acquisition and the firing of a defensive missile. Its future importance could increase, however, in relation to developments in higher speed, low flying weapons.

The relative merits of increased radar horizon at the expense of increased radar visibility depend on the particular military role under consideration. For the roles envisaged by the NSR 7069, the Inquiry takes the view that the relative advantages and disadvantages associated with the S102 would largely offset each other. In addition, the Inquiry believes that, should an increased radar horizon have been required for the Type 23, then this could have been achieved by relatively modest design changes without incurring the same penalty on radar signature as is the case with the S102.

The Inquiry has investigated the influence of seakeeping behaviour on the surveillance radar with the conclusion that, although the S102's shorter roll period would give rise to a more onerous motions environment, the different characteristics could be accommodated without any unacceptable loss of performance. In addition, no significant re-design or increased maintenance penalty is anticipated.

Little evidence has been submitted either for or against the Sirius concept with regard to infra-red and magnetic signatures. The Inquiry has, nevertheless, given due consideration to the main factors affecting these characteristics and concludes that there is no significant advantage to either the Type 23 or S102 designs. There is, however, a slight disadvantage to the Sirius hull for both signatures arising from its greater powering requirements. In the case of infra-red emissions, the increased power at any given speed will produce increased waste heat in the form of exhaust gases and thus require greater quantities of cooling air, both for exhaust gas mixing and structural cooling. The cost implications of this are included in the ship's systems cost evaluation covered in Section 8 of this chapter. Assuming that the increased diesel-electric propulsive power, identified in Section 2 of this chapter as being necessary to meet the NSR 7069 endurance and maximum towed array speed requirements, is provided in the S102, then there would be increased magnetic fields associated with both the larger electric propulsion motors and the increased power generation requirements. In the absence of any de-gaussing considerations, this would result in some increase in overall magnetic signature for all operating modes involving electric propulsion.

7.5   Conclusions

The S102 design can satisfactorily accommodate all the weapon systems required by the NSR 7069. No significant overall advantage, with respect to weapon effectiveness or layout efficiency, has been identified for the S102 or Type 23.

The higher reserve stability associated with the Sirius hull form would provide greater flexibility for increasing weapon systems and armament top weight. Such flexibility may be considered important with regard to subsequent armament refit with future weapon developments. However, space is likely to be the limiting factor for both design concepts and, in the Inquiry's view, development trends are likely to lead to lighter rather than heavier weapon systems.

The different seakeeping characteristics between a Sirius and conventional hull form are considered unlikely to lead to any significant advantage or disadvantage with respect to weapon performance or maintenance requirements.

The S102, following the single design iteration, would be unable to achieve the NSR 7069 required speeds given the machinery configuration proposed by TGA. To achieve these speeds additional gas turbines, larger electric motors and greater diesel-generator capacity would have to be fitted. Such modifications would have a marginal but disadvantageous effect on magnetic and infra-red signatures for the S102 compared with the the Type 23.

The higher profile of the superstructure would make the S102 more susceptible to radar detection at longer range than is the case for the Type 23. However, this disadvantage would be offset against the corresponding increase in radar horizon and the consequent improvements in target acquisition and reaction times. These improvements could be significant for the defensive capability against future developments in sea skimming missile performance.

Propeller cavitation inception speeds would be lower for the S102 than for the Type 23 and, for this reason, it is considered that the S102 would be unable to satisfy the NSR 7069 radiated noise targets over the upper end of the quiet towed array speed range.

The greater powering requirement of the S102, in comparison with the Type 23, would imply a greater radiated noise signature at all speeds up to the maximum specified by the NSR 7069.

The self-noise characteristics at the bow mounted sonar would be greater on the S102 than on the Type 23 due to increased bow splash, greater incidence of bow flare impact, shorter noise transmission paths to machinery items, higher propeller noise generation and closer proximity of the propellers. This increase in self-noise would be mitigated to some extent, depending on ship speed and sea-state, by the better relative bow motion, bow slamming and bow emergence characteristics of the S102.

In overall terms the Inquiry concludes that, since the effectiveness of an ASW frigate is dependent, first and foremost, on its ability to detect and locate submarines, the S102 would be unable to meet fully the primary function required by the NSR 7069 due to exceedance of noise targets over the towed array upper operational speed range. In addition, even over that part of the speed range where the noise targets could be achieved, the S102's performance, due to its greater radiated noise levels associated with its greater power requirements, would be inferior to that of the Type 23 frigate.

CHAPTER 6

ASSESSMENT OF THE S102 DESIGN

SECTION 8
Construction Costs and Build Time

8.1   Introduction

TGA have claimed that a frigate based on their S90 hull form would be substantially cheaper to build than such a vessel based on a conventional hull form. They have indicated that the major cost saving would result from the fact that the vessel could be built using a commercial strength standard rather than a naval standard. TGA believe that the adoption of a commercial strength standard would allow cheaper, lower grade steel to be used and would also enable the vessel to be built using commercial building standards which are less labour intensive than corresponding naval building standards. In addition, as the accommodation and ship systems could be concentrated more centrally in the vessel, the length and complexity of the ship systems would be reduced and thus their cost. The provision of more 'elbow room' in the S90 hull form would also enable fitting out to be carried out with much greater ease which, in turn, would reduce the labour costs and construction time.

The Hill-Norton Committee identified, based on information provided by Frederikshavn Vaerft A/S (FHV), that the potential cost savings arising from the factors described above could amount to 26.2% of the unit cost of the Type 23 (as quoted by the MoD in October 1983) for a vessel of the S90's proportions. The Committee concluded that if savings even approaching this magnitude could be confirmed, the effect on the frigate force of the Royal Navy would be highly significant.

In order to assess these claims, the Inquiry has compared the difference in construction costs and build time of the S102 and the Type 23. Although the Type 23, as a design, is considerably more advanced than the S102, the Inquiry considers that the substantial cost savings claimed by TGA should be identifiable from such a comparison.

In comparing the S102 and Type 23 construction costs, the Inquiry has examined only those costs which can be considered to be dependent on the hull form adopted. It should be noted that there are a number of other factors which are not hull form dependent but which do have a considerable effect on the construction cost of a warship, some of these being:

> The Government's procurement policy.
> Operating role including required crew complement, speed and mission profiles.
> Number of ships ordered.
> Shipyard selection.
> Strength and construction standards.
> Labour costs (i.e. region or country of build).
> Working practices and labour relations.
> Climate.
> Level of sub-contractor involvement.

Shipyard's experience of building warships and its technological capabilities.

Workforce competence.

Production methods (e.g. use of modular construction and pre-outfitting techniques).

Planned or timely delivery of materials and equipment.

Quality assurance requirements (extent and type of inspection, verification and documentation).

Security requirements.

Overhead costs of shipyard and sub-contractors.

The potential for cost savings in the above areas is recognised and it is understood that, in the case of the MoD and UK naval shipbuilders, measures are being implemented to reduce these costs where possible. However, although these items do have a major influence on the construction cost of a particular warship, they will not be significantly different for two vessels built in the same shipyard to the same specification which only differ in their hull form and proportions, since such items are independent of hull form.

Since the Type 23 frigate is being built in the UK, the Inquiry has based its construction cost comparison on the understanding that the S102 would also be built in this country. In order to quantify those costs which differ due to hull form alone, it is essential, in addition to comparing vessels which meet the same specification (in this case the NSR 7069), that the same rates for labour, overheads, etc, are applied in connection with the construction of each vessel.

8.2   Construction Cost Components

The total construction cost of a naval vessel is usually referred to as the Unit Production Cost (UPC). The Inquiry has identified that the MoD sub-divide this UPC into the following major cost groups:

Group 1.	Hull	Group 5.	Auxiliary Systems
Group 2.	Propulsion	Group 6.	Outfit & Furnishings
Group 3.	Electrical	Group 7.	Weapons
Group 4.	Control & Communication		

Each of these groups consists of:

i)   the material/equipment purchase cost,

ii)   the labour (and overhead) cost associated with the fabrication or installation of the material or equipment.

For consistency, the Inquiry has adopted the MoD's breakdown of the UPC and has examined how the material, equipment and associated labour costs would differ between the S102 and the Type 23 for each of the seven cost groups identified above.

The purchase cost of material and equipment has been determined from manufacturers' data where possible. In the absence of such information, data from the MoD for the Type 23 frigate has been used. This data has been independently verified where possible.

The Inquiry has calculated the direct labour costs based on a rate of £5.00 per manhour. Associated overhead costs have been taken at the rate of 130% of the direct labour cost. These basic rates include salaries and other ancillary payments and they are also intended to be representative of the average costs of both blue and white collar workers. It should be noted that individual UK naval shipyards may well have different manhour and overhead charges from these. However, such differences will have little effect in a comparative costing exercise.

It should be noted that the methods used by the Inquiry to estimate the group cost differentials cannot be considered to be rigorous. However, the Inquiry believes that they are adequate in providing a guide to the order of difference likely to be found for ships which differ only in their hull form and proportions.

8.3   The Construction Cost of the Type 23 Frigate

Based on the MoD cost estimates for the Type 23 frigate, the Inquiry has estimated the contribution which each of the cost groups identified in Section 8.2 makes to the total cost of a Type 23 frigate, built in a UK shipyard, at 1986/87 prices. These contributions, expressed as a percentage of a Net Unit Production Cost (NUPC), are as shown in Table 6.8.1.

The NUPC has been estimated by the Inquiry by deducting all first of class, development, lead shipyard and contingency cost components together with VAT and estimated profit margins from the UPC provided by the MoD. This NUPC has been taken to represent the price of all materials, equipment and associated labour costs incurred in the build of a Type 23 frigate.

Group	Materials & Equipment %	Labour + Overheads %	Total % of NUPC
1. Hull	1.6	11.4	13.0
2. Propulsion	6.2	2.5	8.7
3. Electrical	5.6	6.8	12.4
4. Control & Comms.	5.3	1.4	6.7
5. Auxiliary Systems	6.8	6.3	13.1
6. Outfit & Furnishings	6.6	7.8	14.4
7. Weapons	31.3	0.4	31.7
Total	63.4%	36.6%	100.0%

Table 6.8.1   Group Cost breakdown for Type 23 Frigate (expressed as a percentage of the NUPC)

The percentage group cost breakdown given in Table 6.8.1 is intended to be representative of the contribution each cost group makes to the NUPC. Individual shipyards may have slightly different breakdowns to those given in Table 6.8.1. However, the Inquiry considers that such differences will be small in magnitude.

8.4   Comparison of the S102 and Type 23 Group Costs

For each group detailed in Table 6.8.1, the Inquiry has assessed the cost differentials between the S102 and Type 23 resulting from the adoption of the two different hull forms. These differentials have been expressed as a percentage of the Type 23 NUPC.

8.4.1   Hull - Cost Group 1

i)   Material Purchase Cost

The following items are included in the purchase cost for this group:

> Gross steel material (plate and profile)
> Gross aluminium material (plate and profile)
> Castings and forgings
> Watertight, weathertight and gastight doors
> Fastenings and side scuttles
> Delivery costs of bought in items (for the Group)

From a review of these items, only the quantity of steel material used in the hull construction will be significantly affected by hull form.

The other items will not differ appreciably between the S102 and the Type 23.

Based on the estimated steelweight of each design (Chapter 5, Section 3.2) and the grades of steel to be used, the cost of the net steel material has been estimated based on British Steel Corporation's March 1987 prices.

As TGA requested the Inquiry to modify the scantlings of the S102 obtained using the LR 100A1 commercial standard to give equivalence with the Type 23 (see Chapter 5, Section 2.2.3), the material cost for the S102 is, therefore, based on a steelweight which is less than that which would be obtained if the LR 100A1 commercial standard had been used.

The net steel material cost for each design has been estimated as:

Type 23	0.40% of the NUPC
S102	0.35% of the NUPC

If the LR 100A1 standard had been adopted for the S102, then the steel material cost would have increased to 0.38% of the NUPC of the Type 23.

It is evident from these figures that the difference in the steel material cost due to a variation in hull form is small and the reduction in the NUPC due to the difference in the steel order for the S102 compared with the Type 23 is negligible (around 0.05% of the NUPC). Though the differences between the S102 and Type 23 steel orders would be increased by the incorporation of material scrap allowances, the potential savings from the adoption of the S102 would still be a negligible percentage of the total NUPC.

In addition, it should be noted that the adoption of a commercial strength standard, as opposed to a naval standard, for the design considered has little effect on the overall steel purchase price since the resulting scantlings and steel grades do not differ appreciably between a commercial and naval strength standard.

ii)   Labour Cost

Table 6.8.1 indicates that for the Type 23 the major cost component in Group 1 is the labour and associated overhead cost. This cost relates directly to the number of manhours attributed to the actual construction of the hull.

Based on a manhour rate of £5 per hour and associated overhead costs at the rate of 130% of the direct labour cost, the manhours spent on the actual construction of the Type 23 hull have been estimated from data supplied to the Inquiry. This estimate excludes the labour cost associated with the installation of the hull items (e.g. doors and hatches), together with the testing, cleansing and security, etc, included in Group 1.

These manhours are incurred in the handling, cleaning and protecting, cutting, pre-forming, fit-up, welding, assembly and fairing of the steel material used to construct the hull. Of these activities, the amount of welding required has the largest influence on the number of manhours required to construct the hull.

The welding content of a steel hull can broadly be divided into three categories:

a)   The connection of plates to form the shell of the ship and the internal divisions such as decks and bulkheads.
b)   The attachment of stiffening members to these plated areas.
c)   The assembly of panels into erection blocks and their subsequent assembly on the building berth.

Since, for the purposes of welding requirements, the plating thicknesses and steel grades of the two designs are similar, the amount of plate welding (and hence direct labour manhours) required for each design is proportional to the expanded surface areas of their hulls, decks and bulkheads. A comparison of the resulting areas for the S102 and Type 23 indicates that there is an increase of approximately 9.3% in the length of plate welding for the S102 compared with the Type 23.

The welding involved in attaching stiffeners to the plated areas has been estimated using representative structural panels from each design. The resulting comparison indicates that for the S102, with its longitudinal framing system, there is an increase of approximately 8.9% in the fillet welding length compared with the Type 23.

In order to quantify the cost increase due to the additional welding for the S102, the Inquiry has apportioned the time for the activities involved in the construction of the hull as follows:

Stockyard, plate preparation, burning by numerical control	10%
Prefabrication hall - welders	18%
- platers & burners	7%

Erection at berth	- welders	35%
	- platers, burners & drillers	30%
	Total	100%

Based on these figures and the manhour and overhead rates adopted by the Inquiry, the increased welding content in the S102 would result in an increase in labour costs of approximately 0.8% of the NUPC.

However, as the S90 hull form has less double curvature than the Type 23, a reduction in the total labour content of 8% in the prefabrication hall and 3.8% on the berth is considered reasonable to account for the reduced work content for shell structural elements. This results in a saving of 0.44% of the NUPC. Hence, an overall increase in the labour cost of the S102 of 0.36% of the NUPC would be expected when compared with the Type 23.

8.4.2   Propulsion - Cost Group 2

TGA have proposed that a CODLAG propulsion system similar to that fitted in the Type 23 should be installed in the S102, with the exception that Spey SM1C gas turbines should be fitted rather than the Spey SM1A gas turbines installed in the Type 23 (Chapter 5, Section 2.2.2).

The propulsion system for the S102 can be summarized as follows:

Ship Machinery	Manufacturer's Continuous Rating
2 × Spey SM1C Gas Turbines	2 × 18 MW
2 × GEC Brush Electric Motors	2 × 1.5 MW
4 × Paxman Diesel-Generators	4 × 1.3 MW

i)   Purchase Cost

The fitting of the SM1C turbines in the S102 rather than the SM1A turbines would result in an additional purchase cost of 0.19% of the NUPC for the units themselves compared with the Type 23.

As indicated in Section 2 of this chapter, the S102 would not achieve the maximum speed required by the NSR 7069. In addition, the power provided by the electric motors would be insufficient for the vessel to achieve either the NSR required maximum quiet towing speed or the endurance speed. Section 2.6 discussed possible machinery configurations which could be fitted in order that the S102 could achieve the NSR required speeds.

To achieve the maximum NSR speed it was suggested that a practical configuration would be to install four Spey SM1A gas turbines. The additional purchase cost, compared with the Type 23, for the extra two Spey SM1A turbine modules and their associated gas turbine change units would be in the order of 3.91% of the NUPC. However, the total additional cost involved as a result of such a machinery arrangement would require to be assessed by a major re-design of the vessel, possibly involving an increase in the length of the ship, to accommodate the extra turbine units. Such a re-design would probably result in an increase in cost for a number of the other cost groups.

In order to achieve the NSR towed array speed and the endurance speed using the electric motors alone, larger motors would have to be fitted to the S102 than those fitted in the Type 23. The required motor sizes (see Section 2.6 of this chapter) for the S102 result in an approximate increase of 0.67% (excluding the recovery of development costs) of the NUPC in the purchase price of the more powerful electric motors, thyristor converters and the increased diesel-generator capacity required to provide the necessary power.

It should be noted that the above assessment is based on a performance prediction factor $(1+x)$ of 1.0 (see Chapter 4, Section 4.4.5). The effect on the purchase cost of machinery, if this factor was taken to be equal to 0.9, has been assessed by the Inquiry. The results of this assessment indicate that although the deficiency between the speeds of the S102 and those required by the NSR would decrease, the S102 would still require larger electric motors and additional gas turbines compared with the Type 23, and that the effect on the increased purchase cost of the propulsion system for the S102 would be negligible.

If a reduction in the NSR maximum speed was considered acceptable by the Naval Staff, then it would obviously be necessary to compare the Type 23 at the same top speed as that achieved by the S102. This would result in a significant reduction in the power requirements for the Type 23 which would reduce the propulsion system purchase cost accordingly. However, the Type 23 would also require a re-design in order to assess the reduction of the other group costs which would occur if an alternative machinery arrangement to that already fitted was installed in the Type 23.

ii)   Labour Costs

In the absence of a detailed engine room layout for the S102, it is not possible to quantify precisely the cost differentials for the installation of the propulsive machinery. However, the dimensions of the turbine and motor rooms are similar at the inner bottom level for each design. On moving upwards from the tank top, the S102 gains space at the sides at a greater rate than the Type 23. However, this does not significantly improve accessibility from the outboard side for a two-turbine arrangement (see Figure 6.3.1). Access from the inboard sides and the ends is similar for both designs. Therefore, the Inquiry considers that the machinery installation costs (and time) for the propulsion arrangements now proposed would not differ significantly between the two vessels.

If the required number of gas turbine units to achieve the NSR maximum top speed were installed in the S102, there would obviously be a significant increase in the installation cost for the S102.

8.4.3   Ship Systems - Cost Groups 3, 4, 5

The cost differentials for Group 3 (Electrical), Group 4 (Control and Communication) and Group 5 (Auxiliary Systems) have been considered under the collective heading of Ship Systems. Within this group, the purchase and labour costs fall into the following two categories:

a)   Purchase and associated installation cost of the equipment itself.
b)   Purchase cost of the cables, piping and trunking associated with the respective equipment and the associated installation cost.

8.4.3.1   Equipment

i)   Purchase cost

To satisfy the NSR 7069, all the electrical, ship and weapon control, communication and auxiliary systems equipment have been taken to be identical for the both the S102 and the Type 23. As a result, the purchase cost of such equipment will not vary between the two vessels.

ii)   Labour cost

As stated in Chapter 5, Section 5, the compartmental floor areas in the Type 23 have been taken as the minimum required to be allocated in the S102. As the objective of the S102 design development was to provide the minimum space sufficient to accommodate all the spaces and equipment relating to the NSR, the compartmental floor areas allocated in the Type 23 have been allocated in the S102. As a result, there is no increased 'elbow room' within the respective compartments and since the equipment is the same for both designs, there will be no significant difference in cost or time between the S102 and the Type 23 for the installation of the equipment itself on account of similar accessibility.

8.4.3.2   Cables, Piping and Trunking

i)   Purchase Cost

The purchase costs of the cables, piping and trunking for the Type 23 ship systems have been deduced from data supplied by the MoD.

The differences between the lengths of cables, piping and trunking associated with the individual components of the S102 and Type 23 ship systems have been estimated by the Inquiry from a consideration of the relative main dimensions and enclosed volumes of each design and the relative locations of the relevant compartments.   Other factors, such as the implication of the increased propulsive power for the S102 on the fuel, lubricating and cooling systems, have also been taken into account in assessing the differences in lengths and capacities of the various systems.   From the Inquiry's assessment of the relative differences, cost variation factors have been derived which, when multiplied with the respective material purchase costs determined for the Type 23, give the purchase costs for the S102. Using these factors, the purchase cost of the cables, piping and trunking for the S102 has been estimated to be 0.8% of the NUPC more than the Type 23.

It should be noted that the longitudinal locations of the power generation, surveillance and communications, weapon control and ship control compartments are similar in both ships.   Under these circumstances, the greater transverse and vertical separations in the S102 tend to dominate the system lengths without any compensatory effect from the shorter length dimension.

In addition, the greater enclosed volume of the S102 compared with the Type 23 would result in the air treatment and filtration units being increased in size compared with the Type 23 in order that an adequate quantity of warmed or cooled filtered air is supplied throughout the vessel. This would further increase the cost of the S102 compared with the Type 23.

TGA have stated that it is a fundamental part of their concept to be able to trim the S102 in order to reduce its resistance, particularly at low speeds. They have proposed that the trim is altered by means of rapid fuel transfer between tanks. The Inquiry has not assessed the increased cost that would be incurred if the S102 fuel transfer system was enhanced so as to be able to achieve the rapid and reliable fuel transfers required to trim the vessel. However, the provision of such a capability would obviously increase the cost of the S102 compared with the Type 23 (see Section 2.9 of this chapter for discussion of effect of trim on the resistance of the S102).

ii)   Labour Cost

Although the S102 encloses more volume than the Type 23, this additional volume has not significantly increased the 'elbow room' (see Section 3.2 of this chapter) within the vessel to enable easier installation of the cables, piping and trunking. The provision of an alternative main access route would help improve the flow of personnel, materials and equipment within the ship during construction and outfitting. However, modern modular and pre-outfitting construction techniques, in which small blocks are outfitted on the berth using 'open sky' access techniques (i.e. compartments are accessed directly from above prior to the decks being put in place), would almost eliminate this advantage. Therefore, the Inquiry does not consider that there would be a reduction in the labour costs for the installation of the necessary ship systems within the S102 compared with the Type 23. In fact, based on the increased length of cable runs, piping and trunking in the S102, the Inquiry considers that the labour cost would increase. Using similar cost variation factors to those applied to the purchase cost of the cables, piping and trunking, it has been estimated that the installation labour cost for the S102 compared with the Type 23 would be increased by approximately 1.1% of the Type 23 NUPC.

8.4.4   Outfit & Furnishings - Cost Group 6

This Group includes such items as paint, deck coverings, cabin furnishings, workshops, etc.

As indicated in Section 8.4.1, the surface area of the S102 is about 9.3% greater than that of the Type 23. Based on data provided by the MoD, the Inquiry has estimated that it will cost an additional 0.17% of the NUPC to paint the S102 compared with the Type 23.

As the compartmental sizes are similar in the S102 and the Type 23 and the crew complement and weapons are identical, the difference between the costs associated with the outfit of the individual compartments in the S102 and the Type 23 is unlikely to be large. However, the double passageways of the S102 are estimated to increase the associated outfit costs by about 0.08% of the Type 23 NUPC above that for the single passageway of the Type 23.

8.4.5   Weapons - Cost Group 7

As the weapon fit is identical for the S102 and the Type 23, the purchase cost of the weapons will not vary between the two vessels.

The cost of installing the weapons will also not differ (apart from the length of the cables, piping and trunking that link the weapons to the various control systems. This aspect has been considered under Section 8.4.3).

8.5   **Comparison of the Construction Cost of the S102 and Type 23**

The group cost differentials discussed in Section 8.4 are summarized in Table 6.8.2 by comparing the cost group percentage breakdown of the NUPC for the Type 23 frigate (from Section 8.3) with the appropriate values derived for the S102.

Group	Purchase Cost Type 23	Purchase Cost S102	Labour Cost Type 23	Labour Cost S102	Total Type 23	Total S102
1. Hull	1.6	1.6	11.4	11.7	13.0	13.3
2. Propulsion	6.2	6.4	2.5	2.5	8.7	8.9
3. Electrical	5.6		6.8		12.4	
4. Control & Comms.	5.3	18.6	1.4	15.6	6.7	34.2
5. Aux. Systems	6.8		6.3		13.1	
6. Outfit & Furnish.	6.6	6.7	7.8	7.9	14.4	14.6
7. Weapons	31.3	31.3	0.4	0.4	31.7	31.7
Totals (%)	63.4	64.6	36.6	38.1	100.0	102.7

Table 6.8.2   Group Cost Comparison between the S102 and Type 23 Frigate (expressed as a percentage of the Type 23 NUPC)

Table 6.8.2 indicates that the NUPC for the S102 will be 2.7% more than that of the Type 23 at 1986/87 prices. As indicated in Section 8.2, the methods used by the Inquiry to estimate the group cost differentials cannot be considered as rigorous and, therefore, 2.7% must be considered as an approximate increase.

However, as the S102 requires more gas turbine units and larger electric motors to be installed in order that it can meet the NSR 7069 speed requirements, the Inquiry considers that to assess the true difference between the NUPC for the S102 and the Type 23, it would be necessary to re-design the S102 so that sufficient space was provided to accommodate the additional machinery necessary for it to achieve the NSR speeds. The overall cost differential between the S102 and Type 23 would, in the Inquiry's opinion, increase substantially as a result of such a re-design. The purchase costs of additional turbines and electric motors alone, for one feasible machinery configuration, indicate that the S102 would incur a further cost increase of approximately 4.6% of the NUPC compared with the Type 23. This would result in a total increase of 7.3% of the NUPC compared with the Type 23.

If the Naval Staff accepted a lower maximum speed, a re-design of the Type 23 to meet the lower speed requirement would obviously be necessary before assessing the difference between the NUPCs for the two vessels. However, since considerably less power would be required, a significant reduction in cost would be anticipated for the Type 23.

The Inquiry has examined the basis of the potential 26.2% saving in the UPC identified in Paragraph 20 of the Hill-Norton Committee Report arising from the adoption of the S90 in preference to the Type 23. As indicated in Chapter 4, Section 3, the S90 was found to be too small to accommodate all the necessary spaces and equipment required by the NSR. Therefore, the figures for the S90 presented in Paragraph 20 cannot be realistically compared with those for the Type 23, as the S90 does not achieve the capability required by the NSR. In addition, it is necessary to have carefully constructed and consistent definitions when comparing cost breakdowns from different sources. The comparison of a breakdown for the Type 23 based on a typical percentage breakdown given by the Hull Committee of the DSAC for a conventional RN frigate with that of a detailed shipyard estimate for a specific ship, can lead to the situation where like is not being compared with like.

The Inquiry, in comparing the construction costs of the S102 and Type 23, has assumed that both vessels are built in the same shipyard to the same strength and construction standards. It has, therefore, sought to ensure that a valid and independent basis for its cost comparison is made.

With reference to the hull structure cost comparison between a Sirius design and the Leander given in Paragraph 18 of the Hill-Norton Committee Report which indicated a 56% saving in the hull construction cost for the Sirius design, the Inquiry concludes that again such a comparison must be treated with caution. The Leander is a very old class of ship incorporating a number of relatively expensive structural details such as a rounded gunwale and complicated brackets. The Type 23, on the other hand, has a considerably simpler form of construction and will, therefore, be relatively cheaper to construct than the Leander. Although FHV (now known as Danyard) indicated to the Inquiry that they would still consider that the Type 23 would cost considerably more to build than the S102 in Denmark, due to increased elbow room and simpler construction arising for a vessel based on the Sirius concept, the Inquiry's independent findings do not substantiate this. A number of British shipyards have been approached and they have all indicated that they do not consider that, given the same strength and construction standards, there would be any significant difference in the hull construction cost of a short/fat vessel and a long/thin vessel both designed to meet the same specification and built in the same shipyard. The most favourable estimate for the S102 represented a relative decrease in the hull construction cost of 7%, this being approximately equivalent to 0.6% of the Type 23 NUPC.

Since the cost savings identified in the Hill-Norton Committee Report were central to their overall conclusions, the Inquiry, in addition to its own extensive investigation, has made several attempts to obtain specific information from Danyard concerning the precise grounds on which they based their anticipated savings in the construction cost of the S90 hull in comparison to a 'long/thin' hull. These attempts have been unsuccessful and, in response to the latest approach to Danyard, the Inquiry has been informed that the member of their staff responsible for providing the previous information is no longer in their employment and that they are not currently in a position to either elaborate on or modify the views expressed by him in this matter.

8.6   Conclusions

The Inquiry has assessed the construction cost differentials of the S102, a vessel based on the S90 hull form, and the Type 23, a vessel based on a conventional hull form. Although both designs are aimed at meeting the same NSR 7069, it should be noted that the S102 does not achieve all the requirements. Both vessels have been costed assuming that the manhour and overhead rates are the same for each vessel. Only those costs which are considered to be affected by the hull form adopted have been examined.

This assessment has indicated that, rather than being cheaper to build than a frigate based on a conventional hull form, a frigate based on the S90 hull form would be more expensive to build. The Inquiry's assessment indicates that the S102, a design which will not meet the NSR required speeds, would cost approximately 2.7% of the Type 23 NUPC more to build. The real difference between the construction costs of the S102 and the Type 23 would be substantially more than 2.7% if the S102 was re-designed to meet the NSR speed requirements. The extra propulsion unit costs alone, for a proposed arrangement which would provide sufficient power for the S102 to achieve the required speeds, indicates a further minimum cost of 4.6% of the Type 23 NUPC, leading to a total minimum increase of 7.3% of the NUPC compared with the Type 23.

With reference to those aspects which TGA believe would provide cost savings should their hull form be adopted in preference to a more conventional hull form for vessels of frigate size, the Inquiry concludes that:

i)   The effect of the strength standard adopted, and the steel grades incorporated, on the steel construction cost is negligible relative to the total cost of the ship. In addition, strength standards are not hull form dependent and whatever standard is used is as applicable to the Type 23 as it is to the S102.

ii)   The adoption of commercial building practices would reduce the construction cost differentials between the S102 and the Type 23. However, the use of such practices is again not hull form dependent and it should be noted that a form of construction which is largely consistent with commercial methods has been adopted on the Type 23.

iii)   The relative longitudinal locations of the major ship systems are similar in both the S102 and Type 23 designs. However, a comparison of the transverse and vertical locations indicates that the compartments are spaced further apart in the S102 than in the Type 23. Therefore, the cables, piping and trunking associated with such compartments would be longer in the S102 than in the Type 23 and would, therefore, cost more. In addition, the greater enclosed volume and higher power requirements of the S102 results in certain of the ship systems also costing more for the S102 when compared with the Type 23.

iv)   Although the S102 design encloses more volume than the Type 23 design, this additional volume has not significantly increased the 'elbow room' within the vessel. The provision of an alternative main access route would improve the flow of men, materials and equipment within the ship during construction and outfitting. However, this would only be of benefit in a programme of building which involves outfitting after substantial completion of the hull structure has taken place. Modern modular and pre-outfitting techniques in which small blocks are outfitted on the berth using 'open sky' access techniques (i.e. compartments are accessed directly from above prior to the decks being put in place) would almost eliminate this advantage.

With regard to construction time differentials, the Inquiry considers that, as there is no significant increase in 'elbow room' enabling more people to work in a given compartment or enabling the installation and outfitting to be carried out more easily and quickly, the build time would not be reduced for the S102. In contrast, due to the increased labour content in a number of areas, the Inquiry considers that the build time would be marginally increased.

CHAPTER 6

ASSESSMENT OF THE S102 DESIGN

SECTION 9
Through Life Costs

9.1   Introduction

TGA claimed, with their original S90 design proposal put forward to the MoD in 1983, that the through life costs would be substantially less for the S90 compared with a conventional frigate of similar displacement and performance.   However, this reduction was based on the use of diesel engines rather than the gas turbines currently installed in RN frigates. TGA considered that the ability of the diesel engines to operate on residual fuel oil, which is cheaper and more widely available than the 'Dieso' used by the Royal Navy, would mean that the S90 would not normally have to re-fuel at sea from Royal Fleet Auxiliary (RFA) tankers and this, they contended, was an essential feature of the S90 design proposal which would reduce running costs still further.

However, as TGA now propose a CODLAG propulsion system for the S102, a reduction in fuel costs due to using diesel engines can no longer be considered an implicit feature of the Sirius design concept.

With reference to other areas where the through life costs of a vessel designed according to the Sirius design concept may be reduced, the Hill-Norton Committee Report indicated in Paragraph 30 that cost savings may arise due to the more convenient hull proportions of such a vessel for the replacement of accommodation, equipment, systems, weapons and machinery items. In addition, the heavier and less stressed commercial type structure would require less frequent maintenance and repair and fewer maintenance manhours.

Although the NSR 7069 contains details of the through life plan for an ASW frigate built and operated in accordance with this NSR, there is no associated target through life cost. Therefore, the Inquiry has assessed the through life cost of the S102 using the NSR 7069 through life plan and associated mission profiles[1] and has compared this cost with that of the Type 23 using the same through life plan and mission profiles.   The resulting cost differentials between the S102 and the Type 23 have been expressed as a percentage of the Type 23 through life cost.

9.2   Through Life Cost Components

The Inquiry has examined only those components of the through life cost which can be considered to be dependent on the hull form adopted. Other costs such as infra-structure costs (e.g. management and training personnel, shore-based specialists, reserve staff and shore-based training facilities),

---

1.   Mission profiles indicate the amount of time that the vessel is expected to operate at a particular speed in a specified operational role

although affecting the through life cost, have been taken to be the same for both vessels.

The Inquiry has established, based on the through life plan given in the NSR 7069 and further data supplied by the MoD, that the major components of the through life cost which may be affected by the hull form of an ASW frigate built and operated in accordance with the NSR 7069, can be divided into two groups:

i)   Operational Running costs:

        Ship's company costs (wages, food, etc)
        Propulsion fuel oil
        Generator fuel oil for the hotel load
        Stores

ii)   Maintenance, Repair and Refit costs:

        Running hours based maintenance and repair (i.e. turbine and generator overhauls).
        Calendar based maintenance, repairs and refit (i.e. those items dealt with during dry-docking and refit periods).

For both these groups, the major factor influencing the cost differentials between the S102 and the Type 23 is the machinery configuration installed and the power it delivers.

A problem encountered by the Inquiry in trying to assess the S102 and Type 23 through life cost differentials was that the NSR through life plan assumes that the vessel will achieve the required NSR speeds. As indicated in Section 2 of this chapter, the S102 does not achieve these required speeds with the machinery installation proposed by TGA (i.e. two 1.5MW electric motors and two SM1C gas turbines). This makes a comparison with the Type 23 very difficult for those costs which are determined on the basis that the installed power is sufficient to achieve the appropriate speeds.

To enable a comparison to be made, the Inquiry has, therefore, made two assumptions in determining those costs which are associated with the installed power, namely:

i)   For assessing the operational running costs (i.e. the fuel oil costs), the appropriate speed/power relationships for the S102 and Type 23 for the range of speeds indicated in the NSR mission profiles have been taken. This assumes that the necessary power can be fitted in the S102 at its current size and displacement.

ii)   For assessing the maintenance and repair costs which are related to the number and size of the propulsion units (e.g. gas turbines) required to deliver the necessary power associated with item (i), it has been assumed that the S102 is fitted with two 2.3MW electric motors and four Spey SM1A gas turbines, this being considered to be the most practical configuration capable of providing sufficient power for the S102 to achieve the required NSR speeds at its current size and displacement (see Section 2 of this chapter).

These two assumptions form the basis upon which the Inquiry has made its assessment of the comparative through life costs of the S102 compared with the Type 23.

If the Naval Staff were to accept the lower speeds achieved by the S102 with TGA's proposed machinery configuration, then the NSR mission profiles would require to be adjusted accordingly and, for a valid comparison to be made with the Type 23, a re-assessment of the Type 23 would be necessary since it requires less power to be installed to meet these lower speeds.

The Inquiry has made an assessment of the effect on those costs which are dependent on the installed power should the lower speeds that the S102 can achieve with TGA's proposed machinery configuration be considered acceptable. This assessment is presented in Section 9.7 of this chapter.

9.3   Anticipated Through Life Costs for the Type 23

From data supplied by the MoD which relate to the Type 23 and other appropriate RN ships, the Inquiry has deduced the through life cost of a Type 23 frigate which is built and operated in accordance with the through life plan defined in the NSR 7069.

The cost breakdown, expressed as a percentage of the total through life cost, is given in Table 6.9.1.

It should be noted that the transmission system and the electric propulsion motors are not overhauled during the life time of the vessel unless premature failure occurs. The electric motors are maintained by the ship's company alone.

	Total %
Operational Running Costs	
Ship's company costs (wages, food, etc)	47.8
Propulsion fuel oil	10.2
Generator fuel oil for hotel load	3.0
Other stores (excl. ammunition)	7.7
Maintenance, Repair and Refit Costs	
Gas turbine overhauls	3.3
Generator set overhauls	2.0
Dry-docking and essential repairs	4.3
Restorative refit	18.8
Fleet Maintenance Group[2]	2.9
Total	100.0 %

Table 6.9.1   Percentage Through Life Cost Breakdown for the Type 23 Frigate

The Inquiry has assessed the cost differentials between the S102 and the Type 23 which result from the adoption of the two different hull forms for the items identified in Table 6.9.1.

9.4   Comparison of the S102 and Type 23 Operational Running Costs

The Inquiry has assumed that the ship's complement for the S102 and the Type 23 would be identical and, therefore, costs relating to the ship's company (e.g. food, wages, stores, etc) would be the same for both vessels. It should be noted that, although the S102 requires more gas turbine units than the Type 23 to achieve the required maximum speed, the Inquiry has assumed that the increased number of turbine units will not lead to an increased ship's complement.

As the weapon fit is identical for both vessels, the ammunition costs have also been taken to be the same.

Therefore, the differences between the operational running costs of the S102 and the Type 23 will arise from the difference between the fuel oil costs for the two vessels. The fuel oil cost is determined from the mission

---

2.   The Fleet Maintenance Group are shore-based personnel who help the ship's company during overhauls of equipment such as turbines and generators.

profiles, the fuel consumption, the replenishment frequency and quantity and the cost of the fuel as supplied to the ship.

9.4.1   Mission Profiles and Operational Roles

The utilisation of propulsive power depends upon the adopted mission profiles, i.e. the speed/time relationships planned for the operational roles of the vessel. The NSR 7069 specifies two main ASW roles. The MoD envisage a third general purpose role which may be required in the future. Although the Inquiry has noted this future potential role, since it is strictly outside of the Inquiry's terms of reference as it is not contained in the current NSR, the Inquiry has ignored this third role in its main assessment.

9.4.2   Fuel Consumption and Replenishment

The consumption of fuel oil is clearly dependent on the installed propulsion system, the delivered horsepower and the time interval over which that power is required (which in turn depends on the mission profiles).

For the comparative assessment of the fuel consumption of the S102 and the Type 23, it has been assumed that both vessels are in a nominal half oil condition. The appropriate speed/power relationships for each vessel have been determined for this condition (it should be noted that for the S102 it has been assumed that optimum trim can be achieved for each speed) and the respective fuel consumptions calculated accordingly.   The Inquiry considers that, for a comparative exercise, this assumption is acceptable.

For each mission profile, the percentage increase in the total fuel consumption of the S102 compared with the Type 23 (including a fixed allowance for hotel power generation) has been estimated to be as follows:

	% increase for S102 compared with the Type 23
Role 1	34.6
Role 2	57.1
Roles 1 and 2	48.5

It should be noted that these figures would increase marginally due to a variation in the hotel power load which depends upon the operational mode (for example, the 'quiet' or 'normal' running load) of the vessel.

Assuming that the S102 and Type 23 are carrying their design fuel load on departure at the appropriate deep displacement then, with 95% fuel pumpable, the minimum numbers of re-fuels per mission are calculated to be:

	Type 23	S102	Increased no. for S102
Role 1	1	1	0
Role 2	2	3	1
Roles 1 and 2	3	4	1

Hence, the nominal frequency of visits by RFA tankers (or visits to bunkering stations) would be higher for the S102 than for the Type 23; the quantity of fuel to be delivered would be about 48.5% greater. In practice, the frequency of re-fuelling would considerably exceed the values indicated above since, in general, current frigates are re-fuelled before onboard stocks fall below about 50%. It should be noted that the S102 in the 50% fuel-used condition has insufficient fuel remaining to obtain the necessary trimming moment to achieve optimum LCG locations (see Chapter 5, Section 3.3).

The increased replenishment frequency and quantity of fuel oil that is required by the S102 compared with the Type 23 would obviously require the RFA fleet infra-structure and associated costs to be re-assessed, particularly if the Sirius design concept was to be adopted for all warships up to and including destroyer class.

9.4.3 The Cost of Fuel Oil Supplied Onboard RN Ships

The Inquiry has taken, for the purposes of the comparison of the S102 and Type 23 designs, a cost of £150/tonne for the fuel oil delivered onboard each ship. This figure includes an allowance for the associated distribution cost.

9.4.4 Comparison of Fuel Oil Costs for the S102 and Type 23

Based upon the mission profiles for Roles 1 and 2 and using the calculated speed/power relationships for each design together with the variable hotel load consumption, comparative fuel cost calculations have been carried out. It is estimated that the larger quantity of fuel oil used by the S102 would cost approximately 49.5% more than the fuel used by the Type 23 for the corresponding missions and time period.

This increased cost for the S102 must, however, be considered as an absolute minimum increase since:

i)   It has been assumed that the optimum trims required to minimise the hull resistance of the S102 have been achieved. However, these trims cannot be achieved without radical changes to the design (see Chapter 5, Section 3.3). If the optimum trim conditions were not achieved by subsequent design iteration, an increase in resistance would occur.

ii)   It has been assumed that the additional gas turbines and larger electric motors and generators can be accommodated within the current size and displacement of the S102. In reality, to accommodate this machinery configuration would require either an increase in the size of the S102 or an increase in its displacement. An increase in ship size or displacement could result in an increased power demand over the entire speed range.

iii)   The rate of fuel consumption of the S102 at all speeds up to the NSR maximum required speed is significantly greater than that of the Type 23. Nevertheless, it has been assumed that the existing and planned RFA fleet would be adequate to supply fuel at this increased rate. It is possible, however, that additional RFA's, or more intensive use of the existing RFA fleet, would result in increased infra-structure costs.

iv)   Fuel costs for hotel load power generation have been considered to be the same for each vessel.

9.5   Comparison of the S102 and Type 23 Maintenance, Repair and Refit Costs

The differences between the maintenance, repair and refit through life costs for the S102 and the Type 23 have been assessed by examining the differences in those costs which are:

i)   Running hours based (e.g. gas turbine overhaul)
ii)   Calendar based (e.g. dry-docking and refit).

9.5.1 Running Hours Based Maintenance and Repair

9.5.1.1 Gas Turbine Maintenance and Repair

The maintenance of gas turbines involves:

i)   Overhaul. The gas turbine change units are removed (with the assistance of the Fleet Maintenance Group) and sent to the manufacturer for renovation.
ii)   Continuous maintenance and repair by shipboard personnel.

The frequency of routine overhauls is related to the running hours of each turbine unit. However, an allowance must also be made for unscheduled replacements resulting from premature failure.

Based upon the running hours for the various mission profiles, the costs of overhaul and repair of the gas turbine units have been deduced for the life of each ship. For the S102, the running hours based maintenance costs associated with the four SM1A gas turbines would be approximately 80% more than the corresponding costs for the Type 23 fitted with the two SM1A gas turbines.

Although the S102 requires more turbines, it has been assumed that no additional crew members would be required. However, the frequency of removal for overhaul of gas turbine change units would be increased substantially. An associated increase in the Fleet Maintenance Group manpower levels would be required and the percentage increase in these costs for the S102 compared with the Type 23 has been estimated to be 13%.

It should be noted that no allowance has been made for the effects of inflation, nor for the provision of spare turbines for either ship. These factors could further increase the maintenance cost differential between the S102 and the Type 23 given the increased number of turbine units required for the S102.

9.5.1.2   Diesel-Generator Systems

In order to provide sufficient power to drive the larger electric motors fitted in the S102, increased diesel-generator capacity is required. To provide this additional capacity, the Inquiry would propose the installation of an extra generator of the same rating as those already fitted (see Section 2.6 of this chapter). It has been estimated that the extra generator would result in a 25% increase in the running hours based maintenance cost of the diesel-generators for the S102 compared with the Type 23 over the life of the ship.

9.5.1.3   Electric Propulsion Motors

The electric propulsion motors are not normally overhauled during the life of the ship unless premature failure occurs. However, maintenance by the ship's company of the larger motors, converters and switch gear is expected to require more manhours for the 2.3MW motors fitted in the S102 than for the 1.5MW motors fitted in the Type 23. However, any additional cost would be absorbed into the ship's company costs.

9.5.2   Calendar Based Maintenance, Repair and Refit

A feature of the S102 which may reduce the maintenance, repair and refit costs is the improved access provided by the twin passageway system. The actual cost benefits, however, could only be estimated by means of a detailed refit planning study or by an actual refit. The main benefit arising from this feature would be reduced labour costs.

However, it should be noted that there is no significant increased 'elbow room' in the individual compartments of the S102 compared with the Type 23 (see Section 3.2 of this chapter). Therefore, the replacement of equipment within compartments, for example, would require the same amount of labour for both vessels and, therefore, the costs associated with such activities would be similar.

The major items of calendar based maintenance are completed during refit and docking periods. Based on data provided by the MoD relating to the projected maintenance of typical items through the life of a Type 23 frigate, the Inquiry has identified the items which will be affected by the hull form.

The Inquiry considers that the frequency of maintenance of these items would be identical for both vessels. However, the amounts of materials and labour involved could vary.

9.5.2.1 Steelwork Related Items

The scantlings of the S102 and the Type 23 are similar and deterioration due to wear-and-tear and or corrosion would be expected to occur at similar rates for both ships. However, as the plated area of the S102 exceeds that of the Type 23 by 9.3% (see Section 8.4.1 of this chapter), inspection and repair would be expected to increase accordingly for the S102 compared with the Type 23.

Steelwork preservation material and labour costs would also be expected to be greater for the S102 due to the increased area of plating compared with the Type 23.

Although the S102 may have a greater margin against fatigue damage (see Section 3.5 of this chapter), this would only reduce the level of repair associated with fatigue cracking, compared with the Type 23, if the strength standard adopted incorporated inadequate safety factors against such damage. Therefore, the Inquiry considers that, for the proposed life span, there would be no appreciable difference in the level of repair associated with fatigue cracking for the S102 and Type 23 provided that the strength standard adopted incorporates adequate safety factors against such damage.

As the S102 has larger fuel tanks than the Type 23, fuel tank re-coating would be more expensive. However, as re-coating is carried out only once during the life of the vessel, unless premature deterioration of the coatings occurs, this increase in cost is unlikely to have a significant effect on the through life cost differentials.

9.5.2.2   Ship Systems Related Items

In general, the piping, cabling and trunking associated with the ship systems, as indicated in Section 8.4.3 of this chapter, would be more extensive in the S102 than the Type 23.   Therefore, the materials and labour content for maintenance, repair and refit of these systems would be expected to be greater for the S102.   In particular, the air filtration, treatment and distribution systems, being larger in the S102 due to the increased volume, would be expected to cost more to repair and maintain.

Gas turbine and diesel-generator intakes and exhausts would be larger and or more numerous in the S102 if sufficient machinery was installed for the vessel to achieve the NSR required speeds.   Therefore, the maintenance of these items would involve additional costs for the S102 compared with the Type 23.

9.5.2.3   Summary of Cost Differences for Calendar Based Maintenance, Repair and Refit

Insufficient data was available for a reliable comparison to be made of the cost of maintaining the steelwork and ship system related items.   However, it is the Inquiry's opinion that, for these calendar based maintenance items, the potential cost saving for the S102 due to its twin passageway system would be offset by the increased costs identified in Sections 9.5.2.1 and 9.5.2.2.   Therefore, the Inquiry cannot identify any significant difference between the calendar based maintenance, repair and refit cost for the two vessels.

9.6   Comparison of the Through Life Costs of the S102 and Type 23

Based on the foregoing analysis and discussion, the Inquiry has estimated the through life operational running costs and the maintenance, repair and refit costs for the S102 and has compared these costs, in Table 6.9.2, with the Type 23 through life cost breakdown given in Table 6.9.1 of Section 9.3.

It should be noted that any extra labour costs incurred in the repair and maintenance of the additional turbines and propulsion machinery in the S102 undertaken by the ship's staff are absorbed into the fixed ship's complement costs.

The Inquiry has also assessed the effect on the through life cost for the S102 arising from the use of a performance prediction factor $(1+x)$ of 0.9 rather than 1.0 (see Chapter 4, Section 4.4.5).   The effect of this lower value is to reduce the delivered power requirement by 10%.   This has a consequential effect on fuel consumption and operational running costs for the S102. However, as the S102 would still require four SM1A gas turbines to achieve the NSR maximum required speed, the running hours based maintenance cost would not differ significantly. No other aspect of the through life cost of the S102 would be materially affected by a (1+x) of 0.9 and, therefore, the through life cost of the S102 with a (1+x) of 0.9 would be reduced from 110.7% to 109.2% compared with the Type 23.

	Type 23 %	S102 %
Operational Running Costs		
Ship's company costs (wages, food, etc)	47.8	47.8
Propulsion fuel oil	10.2	16.7
Generator fuel oil for the hotel load	3.0	3.0
Other stores (excl. ammunition)	7.7	7.7
Maintenance, Repair and Refit Costs		
Gas turbine overhauls	3.3	6.6
Generator set overhauls	2.0	2.5
Dry-docking and essential repairs	4.3	4.3
Restorative refit	18.8	18.8
Fleet Maintenance Group	2.9	3.3
Total	100.0 %	110.7 %

Table 6.9.2   Through Life Cost Breakdown for the Type 23 Compared with the S102.

9.7   **Assessment with the S102 Operating at its Achievable Speeds**

The preceding assessment of the through life cost differentials between the S102 and the Type 23 has been based on the assumption that the S102 has sufficient installed power to achieve the NSR required speeds at its current size and displacement.

The Inquiry has also sought to identify the through life cost differential of the S102 and the Type 23 assuming that the Naval Staff accept the down-graded speed performance of the S102. In order to do this, it is necessary to modify the NSR mission profiles to reflect the lower speeds achievable by the S102. It was decided, however, to assume that the S102 would be fitted with the two 2.3MW electric motors so that it could achieve those NSR speeds which are required using only the diesel-electric mode of propulsion. As a result, the mission profiles only need to be modified in the upper speed range to reflect the maximum speed achievable by the S102 with two SM1C gas turbines and two 2.3MW electric motors.

In addition to modifying the NSR mission profiles, it was necessary to assume a down-graded machinery configuration for the Type 23 consistent with the reduced power required by the Type 23 to achieve the S102 maximum speed. Therefore, it was assumed that the Type 23 would have a machinery configuration comprising a single SM1C gas turbine and the two 1.5MW electric motors since this would provide the Type 23 with sufficient power to achieve the maximum speed obtained by the S102.

The calendar based maintenance, repair and refit costs have been assumed to be constant. Therefore, the cost differentials arise solely from the fuel oil costs and the running hours based maintenance and repair costs.

Using the procedure described in Section 9.4, the increase in the fuel costs for the S102 compared with the Type 23 would be approximately 36%.

The increase in the running hours based maintenance and repair costs for the S102 compared with the Type 23 with the proposed machinery installations would be approximately 62% for the gas turbines and 25% for the generating sets.

The overall percentage difference between the through life costs for the S102 and Type 23 resulting from this assessment has been estimated to be 8.2%.

It should be noted that if the Naval Staff decided to retro-fit the Type 23 frigate with the two SM1C gas turbines proposed for the S102, then the Type 23 would have the capability of achieving a much higher speed than that required by the current NSR. The machinery configuration required by the S102 to achieve a similar speed would require machinery capable of providing 85% more power than is provided by the machinery fit proposed by TGA. If a mission profile was adopted which included the higher speed achievable by the Type 23 with two SM1C gas turbines installed, then the through life cost differential between the S102 and the Type 23 would be further increased.

9.8   Conclusions

The Inquiry has assessed the through life cost differentials between a frigate based on TGA's S90 hull form (the S102) and a frigate based on a conventional hull form (the Type 23) using the through life plan and mission profiles given in the NSR 7069. As a realistic comparison of these costs is dependent on both vessels achieving the speeds required by the NSR mission profiles, it has been necessary to assume that the S102 would be fitted with additional machinery sufficient for it to achieve the NSR required speeds.

The Inquiry concludes that the through life costs of the S102 would be 10.7% greater than the Type 23. This increase is dominated by the increased power requirements of the S102 and is determined by the increased fuel oil consumption and running hours based maintenance of the S102 propulsion machinery compared with the Type 23.

In the Inquiry's judgement, the increased calendar based maintenance costs for several of the steelwork and ship system related items of the S102 would be offset by an overall reduction in labour costs which would be associated with the improved access resulting from the twin passageway system of the S102.

The Inquiry has also estimated the comparative costs assuming that the S102 achievable speeds were considered acceptable by the Naval Staff. The mission profiles were adjusted and it was assumed that the Type 23 would be fitted with a suitably down-graded machinery configuration to achieve those speeds obtained by the S102. The resulting comparison indicated that the through life cost of the S102 would be 8.2% more than that of the Type 23.

With reference to the comments made by the Hill-Norton Committee on areas where a reduction in the through life cost of a vessel designed according to the Sirius design concept may occur (see Paragraph 30), the Inquiry concludes that:

i)   As no increased 'elbow room' has been identified within the individual compartments of the S102 compared with that in the Type 23 (see Section 3.2 of this chapter), the replacement of equipment, for example, will not be any less labour intensive in the S102 than the Type 23. The provision of the twin access passageway system would improve the movement of personnel and equipment during repair and refit. However, this advantage is offset by the increased maintenance cost of a number of steelwork and ship systems related items for the S102.

ii)   For the proposed life span of both vessels, there would be no appreciable difference between the level of repair associated with fatigue cracking for the S102 and the Type 23 provided that the strength standard adopted incorporated adequate safety factors against such damage (see Section 3.5 of this chapter).

If the unit production cost of both vessels is also taken into account when comparing the through life costs of both vessels, the percentage cost breakdown of the total through life cost for both designs is:

	Type 23 %	S102 %
Unit Production Cost	47.3	50.8
Operational Running Cost	32.1	35.5
Maintenance, Repair, Refit Cost	20.6	22.8
Totals	100.0 %	109.1 %

The above table assumes that four SM1A gas turbines and two 2.3MW electric motors (and associated generator capacity) are fitted in the S102 in order that it might achieve the NSR required speeds. As was indicated in Section 8 of this chapter, the increase in cost of the S102 with this machinery configuration must be considered an absolute minimum since no account has been taken of the increase in ship size and or displacement which is required to accommodate the additional machinery.

Reducing the performance prediction factor $(1+x)$ from 1.0 to 0.9 has indicated that the total through life cost for the S102 would be reduced from 109.1% to 108.2% compared with the Type 23.

Should the Naval Staff require the higher top speed that could be achieved by retro-fitting the Type 23 with two SM1C gas turbines, then the difference in the through life cost of the S102 compared with that of the Type 23 would be further increased.

CHAPTER 7

CONSIDERATION OF
THORNYCROFT, GILES AND ASSOCIATES LTD
RESPONSE TO THE S102 DESIGN

1.   **Introduction**

Following the Inquiry's development of the S102 and TGA's agreement that this design provided a reasonable basis, as far as size and general layout was concerned, on which to compare the S90 hull form against the NSR 7069 and, in addition, the Type 23 frigate design, the Inquiry formulated initial findings on each of the key issues discussed in Chapter 6.

The Inquiry discussed these preliminary findings with TGA to ensure that no fundamental point or important source of information which TGA were aware of had been overlooked and, in addition, to allow TGA to respond with any relevant comments for further consideration.

TGA's response to the Inquiry's initial findings was to propose a further design iteration which they considered would provide a better ship in relation to the NSR requirements than the S102, particularly in terms of its achievable speed. This vessel, referred to as the S115, was a development of the S110 design study previously undertaken by TGA during the Inquiry's development of the S102 (see Chapter 5, Section 4).

TGA maintained that they did not consider it reasonable, in view of the S102's speed deficiency relative to the NSR, to keep the same length to breadth (L/B) ratio as the S90 hull form and preserved in the development of the S102. They therefore proposed, with this further iteration, to alter the S90 hull form and, in particular, to increase the L/B ratio. TGA informed the Inquiry that the S115 represented the limit of the Sirius concept for the purposes of meeting the NSR.

The Inquiry agreed with TGA that an analysis using empirical methods should be carried out to ascertain whether the speed requirements of the NSR would be met by the S115 with the machinery arrangement previously proposed. Accordingly, the Inquiry agreed to fund TGA to undertake such a study.

The Inquiry also carried out an independent assessment of the power requirements of the S115. In addition, as a consequence of its detailed development and subsequent comprehensive assessment of the S102 in relation to the NSR and the Type 23, together with its examination of the original S90 proposal and the S110 study, the Inquiry was able to make a valid qualitative assessment of the S115 compared with the S102, the NSR 7069 and the Type 23 frigate design. This chapter presents the results of this assessment.

In addition to the S115 proposal, TGA also informed the Inquiry that they considered that the Sirius hull form was capable of speeds well in excess of those required by the NSR 7069 and those which could practically be achieved by a conventional frigate hull form. The Hill-Norton Committee also considered that the Sirius hull form could offer a significant increase in top speed over the maximum which could be realised in a conventional hull form of a similar size. They concluded that, if confirmed, this would be a most important military advantage. In view of the Inquiry's terms of reference which require it to identify *any implications for the design of future destroyers and frigates for the RN*, the Inquiry has, based on the data submitted to it, assessed the performance of the Sirius hull form at speeds above those required by the NSR. Section 4 of this chapter presents the Inquiry's findings on this aspect.

2.   **TGA's S115 Proposal**

The S115 proposed by TGA is based on their previous S110 study (see Chapter 5, Section 4). For this study, TGA scaled the length of the original S90 to a similar waterline length to that of the S102. However, the beam was scaled by a smaller factor and, therefore, the L/B ratio was increased from about 5.0 for the S90 and S102 to 5.3 for the S110. TGA stated that this change was to help reduce the power requirement for the S110. In this respect, the S110 cannot be considered to be a geosim of the S90 hull form since the underwater proportions have been scaled by different amounts.

The S115 proposal maintained the same maximum beam as the S110 but increased the waterline length from 95.4m to 103.6m (this further increased the L/B ratio to 5.73). TGA considered that this increase would produce a vessel which would eliminate the S102's speed deficiency in relation to the NSR, or at least reduce it to acceptable proportions. In addition, TGA proposed to modify the afterbody lines of the S115 to reduce the degree of bow down trim required to achieve minimum resistance. The S115, as well as the S110, is not a geosim of the S90 hull form.

A further modification from the original S90 design proposal which TGA proposed for both their S110 and S115 developments, was to reduce the superstructure height by dividing the tall centralised accommodation block of the original S90 design proposal into separate blocks and distributing them in a similar fashion to those on the Type 23, i.e. along the length of the vessel. TGA maintained that the resulting silhouette of their vessel would then correspond, as far as possible, to that of the Type 23 and that the large lateral accelerations which were identified for the S102 at the bridge height would be eliminated.

Figure 7.2.1 gives a qualitative impression of the developments by the Inquiry and TGA of the original S90 design proposal (i.e. the S102, S110 and S115) compared with the Type 23 frigate. In addition, the original S90 proposal is compared with the Leander class frigate, the Hill-Norton Committee having based their comparative study on these two vessels. This figure illustrates that, in comparison with the Type 23, the distinction between 'short/fat' and 'long/thin' is not as pronounced as might have been thought. It should be noted, however, that the underwater hull forms of the Sirius derivatives, the Leander and the Type 23 illustrated in this figure are still very different.

Although TGA proposed that the deep displacement of the S115 be taken as 4220 tonnes for the purposes of predicting the power of the S115 (112 tonnes more than that of the S102), the Inquiry concluded that the deep displacement of the S115 would be similar to the S102 provided that the same method of determining the scantlings as that adopted for the S102 (see Chapter 5, Section 2.2.3) was used. Therefore, the Inquiry has adopted the lower deep displacement, corresponding to that of the S102, for its assessment of the S115.

3.   **Assessment of the S115 Proposal**

   3.1   **General**

   The following sub-sections detail the Inquiry's findings as they relate to the S115 in comparison with the S102, the NSR 7069 and the Type 23 design. These sub-sections reflect the order in which the respective key issues are addressed in Chapter 6 in relation to the S102.

   3.2   **Speed, Power and Endurance**

   3.2.1   Achievable speeds

   Since the S115 is not a geosim of the S90, and as no model tests have been performed for the S115, both TGA and the Inquiry have had to use empirical methods to estimate the speeds which might be achieved by the S115 (see Chapter 4, Section 4.1 for a discussion of power prediction methods). Although such methods are approximate, they are used during the early design stages since they provide an adequate preliminary estimate of the likely required power and achievable speeds. The methods adopted by TGA and the Inquiry do utilise the S90 model tests; however, they cannot predict the required power and the resulting speed as accurately as the method used for the S102, this vessel being a geosim of the S90.

   Independently, TGA and the Inquiry predicted similar power requirements for the S115 to achieve a given speed. It was agreed that with a performance prediction factor $(1+x)$ of 1.0, the S115 would still fall short of the NSR maximum required speed when fitted with two SM1C gas turbines and the two 2.3MW electric motors required for the S102 to achieve the NSR endurance speed. It should be noted that with the reduction in the resistance of the S115 compared with the S102, the required rating of the electric motors would be reduced to 2.1MW.

TGA maintained, however, that with a 5% reduction in resistance which they considered could be achieved by subsequent minor modifications to the hull form following tank testing, and using a performance prediction factor of 0.9, the S115 would achieve the maximum required NSR speed.

The Inquiry cannot endorse the use of either of the above assumptions in determining the achievable speeds of the S115.

Although it may be possible to achieve a 5% reduction in measured resistance by 'tuning' the hull form following tank testing of a basic hull model, such a reduction cannot be considered applicable to preliminary powering estimates derived by extrapolation from other model test data. Furthermore, the Inquiry considers that, at the preliminary design stage, it is not prudent to assume that the power requirements would be reduced, especially as no design margins have been incorporated as would be normal given the preliminary nature of the S115.

With reference to the selection of an appropriate performance prediction factor, as indicated in Chapter 4, Section 4.4.5, a value of 1.0 has been chosen by the Inquiry as approximating to the likely value which would be used by a towing tank given the available correlation factor data for this type of hull form. Although the Inquiry has also selected a lower bound of 0.9, this value has been used by the Inquiry to assess the sensitivity of the required power and resulting costs for a vessel based on the S90 hull form to the value of the performance prediction factor chosen. Bearing in mind that performance prediction factors are used to ensure that the full scale performance does not fall short of requirements, the Inquiry does not consider that a factor of less than unity can prudently be used based on the evidence examined. It should be noted that the only reliable ship/model correlation factor for a similar vessel was that obtained from the 'Havornen' correlation exercise, i.e. 0.97.

The Inquiry has estimated that the shortfalls in speed of the S115 in relation to the NSR requirements, with the original TGA machinery proposal (i.e. two 1.5MW electric motors and two SM1C gas turbines), would be:

i)   Maximum quiet speed with the towed array sonar deployed - 1.2 knots (0.8 knots with $(1+x) = 0.9$)

ii)   Endurance speed - 1.1 knots (0.7 knots with $(1+x)$ = 0.9)

iii)   Maximum speed - 1.3 knots (0.4 knots with $(1+x)$ = 0.9)

With suitably sized electric motors to achieve the NSR endurance and maximum quiet speed with the towed array sonar deployed (i.e. with two 2.1MW electric motors), the maximum achievable speed of the S115 with two SM1C gas turbines would be approximately 0.8 knots short of the NSR required maximum. However, with a $(1+x)$ of 0.9, the S115 would achieve this speed with the two 2.1MW motors.

3.2.2   Power

In terms of the delivered power required to achieve a given speed, the Inquiry considers that the S115 requires approximately:

i)   32% (21% with $(1+x)$ = 0.9) more power than the Type 23 to achieve the NSR required maximum quiet speed with the towed array sonar deployed.

ii)   44% (30% with $(1+x)$ = 0.9) more power than the Type 23 to achieve the NSR required endurance speed.

iii)   69% (50% with $(1+x)$ = 0.9) more power than the Type 23 to achieve the NSR required maximum speed.

The Inquiry considers that even with suitably sized electric motors to enable the S115 to achieve the NSR endurance and maximum quiet speed with the towed array sonar deployed, the S115 would still require additional gas turbine units to the two proposed SM1C units in order that it might achieve the NSR maximum speed.

Figure 7.3.1 shows the effect of L/B ratio on the delivered power required to achieve the NSR maximum speed. The S102 and the Type 23 values have been calculated from model experiments, whilst the S115 value was determined by applying L/B ratio correction factors, derived from the NPL round bilge high speed series (Reference 7.1), to the S90 model test results.

3.2.3   Endurance

The power required to propel the S115 at the NSR endurance speed has been estimated to be approximately 9% less than that required for the S102. Therefore, with the same design fuel load as the S102, the S115 would be expected to have an endurance range increased by 9%. This range would satisfy the minimum requirement of the NSR but would still be substantially lower than both the range of the Type 23 and the desired target value stated in the NSR 7069.

3.2.4   Summary

The performance of the S115, with respect to speed for a given power, lies between that of the S102 and the Type 23. Although the performance of the S115, with respect to its achievable speeds in relation to the NSR, is better than the S102, the Inquiry considers that this improvement is not sufficient to comply with the NSR requirements or to approach the performance of the Type 23. In particular, the S115 still requires considerably more power than the Type 23 to achieve a given speed.

TGA maintain that with a 5% reduction in resistance along with a performance prediction factor of 0.9, the S115 would achieve the NSR maximum speed. Although the Inquiry agrees that, with these assumptions, the S115 could achieve the required maximum speed, it does not consider that such favourable assumptions are realistic and cannot endorse their use.

3.3   Space, Layout, Structural Design and Weight

3.3.1   Area, Volume and 'Elbow Room'

As indicated in Chapter 5, Section 4, the S110 was judged by the Inquiry to be deficient in usable internal deck area by about 200m^2. Although the S115 has not been the subject of any design development, the Inquiry considers that with the increase in length over the S110, adequate additional deck area would be available to meet the spatial requirements of the NSR 7069 with an acceptable compartment arrangement.

A comparison of the overall dimensions of the S102 and S115 hulls indicated that the enclosed volume would be similar for both designs. However, the volume enclosed by the superstructure of the S115 would be less than that of the S102 due to the superstructure modifications proposed by TGA. Therefore, the total additional enclosed volume of the S115, compared with the Type 23, would be approximately 14%, a reduction of 13% from the 27% additional enclosed volume identified for the S102 when compared with the Type 23.

In terms of accessibility, the reduction in volume and beam of the S115 compared with the S102 may make it difficult to accommodate the two passageway access system to the full extent proposed by

TGA for the original S90 design proposal and incorporated by the Inquiry in its S102 development. It should be noted that for the S110 design, TGA were only able to accommodate a two passageway system on one deck.   Therefore, in terms of accessibility, it is considered that the S115 would probably be inferior to the S102. In terms of available 'elbow room', it is considered that there would be no appreciable difference between the S102 and S115.   In comparison with the Type 23, it is considered that the S115 would, with a single passageway system, have no advantage in terms of accessibility and that the available 'elbow room' would be similar for both designs.

3.3.2   Layout

A major difference between the S115 and the S102 is the de-centralisation of the superstructure block on the S115. A principle feature of the original S90 design proposal was the concentration of the accommodation amidships where, TGA claimed, the advantages of reduced vertical motions could be utilised and this would reduce crew fatigue.

However, for the S115, TGA have proposed that the height of the superstructure be reduced by removing tiers and re-distributing the superstructure in a similar fashion to that on the Type 23, i.e. along the length of the vessel.

3.3.3   Structural Design

The margin against fatigue damage would be reduced for the S115 compared with the S102.   However, as stated in Chapter 6, Section 3.5, it is considered that no significant advantage can be taken of any additional margin above that required by the relevant strength standard.

3.3.4   Steelweight and Displacement

The plating areas for the S102 and the S115 hull (excluding superstructure) are estimated to be similar.   However, with the increase in length of the S115 compared with the S102, the plating and stiffener scantlings may have to be increased which would result in the weight of the hull increasing for the S115 compared with the S102.   However, as the S115 superstructure has been reduced in height and volume, it is considered that the weight of the superstructure of the S115 would be less than that of the S102.   In overall terms, it is considered that the steelweight of the S115 would be similar to that determined for the S102, provided that the same method of determining the scantlings as that adopted for the S102 (see Chapter 5, Section 2.2.3) was used and design margins excluded. In terms of displacement, given that the steelweights for the S115 and S102 are judged to be similar, it is considered that the deep displacement of the two vessels would also be similar.

3.3.5   Summary

It is considered that the S115 would have sufficient area to enable spatial compliance with the NSR to be achieved as does the S102.

The S115 would be less able to accommodate a twin passageway system compared with the S102. If a single passageway system was adopted, then in terms of accessibility, the S115 would be inferior to the S102 but similar to the Type 23. In terms of available 'elbow room', it is considered that the S115, the S102 and the Type 23 would all be comparable. The marked difference between the S115 and the S102 is the division of the superstructure block on the S115 into two and the consequent reduction in height. The Inquiry considers that this is a major departure from the design concept as embodied in the original S90 design proposal.

3.4   Intact and Damaged Stability

3.4.1   Intact Stability

In comparison with the S102, the reduction in breadth of the S115 in association with the changes in length, depth and draught is expected to have the following effect on the hull form related parameters and stability response:-

The freeboard to the uppermost continuous deck would reduce and hence the angle of heel to immerse the deck edge would decrease for the S115 compared with the S102.

The transverse metacentric heights would be reduced. Since GM is reduced, the slope of the righting lever (GZ) curve at the origin would be less and the total area encompassed by the GZ curve would be reduced. A given applied heeling moment would thus produce a greater angle of heel compared with the S102.

The projected area of the S115 hull profile is anticipated to be similar to that of the S102. However, since the S115 wind lever is likely to be smaller, the beam wind heeling moment would be reduced.

The moment to change trim (MCT) would be increased and, therefore, a given trimming moment would produce a smaller change of trim.

3.4.2 Damaged Stability

Assuming that the equivalent subdivision arrangement for the S102 is applied to the S115, it is anticipated that the extent of flooding resulting from weapon damage would increase. This could give rise to greater sinkage, heel and trim after such flooding. Furthermore, the possibility of immersion of the uppermost deck edge would be increased due to a reduction in freeboard and initial stability. However, by modifying the subdivision arrangement, it is anticipated that the aforementioned effects could be reduced.

The increased moment to change trim implies greater longitudinal stability and this may give some benefit to S115 with regard to the avoidance of plunging after damage, although this benefit may be nullified to some extent by reduced freeboard.

3.4.3 Summary

Despite the overall reduction in available stability for the S115 compared with the S102, the reserve of stability inherent in this type of hull form is so large that the proposed change in breadth would not have any serious consequences on its ability to satisfy the intact stability requirements contained in the NES 109.

Although the damaged stability response is more difficult to predict without a full analysis, the large reserve of intact stability associated with such a hull form indicates that, provided due attention is paid to the subdivision arrangement, compliance with the damaged stability requirements of the NES 109 could be achieved.

The S115, whilst having reduced stability compared with the S102, would still be expected to have a greater capability to comply with the intact and damaged stability criteria of the NES 109 than the Type 23.

3.5   Seakeeping

3.5.1 Head Seas Response

Although the increase in length of S115, relative to the S102, would marginally reduce the pitch response, it would also result in an increase in the vertical motions at the fore and aft end.

The combination of higher vertical motions at the fore end and the slightly smaller draught of the S115 would result in a higher probability of bottom slamming compared with the S102, whereas the incidence of deck wetness would be similar for both the S102 and the S115. For both parameters, the incidence of occurrence would still be lower than for the Type 23. The increase in vertical motions at the fore end would also increase the incidence of bow flare impacts. Although it is anticipated that the reduction in beam would mean a slightly finer fore end, the high curvature of the hull below the knuckle line would still cause high bow flare loadings.

As the vertical motions at the fore and aft end would be higher on the S115 than on the S102, and as the superstructure has been re-distributed along the length of the S115, the averaged SMM would be higher for the S115 than the S102. It should be noted that, in this respect, the only significant advantage that the S102 had over the Type 23 was at the high end of the speed range. This advantage would be reduced and the marginal advantage at lower speeds would be even less.

The fact that the bridge has been moved further forward would also mean that the vertical acceleration at the bridge would be higher on the S115 than the S102. As indicated in Chapter 6, Section 5, at the lower speeds there was only a marginal improvement in vertical acceleration at the bridge level for the S102 over the Type 23. Consequently, even less improvement would be expected for the S115 compared with the Type 23.

The Inquiry considers that in head seas, the performance of the S115, compared with the S102, would be inferior.

3.5.2   Beam Seas Response

The natural roll period of a vessel is a function of the radius of gyration of roll in water and the square root of the metacentric height (GM). In approximate terms, the radius of gyration of roll in water can be expressed as a linear function of the beam and therefore the smaller beam on the S115 would result in a lower value. In addition, it is considered that the GM of the S115 would also be reduced in relation to that of the S102. However, the combination of the changes to the GM and radius of gyration will only have a small effect on the natural roll period predicted for the S102 and, therefore, the S115 would still have a much shorter roll period than the Type 23. The lower superstructure would reduce the roll-induced lateral accelerations on the bridge but they would still be higher than those on the Type 23 because of the shorter roll period.

3.5.3   Following and Stern Quartering Seas Response

The Inquiry considers that the large pitch motion indicated for the S102 in following and stern quartering seas would be reduced for the S115 due to the increase in length and reduction in beam. However, it is still considered that the vessel's response on such headings would need to be carefully assessed by means of model tests.

3.5.4   Speed Loss in Waves

The increase in length of the S115, in association with the changes in breadth, depth and draught, is not considered to alter the overall speed loss in waves significantly for the S115 in comparison with the S102. In this respect, the S115 would still maintain an advantage over the Type 23 in terms of speed limitation due to a voluntary reduction. With respect to the maximum achievable speed in rough weather, as was indicated in Chapter 6, Section 5, this is limited by the involuntary speed loss associated with the added resistance in waves and, in this respect, the Type 23 is still considered to be able to achieve a higher absolute speed than the S115 in rough weather, should this be required.

3.5.5   Summary

The overall seakeeping performance of the S115 is considered to be better than that of the S102 due to the improved performance of the S115 in beam to following seas outweighing the reduced performance in head seas. However, the overall seakeeping performance of the S115 is not considered to be better than that of the Type 23.

3.6   **Manoeuvrability**

3.6.1   Turning Performance

The S115 would have a larger tactical diameter, advance and transfer than the S102 (see Figure 6.6.1 for definition of terms). The S115 is likely to have a smaller tactical diameter, advance and transfer than the Type 23, although this would ultimately be dependent upon trim and the size of the rudder and skeg.

It is considered that the S102, S115 and Type 23 would all experience a similar speed loss during turning.
The S115's steady turning rate would be inferior to that of the S102 although probably still better than, or at least comparable to, that of the Type 23.

3.6.2 Directional stability

The S115 would be more directionally stable than the S102. It should be noted that the higher L/B ratio would permit a smaller skeg to be fitted to achieve equal directional stability to that of the S102. Reducing the size of the skeg would also enhance the vessel's manoeuvrability.

3.6.3 Stopping Performance

The stopping performance of the S115 would be worse than that of the S102 although, due to its greater resistance, it would still be better than that of the Type 23.

3.6.4 Summary

The turning and stopping performance of the S115, whilst still maintaining an advantage in absolute terms over the Type 23, would be worse than that of the S102.

3.7 Military Features

The principal hull form related factors which influence the military features aspects were identified in Chapter 6, Section 7 as: radiated noise signature, radar horizon/signature and weapon layout/operational efficiency.

3.7.1 Radiated Noise Signature

The dominant factor in the case of the S115 is considered, as with the S102, to be the propeller thrust loading. This would be lower than that on the S102 but higher than that on the Type 23, and thus the cavitation inception speeds are expected to lie between those of the S102 and Type 23 designs. The S115 is considered unlikely to meet the NSR noise target at the higher towed array operational speeds, but non-compliance is expected over a smaller range than is the case for the S102. In addition, the thrust loadings over the entire speed range, and consequently the radiated noise signature at any given speed, is anticipated to be higher than that of the Type 23 but lower than that of the S102.

3.7.2 Radar Horizon and Signature

The position of the main surveillance radar on the S115 has been maintained at approximately the same height as on the S102. Consequently, the radar horizons would be some 20% longer than the Type 23 and the corresponding advantages identified for the S102 are still applicable. The height distribution of the radar cross-section of the S115, however, represents a small improvement on that of the S102, although it is still inferior to that of the Type 23. The Inquiry's view that a similar increase in radar horizon could be achieved if desired on the Type 23 without the same penalty on radar signature still holds.

3.7.3   Weapon Layout and Operational Efficiency

The available deck area for weapon layout is similar on the S115, the S102 and Type 23 designs. Since a satisfactory layout has been achieved for the highest and lowest L/B ratios, i.e. the Type 23 and S102 respectively, no problem in this respect is anticipated for the S115.

The motions environment for the weapons and their associated sensors is likely to lie between that of the S102 and Type 23 designs principally because the roll period, the relevant height locations and the symmetric responses (pitch and heave) are all anticipated to assume intermediate values. Since no overall operational advantage was identified for either the S102 or the Type 23, none is anticipated for the S115.

3.7.4   Summary

The performance of the S115, with respect to military features, is expected to lie between that of the Type 23 and S102. Consequently, with the exception of radiated noise signature, no significant overall advantage is anticipated for any of the three designs and all are expected to comply with the NSR. In the case of noise, although the S115 is considered to represent an improvement over the S102, this improvement is not anticipated to be sufficient to either comply with the NSR targets or to approach the signature of the Type 23.

3.8   Construction Costs

The effect on the cost groups identified in Chapter 6, Section 8.2, due to adopting the S115 rather than the S102, would be as follows:-

3.8.1   Hull

As it is considered that the steelweight of the S115 would be similar to that of the S102 (see Section 3.3.4), the purchase cost of materials would also be similar for both vessels.

With the reduction in the superstructure height and enclosed volume, it has been estimated that the additional plated area for the S115, compared with the Type 23, would be approximately 5%, a reduction of 4% from the value of 9% identified for the S102. This would result in the welding content for the S115 being reduced below that for the S102. If the relative savings identified for the S102 due to reduced double curvature of the hull form are assumed to still be applicable for the S115 hull form then, with the reduced welding content, the hull group cost is expected to be approximately 0.4% of the NUPC less than that for the Type 23. This compares with the increase of 0.3% of the NUPC identified for the S102 when compared with the Type 23.

3.8.2 Propulsion

The two SM1C gas turbines, as identified in Chapter 6, Section 8.4.2, would cost approximately 0.2% of the Type 23 NUPC more than the two SM1A turbines fitted to the Type 23.

If it is assumed that suitably sized electric motors are fitted (i.e. two 2.1MW motors) in order that the S115 might achieve the NSR required endurance speed and maximum quiet speed with the towed array sonar deployed, the additional cost above that of the Type 23 with two 1.5MW electric motors fitted would be approximately 0.7% of the Type 23 NUPC. Therefore, the total increase in the propulsion group cost for the S115 compared with the Type 23 would be of the order of 0.9% of the Type 23 NUPC.

As indicated in Section 3.2.1, it is considered that the S115 would not meet the NSR maximum speed requirement even with suitably sized electric motors. In order to achieve this speed, additional gas turbine units would need to be installed, increasing the propulsion group cost still further above that for the Type 23.

3.8.3 Ship Systems

Although no layout has been produced for the S115, the Inquiry considers that as the enclosed volume of the S115 is less than that of the S102 and as the superstructure and overall proportions have moved closer to those of the Type 23, this group cost would also move towards that for the Type 23 and hence the excess cost identified in Chapter 6, Section 8.4.3 for the S102 compared with the Type 23 would be reduced.

3.8.4 Outfit and Furnishings

It is considered that there would be a marginal reduction in this group cost for the S115 when compared with the S102.

3.8.5   Weapons

As the weapon fit would be identical for the S115, the S102 and the Type 23, this group cost would also be identical for all three vessels.

3.8.6   Summary

In the Inquiry's judgement, the 2.7% increase in the NUPC identified for the S102 when compared with the Type 23 would be reduced to approximately 1.5% for the S115 when compared with the Type 23. However, as previously indicated, the S115 is still a vessel which does not meet the NSR maximum speed or noise requirements.

If the S115 was fitted with sufficient power to meet all the NSR speed requirements, then, in the Inquiry's opinion, a significant cost increase would be incurred. A four SM1A gas turbine installation, which is a possible practical machinery configuration capable of providing the required power, would increase the minimum overall additional cost, compared with the Type 23, by approximately 5% of the Type 23 NUPC.

3.9   Through Life Costs

The major contributions to the increased through life cost of the S102 compared with the Type 23 were identified in Chapter 6, Section 9 as being the larger fuel cost and increased machinery maintenance and repair.

As indicated in Chapter 6, Section 9.1, to make a realistic comparison with the Type 23 through life cost, it is necessary to assume that the vessel being compared, in this instance the S115, can achieve the NSR required speeds and fulfil the NSR specified mission profiles. As indicated in Section 3.2.1, the S115 would not achieve the NSR maximum speed with the proposed machinery configuration. Therefore, to enable a comparison of the through life cost of the S115 with that of the Type 23, it has been assumed that the S115 has sufficient installed power to achieve the required speed. In this respect, the fuel cost can be assessed using the appropriate speed/power relationship derived for the S115. For assessing the maintenance and repair costs associated with a practical machinery configuration which could provide sufficient power for the S115 to achieve the NSR maximum speed, it has been assumed that the S115 is fitted with additional gas turbine units.

Based on the above assumptions, the Inquiry estimates that the fuel cost for the S115 would be 24.6% more than that for the Type 23.

This compares with the 49.5% additional fuel cost identified for the S102 when compared with the Type 23.

Since additional gas turbine units are required, the maintenance and repair costs for the S115 are considered to be of the same order as those identified for the S102.

Therefore, in overall terms, it is anticipated that the through life support and running cost for the S115 would decrease when compared with the S102 due principally to the reduced fuel cost. However, the through life cost of the S115 has been estimated to still be 7.4% more than that for the Type 23 due to the higher power requirement at every speed and the repair and maintenance of the additional turbines.

With a performance prediction factor $(1+x)$ of 0.9, it would not be necessary to fit the additional gas turbine units to achieve the NSR maximum speed. As a result, the turbine associated maintenance and repair costs would be reduced. In addition, the propulsion fuel cost would also be reduced. However, the Inquiry has estimated that the through life cost of the S115 would still exceed that of the Type 23 by 2.1%.

3.10   Summary of the Overall Cost Differential

Although in comparison with the S102, the S115 would reduce the overall cost differential with the Type 23, the Inquiry has estimated that the S115 would still cost a minimum of 6% more than the Type 23 both to build and to operate. With a performance prediction factor $(1+x)$ of 0.9, this increase in cost relative to the Type 23 would be approximately 2%.

4.   The Sirius Hull Form at High Speed

TGA informed the Inquiry that they considered that the Sirius hull form was capable of speeds well in excess of those required by the NSR 7069 and those which could practically be achieved by a conventional frigate hull form. The evidence that TGA presented to support this claim is principally contained in two graphs, namely:

i)   A non-dimensional comparison of the hull resistance of the US Navy Perry class FFG-7 frigate with that of the Sirius hull form. This graph was originally published as part of the written discussion by Mr D.L. Giles and Commander P. Thornycroft to Reference 7.2, and has been reproduced as Figure 7.4.1. It should be noted that this graph was also reproduced in the Hill-Norton Committee Report as Figure 13.

ii)   A comparison of the brake horsepower against speed of the S90, the Perry class frigate and the Leander class frigate. This graph has been published in Reference 7.3 and has been reproduced as Figure 7.4.2.

The Hill-Norton Committee also considered that the Sirius hull form could offer a significant increase in top speed over the maximum which could be realised in a conventional hull form of a similar size. They concluded that, if confirmed, this would be a most important military advantage. The Inquiry has therefore carefully examined Figures 7.4.1 and 7.4.2 and the data used to derive them.

4.1   Figure 7.4.1 - Non-dimensional Comparison of Hull Resistance

This figure has been discussed in detail in Chapter 4, Section 4.5. An examination of the resistance data available for the Perry class revealed that the Perry class curve plotted in Figure 7.4.1 was incorrect. The correct Perry class data has been re-plotted in Figure 7.4.3 with speed as the horizontal axis. This figure shows that the Sirius hull form is approximately twice as resistful as the Perry class frigate at all speeds for which data exists.

4.2   Figure 7.4.2 - Comparison of the S90, Perry and Leander Class Frigates

Figure 7.4.2 shows the brake horsepower that is required for each vessel to achieve a given speed. In order to calculate this brake horsepower, it is necessary to first determine the effective power and the propulsive coefficient. The Inquiry has examined how these two parameters have been determined for each vessel shown in Figure 7.4.2.

Based on the data obtained by the Inquiry for the Perry class frigate (see Chapter 4, Section 4.5), it is concluded that the effective power that has been used in determining the Perry class curve shown in Figure 7.4.2 is incorrect. Furthermore, the propulsive coefficient used to determine the efficiency of the power conversion has been underestimated by about 25 - 30%.

Upon examining the available data for the Leander class frigate, the Inquiry found that the propulsive coefficient for this vessel has also been underestimated by 25 - 30%. The reason for this is dealt with in Chapter 4, Section 4.6. As a result, the Leander curve shown in

Figure 7.4.2 is also incorrect. It must also be stated that the Leander curve has been extrapolated beyond the maximum speed for which data exists. TGA in Reference 7.3 stated that the Leander line was extrapolated in a manner which was consistent with the Perry class resistance curve. As stated above, the Perry class curve is incorrect; therefore, the extrapolation of the Leander curve is also incorrect.

With reference to the S90 curve shown in Figure 7.4.2, the NMI S90 model test data used by the Inquiry only covers the speed range up to 35 knots. The Inquiry has plotted this data along with the correct Perry class data in Figure 7.4.4. It should be noted that the Perry class data is for a displacement of 3424 tonnes. At the displacement of 2600 tonnes, for which the S90 data is plotted, the brake horsepower of the Perry class would be even lower.

Figure 7.4.4 indicates that up to all speeds for which data is available, the S90 requires considerably more power to achieve a given speed.

4.3   Osprey and Ton Class Comparison

As further evidence that a hull form based on the same concept as their Sirius design philosophy would be less resistful at high speeds, TGA also submitted to the Inquiry a comparison of the shaft horsepower against speed for the Osprey class patrol vessel and the trial results for the Ton class coastal minesweeper. The appropriate figure has been reproduced as Figure 7.4.5.

The Inquiry has examined the data used to produce this diagram and has concluded that the data has been extrapolated beyond its limits. The data used to plot Figure 7.4.5 is shown in Figure 7.4.6. This figure shows that the Ton class is less resistful than the Osprey class at all the speeds for which it was tested. The Inquiry considers that extrapolating beyond available data can be misleading.

4.4   Other Data

The data plotted in Figure 7.4.4 is only available for a speed range of up to 31 knots for the Perry class and up to 35 knots for the S90. As previously stated, the Inquiry considers that extrapolating data beyond the limit of its validity can be misleading. Therefore, in order to make a rational comparison of the Sirius hull form with measured and tank test data from conventional frigate and naval hull forms at higher speeds, additional data (in the form of effective powers) has been obtained from the MoD and this has been plotted in Figure 7.4.7 for similar displacements.

This figure shows that for speeds up to 45 knots the Sirius hull form is still more resistful than conventional and naval frigate hull forms. Above 45 knots there is insufficient data to draw any firm conclusions.

At speeds approaching 45 knots and above, vessels other than displacement monohull ships, for example hydrofoils, hovercraft and surface effect ships, represent potential alternative solutions and would therefore also require to be evaluated in relation to a requirement defined for either a very fast frigate or destroyer.

Figure 7.4.8, adapted from Reference 7.4, shows the 'transport efficiencies' of various types of vessel along with the derived transport efficiencies for the S102, S115 and Type 23. A high efficiency means that a greater weight can be propelled at the same speed for a lower power. This figure indicates that the trends for achieving higher speeds are away from displacement monohull vessels, whether they be conventional or Sirius shaped hull forms. However, Figure 7.4.8 is only a preliminary guide and detailed studies of all aspects of the requirement would need to be undertaken before a definite conclusion on the best configuration could be arrived at.

It should also be recognised that a high speed monohull concept is not necessarily consistent with maintaining high speed in progressively worsening sea conditions. Reference 7.4 addresses this problem and has published limiting speed data for a range of vehicle types and weights in progressive sea-states. Figure 7.4.9 reproduces this data for vessels of 1000 and 5000 tonnes from which it can be seen that careful evaluation of other alternatives to a monohull would need to be undertaken if operation at high speeds in high sea-states is required.

The Inquiry also foresees that there would be considerable difficulty in finding a machinery configuration which could realistically deliver the substantial amounts of power that would be required to drive a Sirius hull form at high speeds and still produce a vessel with the equivalent military capability of current frigates and destroyers.

4.5   Summary

The Inquiry has assessed the claim that the Sirius hull form offers the advantage of being capable of speeds well in excess of those which could be achieved by more conventional frigate hull forms. The evidence presented by TGA to support this claim has been found to be in error and the correct data shows that the Sirius hull form is substantially more resistful than a conventional hull form up to speeds for which data is available (approximately 45 knots).

Above such speeds, the Inquiry considers that other marine vehicles would need to be carefully evaluated in addition to a displacement monohull vessel, particularly in relation to transport efficiency and operation at high speed in other than calm water conditions.

5.   Conclusions

The Inquiry has carried out a thorough assessment of the S115 proposal put forward by TGA as representing the limit of the Sirius design concept for the purposes of meeting the NSR 7069. Although TGA have maintained that the S115 should be progressed to a similar state of development and be assessed at the same level of detail as the S102, the Inquiry considers that this is unnecessary. The Inquiry's assessment has been based on the comprehensive database and knowledge gained through the evaluation of the original S90 proposal, the detailed development of the S102 and its subsequent assessment both against the NSR and the Type 23 and the examination of the S110 study. Therefore, the Inquiry considers that the conclusions it has drawn with respect to the S115 would not be materially altered by developing the S115 to the same level of detail as the S102.

As a result of this assessment, the Inquiry concludes that the S115 goes further towards meeting the NSR 7069 requirements than the S102 and, in this respect, is a better solution to these requirements than the S102.

However, although the S115 reduces the S102's speed deficiency in relation to the NSR speed requirements, the Inquiry concludes that the S115 would still not meet the NSR maximum speed requirement with the machinery configuration proposed. In addition, due to the greater power requirement, relative to the Type 23, the vessel would not meet the NSR noise targets over the upper operating quiet towed array speed range. In all other respects, the Inquiry considers that the S115 would meet the NSR requirements, as does the S102.

In comparison with the Type 23, the S115 would still require considerably more power to achieve a given speed (the S115 is estimated to require 69% more delivered power than the Type 23 to achieve the NSR maximum speed). Although the through life cost of the S115 would be lower than that of the S102, due to the reduced power requirement and consequent reduction in fuel cost, this cost would still be greater than that of the Type 23. The construction cost of the S115 would also still be more than the Type 23. Therefore, although the overall cost differential with the Type 23 would be reduced, the S115 would still cost more both to build and operate. It is anticipated that the minimum additional overall cost of an

S115, meeting the NSR speed requirements, would be in the order of 6% more than that of a Type 23 frigate. The seakeeping performance of the S115 in overall terms is considered to be better than the S102, but still worse than the Type 23. In general terms it is concluded that the performance parameters have done no more than tend towards the behaviour of the Type 23. Hence both the advantages and disadvantages of the S102 are maintained but to a reduced degree. The extent of these changes is not such as to require further development of the S115 to quantify them in comparison with the Type 23. In the Inquiry's judgement the Type 23 is still both a cheaper and more effective solution to the NSR 7069 than the S115.

The Inquiry has also assessed the claim that the Sirius hull form offers the advantage of being capable of speeds well in excess of those which could be obtained by more conventional frigate hull forms. The Inquiry concludes that this claim is unfounded and that, in fact, the contrary is true up to speeds for which data is available (approximately 45 knots). At speeds approaching 45 knots and above, the Inquiry considers that other marine vehicles would need to be carefully evaluated in addition to a displacement monohull vessel, particularly in relation to transport efficiency and operation at high speed in other than calm water conditions.

References

7.1   'The NPL High Speed Round Bilge Displacement Hull Series', Maritime Technology Monograph No.4, RINA, 1976.

7.2   Bryson, L.: 'The Procurement of a Warship', Trans.RINA, Volume 127, 1985.

7.3   Giles, D.L.: 'Short and Fat - The Shape of Things to Come?', ATI European Naval Forecast Conference, 14-15th May 1987.

7.4   Eames, M.C.: 'Advances in Naval Architecture for Future Surface Warships', Trans.RINA, Volume 123, 1981.

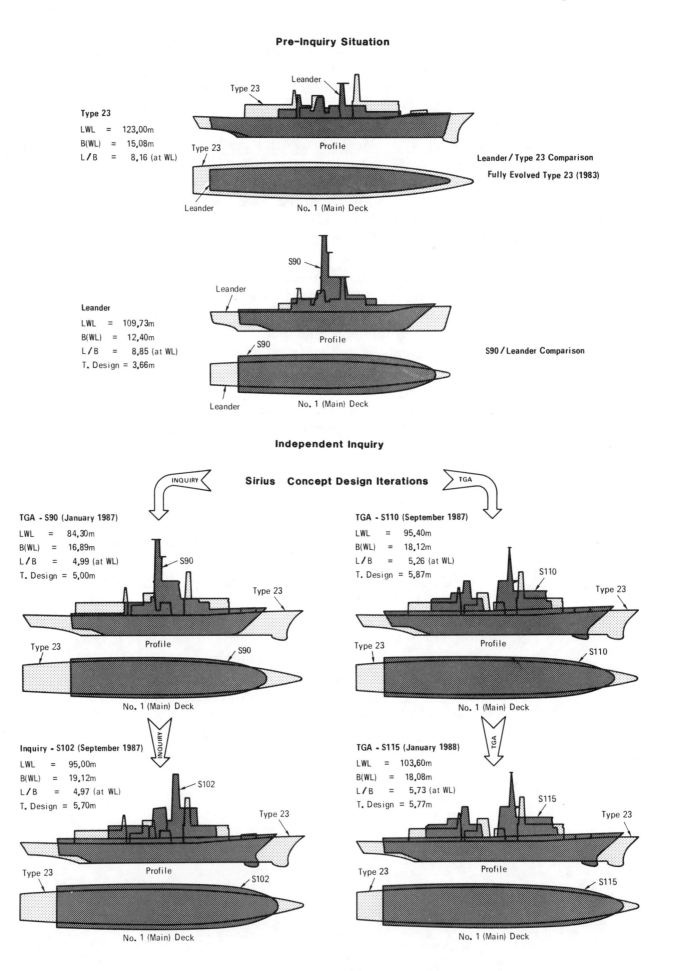

FIGURE 7.2.1   DEVELOPMENT OF THE INITIAL S90 PROPOSAL

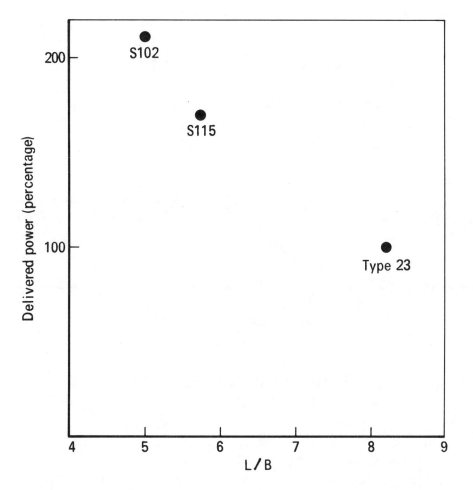

FIGURE 7.3.1   VARIATION OF DELIVERED POWER, WITH L/B RATIO,
TO ACHIEVE THE NSR MAXIMUM SPEED IN THE DEEP
DISPLACEMENT CONDITION

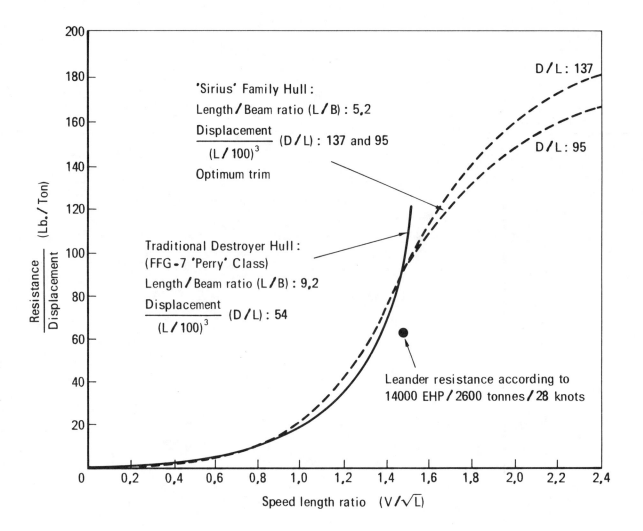

FIGURE 7.4.1   REPRODUCED FROM REFERENCE 7.2

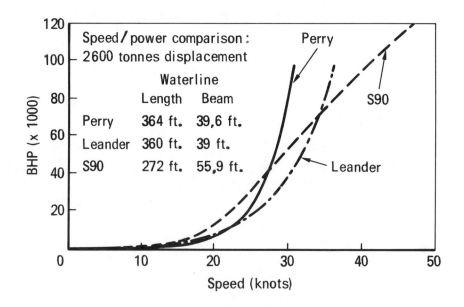

FIGURE 7.4.2   REPRODUCED FROM REFERENCE 7.3

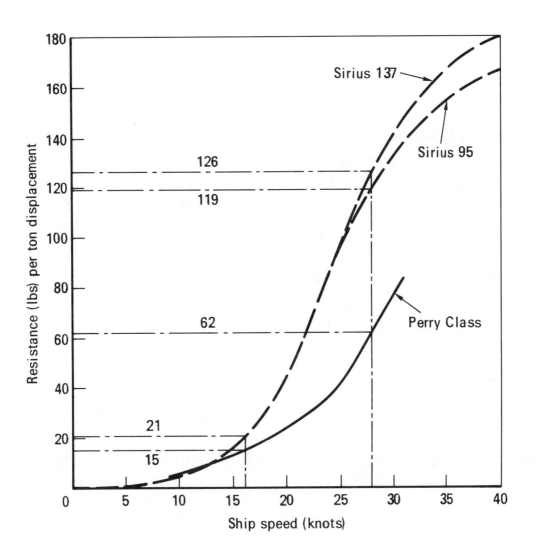

FIGURE 7.4.3

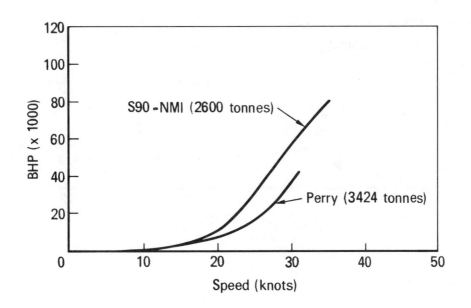

FIGURE 7.4.4

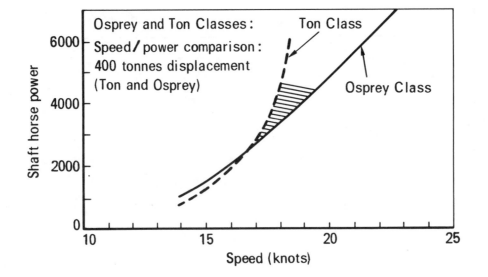

FIGURE 7.4.5   REPRODUCTION OF FIGURE SUBMITTED BY TGA TO
               THE INQUIRY

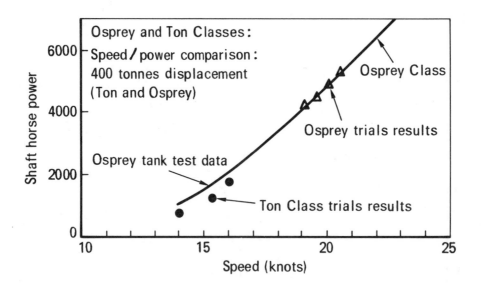

FIGURE 7.4.6

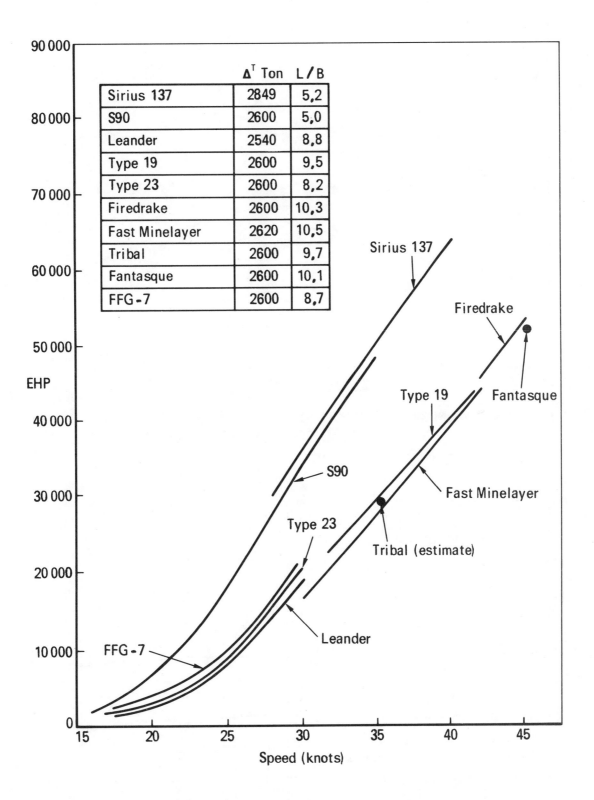

FIGURE 7.4.7   COMPARISON OF EFFECTIVE HORSEPOWERS AT
                            SIMILAR DISPLACEMENTS

Note: Sirius 137 corresponds to vessel illustrated in Figure 7.4.1

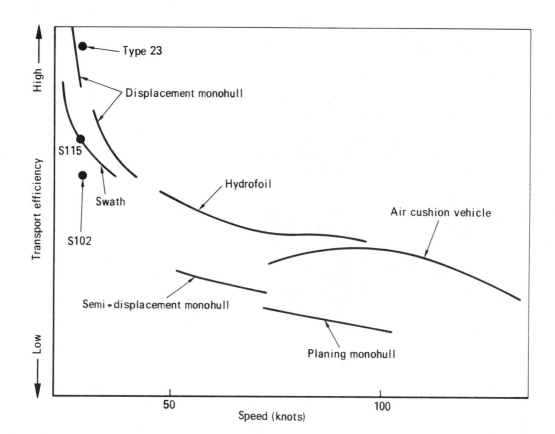

FIGURE 7.4.8   CALM WATER TRANSPORT EFFICIENCY VERSUS SPEED
FOR 4000 TONNES DISPLACEMENT - ADAPTED FROM
REFERENCE 7.4

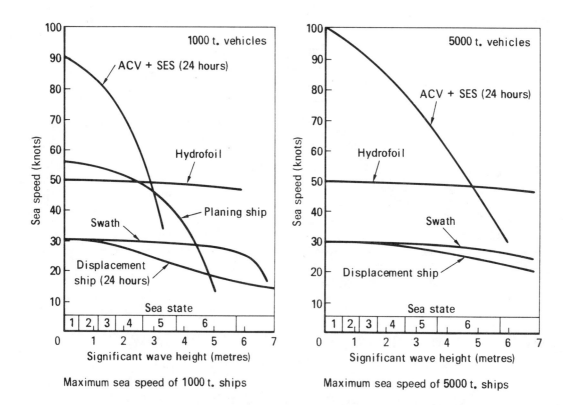

FIGURE 7.4.9   REPRODUCED FROM REFERENCE 7.4

Note: ACV - Air Cushion Vehicle
SES - Surface Effect Ship

CHAPTER 8

PRINCIPAL CONCLUSIONS AND RECOMMENDATIONS

SUMMARY OF PRINCIPAL CONCLUSIONS AND RECOMMENDATIONS

It is the Inquiry's firm conclusion that the Sirius design concept is unable to produce as good a solution to the NSR 7069 as the Type 23 and that the MoD were correct in their rejection of the S90 design proposal in 1983. The Type 23 solution is cheaper both to build and to operate and has a better overall performance than can be achieved by a vessel based on the Sirius concept. The Inquiry further concludes that the advice given to the MoD by YARD along with that by the Hull Committee of the DSAC in 1983 was also correct with respect to their overall conclusions.

The Inquiry concludes that the hydrodynamic performance of a Sirius type hull form can be adequately assessed by conventional naval architectural techniques. The claim that a Sirius hull form does not obey conventional principles has been based on data being incorrectly interpreted. In particular, the Inquiry finds that in regard to the propulsive performance of the S90 hull form, it requires substantially more power to achieve a given speed than that suggested by the Hill-Norton Committee.

The Inquiry's terms of reference require it, after considering the advantages and disadvantages of the S90 hull form in relation to the NSR 7069, to identify any implications for the design of future destroyers and frigates for the Royal Navy. Based on its assessment of the claimed exceptional hydrodynamic performance of a Sirius hull form, along with its comparison of the S102 and S115 against a specific frigate requirement, namely the NSR 7069, the Inquiry has concluded that there are no identifiable implications for the design of future destroyers and frigates for the Royal Navy arising from the Sirius design concept, as far as it is able to foresee the likely role and operating requirements for future warships of this type.

Accordingly, the Inquiry considers, and would recommend, that no further action is required to assess the applicability of the Sirius concept for future frigate and destroyer design.

1.   PRINCIPAL CONCLUSIONS

TGA's Sirius design concept is based on the proposition that hull forms which are commonly used for smaller successful working craft can, with advantage, be scaled up in size and used for much larger vessels.   For frigates and destroyers, TGA claim that the adoption of their design concept would produce a vessel which would have substantial advantages compared with such a vessel based on current frigate and destroyer design philosophy. Paragraph 2 of the Hill-Norton Committee Report summarizes TGA's claims:

> 'It is claimed that a radical alternative {to a current conventional design}, in the shape of a short/fat hull form, would provide very substantial advantages in building and maintenance costs, in construction time, and in simplicity of layout, with no operational penalties. Indeed, it is further claimed that such vessels would be more stable, with better sea-keeping and manoeuvring performance, more commodious between-decks space and thus better accommodation, and that they would be able to carry a greater weapon outfit.'

Before such claims can be assessed, it is necessary to translate the concept into a design which meets a defined requirement. The design of any ship, whether it be a warship or a merchant ship, requires a balance to be achieved between a number of operational, technical and economic factors. These factors are often in direct conflict with each other and, as a result, the success or otherwise of a design is determined primarily by the overall balance that is finally reached between the various parameters which influence it. Therefore, the suitability of a concept cannot be effectively judged until a design, which meets a specific requirement, has been developed to the point at which the overall balance, or compromise, of the various parameters can be assessed. If the overall balance is not established by means of a realistic design, then there is a real risk that advantages will be claimed without the extent of the corresponding disadvantages being properly assessed.

The Inquiry's terms of reference require it to assess the S90 hull form against the NSR 7069 for an ASW frigate. Although the S90 design proposal put forward by TGA to the MoD in 1983 was found, by the Inquiry, to be too small to meet this requirement (see Chapter 4, Section 3), the Inquiry has developed a geosim design based on the S90 hull form which is of the minimum size sufficient to meet the spatial requirements of the NSR while still seeking to preserve the features that TGA considered to be inherent in their S90 design proposal. The development of this design, the S102, has been fully described in Chapter 5.

The Inquiry, throughout its assessment of the Sirius design concept has sought to identify those issues which are strongly influenced by the hull form adopted. Although some of the issues raised in the debate leading up to the Inquiry have been vigorously contested by the parties involved, the Inquiry has found that not all of these issues are hull form related. The Inquiry has concerned itself only with those aspects which are principally hull form dependent.

1.1 **Assessment of the S102 in Relation to the NSR 7069 and in Comparison with the Type 23 Frigate**

In order to assess the overall effectiveness of the S102 as a fighting ship, designed to meet the NSR 7069, the Inquiry has adopted the same criteria used by the Hull Committee of the DSAC and the Hill-Norton Committee, namely:

a) The ability of the ship, as a vehicle, to meet the (staff) requirements for performance, seakeeping and so on.

b) The ability of the ship, as a platform, to carry the required weapon systems in the required numbers, with the required operational performance.

c) The ability of the ship, as an integrated unit, to deploy effectively its own weapons and to withstand, to the required limits, the effects of the enemy's weapons.

In order to assess whether or not the S102, compared with a current frigate design, provides a better balance of the contending operational, technical and economic factors, the Inquiry has compared the S102 with the Type 23 frigate, designed by the MoD to meet the NSR 7069. Although the Type 23, as a design, is considerably more advanced than the S102, the Inquiry considers that the major hull form related issues are not dependent on the fully detailed development of either design and, therefore, a valid judgement of the overall balance achieved by both designs can be made.

Chapter 6 presents the Inquiry's detailed findings as they relate to each key issue considered to be important by the Inquiry. These findings have led the Inquiry to the following principal conclusions:

1. The S102 is able to comply with the NSR 7069 in all but two respects; it cannot achieve the speed requirements or fully meet the radiated noise target.

   The S102 fails to achieve any of the NSR required speeds with the machinery configuration proposed by TGA. An increase of 53% in the electric motor power output together with an increase of 41% in the gas turbine power output is required for the vessel to achieve the NSR required speeds. It is considered that without a major re-design of the S102, possibly involving an increase in the size of the vessel, it would not be possible to install this additional power in the S102.

Since the effectiveness of an ASW frigate is dependent, first and foremost, on its ability to detect and locate submarines, the S102 would be unable to fully meet the primary function required by the NSR 7069 due to exceedance of noise targets over the towed array upper operational speed range.

2.   The S102 is able to carry the required weapon systems in the required numbers. With the exception of the operation of the towed array sonar over its upper operational speed range, the S102 is able to deploy effectively its own weapons and to withstand, to the required limits, the effects of the enemy's weapons.

3.   The S102 does not offer any overall operational advantage compared with the Type 23. On the contrary, the substantially greater power that the S102 requires to achieve a given speed (the S102 requires 111% more delivered power than the Type 23 to achieve the NSR maximum speed) is considered to be a major shortfall arising from the adoption of the S90 hull form. Although the S102 does possess greater intact stability than the Type 23, this is not considered to be an advantage in terms of the NSR 7069 as the Type 23 is able to accommodate all the weapons required by the NSR and deploy them effectively. The seakeeping performance of the two designs is similar, although the Inquiry considers that in overall terms the Type 23 is the better all round vessel. The S102 is more manoeuvrable than the Type 23. However, although this is considered to be an advantage, manoeuvrability is not regarded as a principal requirement of the NSR 7069.

It is anticipated that, due primarily to a lower incidence of deck wetness, the S102 would have an advantage over the Type 23 in terms of voluntary speed limitation in rough weather. However, the maximum achievable speed in rough weather is governed by the involuntary speed loss associated with added resistance in waves and, in this respect, the Type 23 would be able to maintain a higher absolute speed than the S102, should this be necessary.

4.   The S102 does not offer any significant improvement in habitability compared with the Type 23. On the contrary, as the total motions environment is considered to be more onerous for the S102, particularly at the lower speeds where a towed array ASW frigate will spend a significant proportion of its time, the S102 is considered

to be inferior to the Type 23 with respect to habitability and crew efficiency.

5.   The construction cost of the S102 would be greater than that of the Type 23. This is primarily due to the greater power requirement, there being no overall decrease in the hull construction cost of the S102 compared with the Type 23. With sufficient propulsion units installed to achieve the NSR required speeds, the Inquiry estimates that the S102 would cost a minimum of 7.3% more than the Type 23 to build. With the machinery configuration proposed by TGA, the Inquiry estimates that the S102 (which would not meet the NSR speed requirements) would cost approximately 2.7% more than the Type 23 to build. The Inquiry's cost estimates have been based on building both vessels in the same shipyard to the same strength and construction standards and exclude all first of class, development, lead shipyard and contingency cost components together with VAT and profit margins.

6.   The through life cost of the S102 would be considerably more than the Type 23 due to the greater power requirement. Assuming that the vessel has sufficient power installed to fulfil the required NSR mission profiles, then the through life cost of the S102 would be a minimum of 10.7% more than the Type 23. If the NSR mission profiles are modified to reflect the lower speed achievable by the S102, then the through life cost of the S102 would be a minimum of 8.2% more than the Type 23 fitted with a suitable down-graded machinery configuration.

7.   The total cost (i.e. the construction cost and through life cost) of an S102 over the intended life span of the vessel, with sufficient machinery fitted to achieve the NSR speeds, would be a minimum of 9.1% more than a corresponding Type 23 frigate. In terms of ship numbers, this means that for every eleven S102 vessels, approximately twelve Type 23 frigates could be procured. The Inquiry has not attempted to assess measures necessary to ensure that the S102 would meet the NSR noise targets. However, such measures, if feasible, would increase the cost differential between the S102 and the Type 23 still further.

8.   The Type 23 offers a better solution to the NSR 7069 than the S102 in terms of its overall performance coupled with cost effectiveness. The Sirius concept, as embodied in the S102 design, does not offer the substantial advantages claimed for it when assessed against the requirements of the NSR 7069.

1.2   **Assessment of the S115 Proposal in Relation to the NSR 7069 and in Comparison with the Type 23 Frigate**

As indicated in Chapter 7, TGA were informed of the Inquiry's initial broad and tentative findings concerning the comparative merits of the S102 in relation to the NSR 7069 and the Type 23. Arising from this, TGA indicated that they would modify the hull form in order to eliminate the S102's speed disadvantage in relation to the NSR requirements, or at least reduce it to acceptable proportions. They subsequently proposed the S115, a longer version of their previous S110 study (see Chapter 5, Section 4). The S115 was considerably longer than the S102 with a narrower beam resulting in an L/B ratio of 5.73 compared with 4.97 for the S102. TGA stated that the S115 was the limit of the Sirius concept for the purposes of meeting the NSR 7069. In addition to lengthening the design, TGA proposed that the superstructure layout should reflect that of the Type 23 to counter the disadvantages of the S102's tall centralised accommodation block. The Inquiry considers this to be a major departure from the design concept as embodied in the original S90 design proposal.

The Inquiry has carried out a thorough, although qualitative, assessment of the S115 (see Chapter 7) and has concluded that the S115 goes further towards meeting the NSR requirements than the S102 and, in this respect, is a better solution to these requirements than the S102. However, in the Inquiry's judgement, the S115 would still not meet the NSR maximum speed requirement with the proposed machinery configuration and would still exceed the NSR noise targets over the towed array upper operational speed range.

In comparison with the Type 23, the S115 would still require considerably more power to achieve a given speed (the S115 is estimated to require 69% more delivered power than the Type 23 to achieve the NSR maximum speed). Although the through life cost of the S115 would be lower than that of the S102, due to the reduced power requirement and consequent reduction in fuel cost, this cost would still be greater than that of the Type 23. The construction cost of the S115 would also still be more than that of the Type 23. Therefore, although the overall cost differential with the Type 23 would be reduced, the S115 would still cost more both to build and operate. It is anticipated that the minimum additional overall cost of an S115, meeting the NSR speed requirements, would be in the order of 6% more than that of a Type 23 frigate. In overall terms, it is concluded that the performance parameters of the S115 (e.g. seakeeping and manoeuvring) have done no more than tend towards those of the Type 23. Hence both the advantages and disadvantages of the S102 would be maintained but to a reduced degree. In the Inquiry's judgement, the Type 23 is still both a cheaper and more effective solution to the NSR 7069 than the S115.

1.3   Assessment of the Sirius Design Concept in Relation to the NSR 7069 and in Comparison with the Type 23 Frigate

Based on the assessment of the S102 and the S115, it is the Inquiry's firm conclusion that the Sirius design concept is unable to produce as good a solution to the NSR 7069 as the Type 23, and that the MoD were correct in their rejection of the S90 design proposal in 1983. The Type 23 solution is cheaper both to build and to operate and has a better overall performance than can be achieved by a vessel based on the Sirius concept. The Inquiry further concludes that the advice given to the MoD by YARD along with that by the Hull Committee of the DSAC in 1983 was also correct with respect to their overall conclusions.

1.4   Assessment of Key Hydrodynamic Issues

The Hill-Norton Committee suggested that the Sirius design concept would not only provide a better solution to a frigate or destroyer requirement, but that it also produced a hull form which would perform better than established principles would predict, particularly in regard to its propulsive performance. As this would have a considerable implication for the design of ships in general, the Inquiry, in addition to assessing the Sirius design concept in terms of providing a design solution to a specific requirement, has given particular attention to those aspects which the Hill-Norton Committee indicated gave special advantages to a Sirius hull form compared with a conventional hull form. These aspects have been covered in detail in the report. However, there are four points which warrant special mention:

1.   The Hill-Norton Committee attached great importance to the existence of significant hydrodynamic lift for a Sirius type hull form, believing that this phenomenon would offset the penalty in hull resistance normally predicted by conventional methods for this type of hull form and would also allow a vessel based on the Sirius design concept to achieve greater speeds than a conventional vessel. The Hill-Norton Committee based their assertion on the belief that the previous assessments of the S90 proposal, undertaken by YARD and the Hull Committee of the DSAC, had rejected the S90 model tests in favour of computer predictions of the required power, these computer predictions taking no account of hydrodynamic lift and, therefore, predicting that the S90 would require considerably more power to achieve the NSR speeds than that claimed by TGA.

The Inquiry has established that this was not the case and that the S90 model tests were used by both bodies in determining the power requirements of the S90 design proposal. The Inquiry also considers that conventional model testing techniques are adequate to predict the resistance of ships whether they are affected by hydrodynamic lift or not, and has based its own assessment of the power requirements of the S90 hull form on the S90 model tests submitted to it by TGA.

Furthermore, the Inquiry considers that at the operating speeds appropriate to the NSR 7069, the S102 and the S115 would not benefit from significant hydrodynamic lift (see Chapter 4, Section 4.3).

2.   The Hill-Norton Committee suggested that many comparisons between model tests and full scale trial results for ships of the Sirius type had indicated that such ships performed very much better than model tests predicted in terms of the power required to achieve a given speed. This implies that a vessel based on a Sirius hull form would benefit from a low correlation factor and would thus require less power than conventional techniques predicted.

The data submitted to the Inquiry showed that the correlation factors for Sirius type hull forms were not outside the range that would reasonably be expected for such vessels and, therefore, the vessel would not benefit from an unusually low correlation factor (see Chapter 4, Section 4.4).

3.   The Hill-Norton Committee claimed that the propulsive coefficient, relating the effective power to the shaft power, would be 30% better for the S90 compared with a Leander class frigate.

The Inquiry considers that this assertion was based on the incorrect interpretation of data. The propulsive coefficients are, in fact, similar for the two vessels (see Chapter 4, Section 4.6).

4.   The Hill-Norton Committee considered that the prediction of the seakeeping performance of a vessel based on a Sirius hull form was the most controversial matter they examined because of the widely differing technical opinions held on this matter. The Committee indicated that they would place greater confidence in the model test prediction of the seakeeping performance of a Sirius hull form, based on the available data, rather than in theoretical computer predictions.

The Inquiry endorses the Hill-Norton Committee's view that seakeeping represents one of the most controversial issues. It is an area with a high level of uncertainty attached to it and is one that relies heavily on subjective judgements in offsetting superior performance in one respect against inferior behaviour in another.

The Inquiry considers that carefully controlled model tests, assuming that they are sufficiently comprehensive, would provide a more reliable basis than a theoretical analysis for the prediction of the seakeeping performance of a Sirius design. It was, however, concluded that the extent of the available experimental evidence in the case of the S90 hull form was, on its own, insufficient to provide the basis of an adequate assessment of the S90 hull form. It was considered, nevertheless, that sufficient reliable experimental data was available to carry out correlation and validation of a suitable theoretical approach with the conclusion that such a theoretical analysis could be used, albeit with caution and in conjunction with the experimental data, for the assessment and comparative evaluation of the seakeeping behaviour of the S90 hull form (see Chapter 6, Section 5).

The Inquiry concludes that the hydrodynamic performance of a Sirius type hull form can be adequately assessed by conventional naval architectural techniques. The claim that a Sirius hull form does not obey conventional principles has been based on data being incorrectly interpreted. In particular, the Inquiry finds that in regard to the propulsive performance of the S90 hull form, it requires substantially more power to achieve a given speed than that suggested by the Hill-Norton Committee.

1.5   Implications for the Design of Future Destroyers and Frigates for the Royal Navy

The Inquiry's terms of reference require it, after considering the advantages and disadvantages of the S90 hull form in relation to the NSR 7069, to identify any implications for the design of future destroyers and frigates for the Royal Navy. Based on its assessment of the claimed exceptional hydrodynamic performance of a Sirius hull form, along with its comparison of the S102 and the S115 against a specific frigate requirement, namely the NSR 7069, the Inquiry has concluded that there are no identifiable implications for the design of future destroyers and frigates for the Royal Navy arising from the Sirius design concept, as far as it is able to foresee the likely role and operating requirements for future warships of this type.

TGA have claimed that the Sirius hull form would be capable of speeds well in excess of those required by the NSR 7069 and those which could practically be achieved by a conventional frigate hull form. The Hill-Norton Committee concluded that, if confirmed, this would be a most important military advantage. The Inquiry has examined the data submitted to support TGA's claim and concludes that the data has been incorrectly interpreted. Up to the speeds for which data exists (approximately 45 knots), the Sirius hull form is considerably more resistful than a conventional frigate hull form and would require substantially more power to achieve the same maximum speed. At speeds approaching 45 knots and above, the Inquiry considers that other marine vehicles, for example hydrofoils and hovercraft, would need to be carefully evaluated in addition to a displacement monohull vessel, since they may provide a better solution to a given requirement at such speeds.

In a role other than that currently performed by a frigate or destroyer, a vessel based on a Sirius hull form might well provide a better balance of all the relevant factors. However, it is necessary, whatever role is being considered, to have a design which has been sufficiently developed against a defined requirement so that the balance of all the factors can be properly judged. The Inquiry considers that such a balance can be determined for a vessel based on a Sirius hull form using normal naval architecture assessment procedures.

2.   RECOMMENDATIONS

A very thorough independent assessment has been carried out of the advantages and disadvantages of the S90 hull form and the associated Sirius design philosophy for the purposes of meeting the NSR 7069 for an anti-submarine warfare frigate. Arising from this assessment, the Inquiry can find no reason to challenge the MoD's preference for the Type 23 frigate.

Although it has been suggested that a prototype based on a Sirius hull form should be built to resolve this dispute, it is the Inquiry's firm opinion that such an exercise is unnecessary as the performance of a Sirius hull form can be adequately evaluated by normal naval architecture assessment procedures.

The Inquiry considers, and would recommend, that no further action is required to assess the applicability of the Sirius concept for future frigate and destroyer design.

APPENDICES

APPENDIX 1

The Inquiry Team

Chairman of the Inquiry	:	H.R. MacLeod
Inquiry Head	:	J.G. Beaumont, B.Sc., C.Eng.
Inquiry Deputy-Head	:	R.A. Goodman, B.Sc., Ph.D., C.Eng.
Inquiry Co-ordinator	:	A. Buckland, B.Sc., C.Eng.
Speed, Power and Endurance	:	D.W. Robinson, B.Sc., C.Eng.
		R. Spencer, B.Sc., M.Sc., C.Eng.
		D.R. Tozer, B.Sc., M.Sc., C.Eng.
Space, Layout, Structural	:	J.A. Morris, C.Eng.
Design and Weight		M.J. Gudmunsen, B.Sc., C.Eng.
Intact and Damaged Stability	:	D.T. Boltwood, C.Eng.
		A.J. Peter, B.Sc., C.Eng.
Seakeeping	:	D.W. Robinson, B.Sc., C.Eng.
		R.A. Dawkins, B.Sc., M.Sc., Ph.D.
Manoeuvrability	:	D.W. Robinson, B.Sc., C.Eng.
		G.D.W. Lewis, B.Sc.
Military Features	:	C.M.R. Wills, MA
		J.S. Carlton, BA, C.Eng.
Construction Costs and	:	J.A. Morris, C.Eng.
Build Time		M.J. Gudmunsen, B.Sc., C.Eng.
Through Life Costs	:	J.A. Morris, C.Eng.
		M.J. Gudmunsen, B.Sc., C.Eng.
Legal	:	J.W. Hickman, LL M
Administrative Co-ordinator	:	A.J.W. Henderson
Administration	:	V.E. Hull
		J.M. Pearcey
		A.P. Rushbrook

APPENDIX 2

Inquiry Advertisement

The following advertisement appeared in 'The Times' on 15th and 17th December 1986, 'The Financial Times' on 16th December 1986, 'Lloyd's List' on 16th and 17th December 1986, 'The Naval Architect' in the December 1986 and January 1987 edition and the 'Marine Engineers Review' in the January 1987 edition.

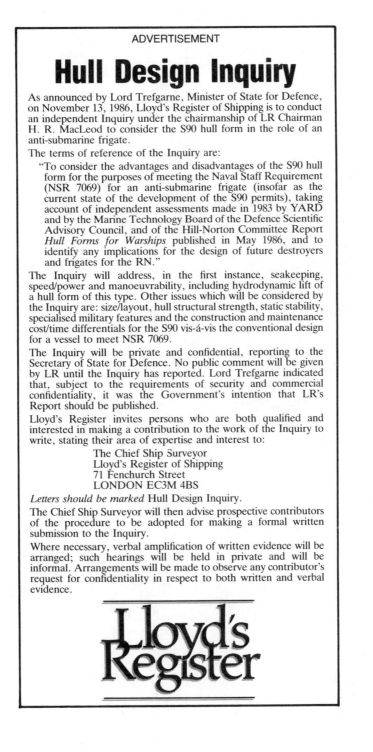

ADVERTISEMENT

Hull Design Inquiry

As announced by Lord Trefgarne, Minister of State for Defence, on November 13, 1986, Lloyd's Register of Shipping is to conduct an independent Inquiry under the chairmanship of LR Chairman H. R. MacLeod to consider the S90 hull form in the role of an anti-submarine frigate.

The terms of reference of the Inquiry are:

"To consider the advantages and disadvantages of the S90 hull form for the purposes of meeting the Naval Staff Requirement (NSR 7069) for an anti-submarine frigate (insofar as the current state of the development of the S90 permits), taking account of independent assessments made in 1983 by YARD and by the Marine Technology Board of the Defence Scientific Advisory Council, and of the Hill-Norton Committee Report *Hull Forms for Warships* published in May 1986, and to identify any implications for the design of future destroyers and frigates for the RN."

The Inquiry will address, in the first instance, seakeeping, speed/power and manoeuvrability, including hydrodynamic lift of a hull form of this type. Other issues which will be considered by the Inquiry are: size/layout, hull structural strength, static stability, specialised military features and the construction and maintenance cost/time differentials for the S90 vis-á-vis the conventional design for a vessel to meet NSR 7069.

The Inquiry will be private and confidential, reporting to the Secretary of State for Defence. No public comment will be given by LR until the Inquiry has reported. Lord Trefgarne indicated that, subject to the requirements of security and commercial confidentiality, it was the Government's intention that LR's Report should be published.

Lloyd's Register invites persons who are both qualified and interested in making a contribution to the work of the Inquiry to write, stating their area of expertise and interest to:

The Chief Ship Surveyor
Lloyd's Register of Shipping
71 Fenchurch Street
LONDON EC3M 4BS

Letters should be marked Hull Design Inquiry.

The Chief Ship Surveyor will then advise prospective contributors of the procedure to be adopted for making a formal written submission to the Inquiry.

Where necessary, verbal amplification of written evidence will be arranged; such hearings will be held in private and will be informal. Arrangements will be made to observe any contributor's request for confidentiality in respect to both written and verbal evidence.

Lloyd's Register

APPENDIX 3

Parties who offered their services or made written submissions to the Inquiry

Adair Research Management Ltd

Anglo-Dutch Engineering Co Ltd (Lips b.v.)

ASEP Associates

British Maritime Technology

A.G. Bischoff

H.S. Bluston

Crossley Engines NEI-APE Ltd

J. Carreyette

Commander R.C. Corlett

Danyard A/S [formerly Frederikshavn Vaerft A/S]

W.D. Ellis

Foundrometers Ltd

Global Maritime

Captain D.J.I. Garstin

Dr R.L. Garwin

Hart, Fenton & Co Ltd

IMC Marine Consultants

Itchen Investments Ltd

J. Koutsovoulos

H. Lackenby

P.N. Ling

Meconsult Ltd

G. Maddicks

A.C. Mitchell

Captain J.E. Moore

A. Mursell

Netherlands United Shipbuilding Bureau

A.L. Oliver

R. Partington

J.F. Purdy

Rumic Ltd

Professor K.J. Rawson

C. Rushton
Saltech Consultants AB (Sweden)
SDRC Engineering Services Ltd
SSPA Maritime Consulting AB (Sweden)
Stone Vickers Ltd
Swan Hunter Shipbuilders Ltd
W. Searle
S.E. Shapcott
A. Silverleaf
P.J. Strain
T. Stuart-Black Kelly
Commander P.T. Thornycroft
G.C. Trout
R.D. Tustin
Vosper Thornycroft (UK) Ltd
WS Atkins Group Consultants
V.A. Webb
A. Whittle

APPENDIX 4

Parties submitting written answers to questions put to them by the Inquiry

Ministry of Defence

Thornycroft, Giles & Associates Ltd

YARD Ltd

Defence Scientific Advisory Council

Admiral of the Fleet The Lord Hill-Norton

British Maritime Technology (now incorporating the National Maritime Institute)

EEL Ltd (formerly the British Hovercraft Corporation)

Stone Vickers Ltd on behalf of TGA

APPENDIX 5

Formal Inquiry Meetings

Party	Meeting Date
Ministry of Defence	2nd & 3rd March 1987
Thornycroft, Giles & Associates Ltd	12th & 13th March 1987
Dr R.L. Garwin	20th March 1987
YARD Ltd	6th & 7th April 1987
Ministry of Defence Weapons Presentation	10th April 1987
Defence Scientific Advisory Council	21st April 1987
Ministry of Defence and Thornycroft, Giles & Associates Ltd	29th April 1987
Admiral of the Fleet The Lord Hill-Norton	29th June 1987
Mr K.L. Kirkman	2nd July 1987
Mr A. Silverleaf	21st July 1987
EEL Ltd	22nd July 1987
Professor K.J. Rawson	22nd July 1987
Netherlands United Shipbuilding Bureau	24th July 1987
Admiral Sir Lindsay Bryson	24th July 1987
Thornycroft, Giles & Associates Ltd	9th September 1987
Captain J.E. Moore	13th October 1987
Thornycroft, Giles & Associates Ltd	5th January 1988
Thornycroft, Giles & Associates Ltd	14th January 1988
Thornycroft, Giles & Associates Ltd	23rd February 1988

APPENDIX 6

Informal Inquiry Meetings

Party	Nature of Meetings and Date
Thornycroft, Giles & Associates Ltd	Discussion of the development of the S90 hull form.
	Dates: 29th April, 1st May, 7th May, 7th July and 7th September 1987. 27th January 1988
Ministry of Defence	Discussion of Type 23 frigate design and S102 development.
	Dates: 15th April, 11th & 12th June, 23rd September and 14th December 1987
YARD Ltd	Discussion and demonstration of YARD's computer program 'PREDICT' used to assess the powering and speed of the S90 design proposal by YARD in 1983.
	Date: 6th February 1987
Maritime Research Institute of the Netherlands (MARIN)	Discussion of Seakeeping, Powering and Noise Aspects.
	Dates: 17th June and 20th October 1987.
SSPA Maritime Consulting AB	Discussion of noise aspects.
	Date: 5th October 1987
Marconi Underwater Systems Ltd	Discussion of noise aspects.
	Date: 7th October 1987

Professor W.G. Price Bishop, Price & Partners Ltd.	Discussion of dynamic stability in waves
	Date: 14th December 1987
British Maritime Technology	Discussion of Model Tests.
	Date: 22nd December 1988
Marconi Radar Systems	Discussion of weapon characteristics.
	Date: 19th January 1988
Hall Russell Ltd	Discussion of Construction Costs.
	Date: 4th March 1988

APPENDIX 7

Inquiry Ship Visits

Ship	Nature of Visit and Date
HMS Broadsword	To obtain an appreciation of a current MoD designed frigate (Type 22) at sea. Date of visit and associated sea trip: 8th April 1987.
HMS Norfolk	To see the first Type 23 frigate during construction at Yarrow Shipbuilders Ltd. Date of visit: 22nd May 1987.
HMS Cornwall	To see a Type 22 frigate nearing completion at Yarrow Shipbuilders Ltd. Date of visit: 22nd May 1987.
Havornen	Danish Ministry of Fisheries Vessel. To obtain an appreciation of a current design based on a TGA hull form at sea. This vessel is an Osprey patrol craft the lines of which were produced by TGA. Date of visit and associated sea trip: 23rd July 1987.

APPENDIX 8

Work undertaken by external parties

Party	Work Undertaken
GEC Electrical Projects Ltd	Provision of data relating to GEC electrical motors for S90 geosim.
KaMeWa	Provision of propeller blade drawings for Southern Cross III.
Maritime Research Institute of the Netherlands (MARIN)	Undertaking model tests of Southern Cross III.
G.G. Mills	Provision of information relating to Peacock Class of vessels.
Paxmans Diesels Ltd	Provision of noise and power data.
Rolls Royce Ltd	Provision of data relating to gas turbine engines designed and produced by Rolls Royce.
Yarrow Shipbuilders Ltd	Provision of cost breakdown for Type 23 frigate.
Marconi Defence Systems	Provision of weapon control data.
Marconi Radar Systems	Provision of weapon control data.
British Aerospace Naval & Electronic Systems Division	Provision of weapon control data.
Plessey Radar Limited	Provision of weapon control data.
J & S Marine Ltd	Provision of weapon control data.
Ferranti Computer Systems	Provision of weapon control data.
McDonnell Douglas Astronautics Company	Provision of weapon control data.
Cockett Marine Oil	Provision of NATO fuel prices.
J. Journee, Delft University	Assessment of added resistance in waves

APPENDIX 9

GLOSSARY

added resistance in waves - Force caused by the action of waves that resists the forward motion of a ship.

advance - A manoeuvring term. The distance by which the centre of gravity of a ship has advanced when the heading has changed by 90°.

amidships - At, or about, the middle portion of a ship.

angle of entry - Angle formed between the centreline and the moulded waterline at the bow.

anti-rolling tank - Tank partially filled with liquid that imparts a roll moment in the opposite direction to the one imparted by the waves.

anti-symmetric ship motions - Sway, roll and yaw.

appendages - Underwater additions to the hull, including such items as rudders, shafting, struts, bossings and bilge keels.

athwartship - see **transverse**.

AVCAT - Aviation turbine fuel.

averaged subjective motion magnitude parameter - A measure of a ship's centre-plane vertical response averaged over the working spaces of the ship.

ballast - Any solid or liquid weight placed in a ship to increase the draught, to change the trim, or to regulate the stability.

baseline - Fore and aft reference line at the upper surface of the flat plate keel at the centreline.

beam - Dimension of a body or ship in a transverse horizontal direction. When not otherwise defined the beam is the moulded dimension, measured amidships at the design waterline.

bilge - Intersection of a ship's bottom and side. May be rounded or angular.

bilge keel - Longitudinal fin fitted at the turn of the bilge to reduce rolling.

Board Margin - A margin to allow for all additions of weight after the final design caused by approved additions to weapon outfit, equipment, stores, fuel, etc., or any other deliberate design change that affects the weight of the ship.

body plan - Drawing consisting of two half transverse elevations drawn for each displacement section having a common vertical centreline, so that the right-hand side represents the sections forward of amidships and the left-hand side represents the sections aft of amidships. On the body plan appear the forms of the various cross-sections, the curvature of the deck lines at the side, and the projections, as straight lines, of the waterlines.

breadth (B) - Largest value of the ship's beam (moulded).

bridge - Top superstructure tier, from which a ship is navigated having a clear view forward and on either side.

broaching - Sudden change in heading produced by a severe following or quartering sea that causes large roll angles or capsize.

bulkhead - Partition walls that subdivide the interior of a ship.

buttock - The intersection of the moulded hull surface with any vertical longitudinal plane not on the centreline.

cavitation - Cavitation is said to occur in a liquid when vapour bubbles form and grow as a consequence of pressure reduction. In the context of propellers, cavitation can occur as a result of the low induced pressures produced when a propeller blade generates lift.

cavitation inception speed - Speed of a fluid at a point, relative to a propeller blade, at which pressure conditions are such that cavitation will just commence.

centre of gravity (G) - The centre through which all weights constituting a ship and its contents may be assumed to act.

centre of gravity, longitudinal (LCG) - Longitudinal location of the centre of gravity.

centre of gravity, vertical (VCG) - Distance of the centre of gravity from the baseline or keel.

chilled water system - Compressors, pipework, etc. circulating a fluid for air conditioning and for controlling the temperature of electronic equipment.

cofferdam - Narrow void space between two bulkheads, decks or floors to prevent leakage between the adjacent compartments.

complement - Ship's company. Number of persons comprising ship's company.

convertor - Device to regulate the voltage, current and phase of electrical power to motors.

correlation allowance coefficient (C_A) - An additional resistance which is added to model test results to increase the accuracy of full scale predictions.

deadrise - see **rise of floor.**

deck - Platform in a ship corresponding to a floor in a building.

de-gaussing - Process of reducing a ship's magnetic signature by passing an electrical current through cables wound round the inside of the ship.

depth, moulded (D) - Vertical distance from the moulded baseline to the underside of the freeboard deck at side.

design margin - A weight contingency included in the displacement of a ship to allow for errors or uncertainties in weight calculations and for unplanned growth of weight.

Dieso - Light marine diesel fuel.

displacement (Δ) - The mass of water displaced by a ship, which is equal to the mass of the ship.

displacement, deep - Displacement of a ship when floating at her greatest allowable draught.

displacement, half oil - Nominal displacement of a ship from which about half the consumable fuel has been removed.

double bottom - Protective compartment at the bottom of a ship bounded by the inner bottom and the shell plating. Used for ballast, fresh water, fuel oil, etc.

downflooding - The ingress of floodwater through an opening into an undamaged space.

downflooding point - Opening through which downflooding occurs.

draught (T) - Distance measured vertically from the water surface to the lowest part of the keel.

draught aft - Draught measured in way of the stern.

draught fwd - Draught measured in way of the bow.

draught, deep - Mean draught when in the deep displacement condition.

draught, design - Mean draught when in the design condition.

draught, load - Mean draught when in the deep displacement condition.

draught, mean - Draught amidships.

efficiency, hull (η_H) - Ratio between the work done on a ship to overcome resistance (P_E) and the work done by the propeller (P_T).

efficiency, open water (η_o) - Ratio between the power developed by the thrust of the propeller (P_T) and the power absorbed by the propeller (P_D) when operating in open water.

efficiency, propulsive (η_D) - Ratio between the effective power (P_E) and the power delivered to the propeller (P_D).

efficiency, relative rotative (η_R) - Ratio of the propeller efficiencies behind the hull and in open water.

efficiency, shafting (η_S) - Ratio between the delivered power (P_D) and the shaft power (P_S); a measure of the power lost in shaft bearings and stern tube.

efficiency, transmission (η_T) - Ratio between the delivered power (P_D) and the installed power (P_I); a measure of the power lost in the shafting, gearbox, uptakes, downtakes, electrical transmission, etc.

elbow room - 'Elbow room' has been interpreted to mean the provision of adequate volumetric space around and between structure and equipment in which no linear dimension is so restrictive as to inhibit the ready access of personnel to work freely.

endurance - Maximum distance a ship can sail without refuelling.

fatigue - Work hardening or embrittlement of ductile materials (e.g. steel) due to successive reversals of load.

flare - Outward curvature of the hull surface above the waterline, usually in the forebody.

Fleet Maintenance Group - Shorebased personnel who help the ship's company during overhauls of equipment such as turbines and generators.

fore - Term used to indicate the portion of a ship lying between amidships and the stem.

form factor (k) - A factor sometimes used to account for hull shape in model experiments.

fouling - Marine biological growths and associated material attached to the submerged surface of a ship's hull.

free surface - Liquid in a partially filled tank or compartment, the surface of which tends to remain horizontal as the vessel heels or rolls.

free surface effect - Reduction in statical stability brought about by the virtual rise in the centre of gravity due to the presence of a free surface.

freeboard - Distance from the waterline to the upper surface of the freeboard deck at side.

Froude Number (Fn) - A relationship between the speed and length of a vessel that is used in scaling model test results to full scale.

general arrangement plan - Drawing which defines the shape and layout of a ship.

geosim - A hull of exactly the same underwater geometrical shape, differing only in size. A contraction of the expression 'geometrically similar'.

girth - Distance around the perimeter of any transverse section or frame, between two selected points. For wetted surface calculations, these two points are generally the waterplane intersections.

gunwale - Intersection of the weather deck and the ship's side.

habitability - Pertaining to the accommodation and comfort of the ship's company.

hatch - Opening for access through a deck.

heading - Instantaneous direction in which the ship is pointing.

heave - Oscillatory vertical translation of a vessel caused by the action of waves.

heel - A static condition produced by enforced rotation about a ship's longitudinal axis. The instantaneous result of rolling, which is an oscillatory motion.

hotel load - Electrical power supplied for lighting and other domestic services.

hull form - Generic term to express the intrinsic three-dimensional shape of a ship's hull (particularly the submerged part).

hull girder - That part of the hull structural material effective in the longitudinal strength of a ship as a whole, which may be treated as analogous to a simple beam or girder.

hydrodynamic lift - Force exerted on a vessel travelling at high speed that lifts it partially out of the water.

hydrophones - Array of sensitive listening sensors.

hydrostatic data - Those properties, usually presented in tabular or graphical form, which relate to the geometric characteristics of a hull form when floating in still water.

inner bottom - Plating forming the top of the double bottom; also called the tank top.

ITTC(1957) Line - A formula used for scaling model test results to full scale.

keel - Fore and aft centreline at the bottom of a ship.

Kempf Manoeuvre - Zig-zag manoeuvre performed to evaluate the ability of the rudder to initiate and check changes in a ship's heading.

knot - One nautical mile per hour.

knuckle - Abrupt change in direction of the hull plating of a ship.

length between perpendiculars - (L_{pp}) Length of a ship between the forward and after perpendiculars. In naval ships the perpendiculars are set up at the extreme ends of the design waterline.

length overall (L_{OA}) - Extreme length of a ship measured between the foremost and aftermost extremities.

length, waterline (L_{WL}) - Length of a ship measured on the still waterplane.

lightweight - Weight of a ship including hull, machinery, outfit and equipment.

lines plan - Drawing depicting the moulded shape of a ship, showing the stations (transverse sections), waterlines and the profile.

load waterline - That line which represents the still water surface when the ship is floating at the deep displacement.

loading condition - List of all variable weights (stores, fuel, etc.) and their dispositions which, together with lightweight, determines the displacement, draught, trim and intact stability characteristics of a ship.

longitudinal - Fore and aft.

longitudinal framing - System of plate stiffening which employs mainly structural members which are laid in the fore and aft direction.

LR 100A1 commercial strength standard - A strength standard defined by the published rules and regulations of Lloyd's Register.

measured distance trial - Trial over a measured distance to determine the speed and power relationship for a ship.

metacentre - Transverse (M_T) and longitudinal (M_L). The point of intersection of the vertical through the centre of buoyancy of a ship in equilibrium with the vertical through the new centre of buoyancy when the ship is slightly inclined.

metacentric height - Transverse (GM_T) and longitudinal (GM_L). The distance between the centre of gravity and the transverse or longitudinal metacentre, measured vertically in the equilibrium position. Positive when M is above G; i.e. on inclination to a small angle a restoring moment arises that acts to return the ship to the vertical.

midship - see **amidships**.

midship section - Drawing showing the structure at a representative cross-section of the hull and superstructure (when appropriate) at or near amidships.

motor room - Compartment containing the electric propulsion motors.

moulded - Adjective used to indicate the generally fair form and dimensions of a hull as determined by the lines to the inside of the shell plating.

nautical mile - The international nautical mile is 1852m.

noise, hydrodynamic - Noise generated by the flow of the water around the hull, its appendages and propeller.

noise, propeller generated - Propeller generated noise derives from the inlet turbulence, the flow of water around the blade surfaces and the wake induced by the blades in the non-cavitating condition. When cavitation occurs this noise source tends to dominate.

noise, radiated - That noise emanating from the vessel by which it can be detected at some remote location.

noise, self - The noise generated by the ship and its systems which may interfere with the vessel's own sensing instruments.

offsets - A series of distances, measured from the centreline at set vertical intervals, to define the shape of the hull of a ship.

outboard - Abreast or away from the centreline towards the side; outside the hull.

performance prediction factor - see **ship performance prediction factor**.

period - Length of time for one complete cycle of a periodic quantity or phenomenon, such as the rolling of a ship from port to starboard and back to port.

period, natural - Time for one complete cycle of the motion resulting when a body is displaced in calm water from its equilibrium position by an external force and then is released.

permeability, surface - Lost waterplane area of a space expressed as a percentage of the gross waterplane area of that space.

permeability, volumetric - Volume within a space that can be occupied by floodwater expressed as a percentage of the total volume of that space.

pitch - Oscillatory rotation of a ship about an athwartship line through a point, usually the centre of gravity, caused by the action of waves.

pitch, propeller (P) - In the context of this report, the pitch of a propeller blade section at radius r is given by $P = 2\pi r.\tan\phi$ where ϕ, the pitch angle, is the angle between the intersection of the chord line of the section and a plane normal to the propeller axis. In simple terms, the theoretical distance that a propeller moves forward, relative to the water, in one revolution.

planing - A vessel that experiences significant hydrodynamic lift is said to be planing.

plunging - For the purposes of stability appraisal, plunging is taken to occur when there is immersion of the uppermost deck at the longitudinal extremities of a vessel.

port - Left-hand side looking forward.

pounding - Impact of a water surface against the side or bottom of a ship hull, whether caused by ship velocity, water velocity or both. Pounding is differentiated from slamming in that the impact, although heavy, is not in the nature of a shock.

power, delivered (P_D) - Power delivered to the propeller.

power, effective (P_E) - Power required to tow a ship, usually without her propulsive device. The power may be for the ship either with or without appendages. If the latter, it is known as the naked hull effective power.

power, installed (P_I) - The power produced by the propelling machinery, before deducting the losses due to uptakes, downtakes, gearbox, electrical transmission, etc.

power, shaft (P_S) - The power delivered to the shafting system by the propelling machinery.

profile - Outline of a ship when projected on the fore and aft vertical plane.

profile, wind - Projected longitudinal area of a vessel above the waterline exposed to the wind.

progressive flooding - Passage of floodwater into an intact space not included in the primary flooding.

propeller, controllable pitch - A propeller having blades that can be rotated about a radial axis so as to change the effective pitch of the blades while the propeller is operating, to make the most efficient use of the available power at all speeds.

quadrant - A propeller is considered to have four quadrants of operation, i.e. two whilst providing ahead and astern thrust with the vessel moving ahead, and two whilst providing ahead and astern thrust with the vessel moving astern.

Quasi-Propulsive Coefficient (QPC) - Coefficient relating effective power (P_E) to delivered power (P_D).

residual fuel oil - Heavy grade fuel oil.

residual righting lever curve - Curve reflecting the difference between the intact righting lever curve and a heeling lever curve representing an external moment tending to displace the vessel from its equilibrium position.

resistance, frictional and residuary (R_F), (R_R) - The two components of ship resistance that are estimated in model test experiments.

resistance, specific - Resistance per unit displacement.

righting energy - Area below the righting lever curve up to a given angle.

righting lever - Horizontal distance between the centre of gravity of a ship and a vertical passing through the centre of buoyancy when the ship is inclined.

rise of floor - Athwartship rise of the bottom from the keel to the bilge.

roll - The rotation of a ship, about a fore and aft centreline, caused by the action of waves.

roll, centre of - Vertical position of a fore and aft centreline about which a ship rolls.

roll damping device - Device for reducing the roll motion of a ship.

rudder - A control surface which by its action or movement controls the steering or the turning of a ship.

scantlings - Dimensions of a ship's frames, girders, plating, etc.

screw - Propeller.

self-propulsion test - Model test in which the model is equipped with a propulsion system.

shaft brackets - Structural supports for propeller shafts on the outside of the hull.

shafting - Propeller shafts.

shaft rake - Angle of the propeller shaft relative to the baseline.

shell envelope - see **shell plating.**

shell plating - Plates forming the outer side and bottom skin of the hull.

ship performance prediction factor - Factor used to increase the accuracy of model test predictions.

ship/model correlation - The correlation between ship power and model test predictions.

side scuttles - Circular windows in a ship's side.

skeg - A fixed appendage fitted to the underwater hull of a ship, generally to increase the lateral area and give increased swing damping and dynamic stability to the hull.

slamming - Heavy impact resulting from a vessel's bottom forward or aft making sudden contact with the sea surface after having risen on a wave.

sonar dome, bow mounted - Dome shaped appendage at the forefoot of a ship, housing a sonar.

sprint and drift - A mode of operation in which a ship travels quickly to a particular point and then continues at low speed from that point in order to conduct some military operation.

stabiliser, active fin - A movable lifting surface fitted to the underwater hull that reduces roll motion by imparting a moment on the ship opposite to that imparted by the waves.

stability, damaged - A measure of a ship's statical flooding characteristics and its residual stability which exists subsequent to sustaining a loss of buoyancy due to penetration from damage to the hull below the waterline.

stability, directional - A vessel is considered to be directionally stable if, after experiencing an instantaneous disturbance (for example, from waves), it returns to its original path and direction with minimal use of the rudder.

stability, straight line - A vessel is considered to be straight line stable if, after experiencing an instantaneous disturbance (for example, from waves), it returns to a straight path.

stability, intact - A measure of a ship's righting capacity in the fully buoyant condition.

stability, residual - A measure of that stability which remains after a reduction caused by external moments or loss of buoyancy.

starboard - Right-hand side looking forward.

stern - After portion of a vessel.

stern gear - General term to include rudders, stocks, shafts, etc.

structural fatigue failure - Damage to material (e.g. cracks) developed as a result of fatigue loading.

superstructure - Erection of a significant size mounted on the weather deck.

surge - Oscillatory longitudinal translation of a vessel in a seaway.

sway - Oscillatory lateral translation of a vessel in a seaway.

symmetric ship motions - Surge, heave and pitch.

tactical diameter - Distance travelled by the centre of gravity of a ship normal to its original approach path in turning through 180°. The tactical diameter is equal to the transfer at 180° change of heading.

tank top - see **inner bottom**.

tankage - Contents of a ship's tanks.

topweight - Weight on a ship notionally concentrated above the centre of gravity.

tow point - Position from which a model is towed in model tests.

towed array sonar (TAS) - An array of sensitive listening sensors (hydrophones) streamed at large distances behind the ship to eliminate self-noise problems.

towing tank - An establishment which tests models of ships.

transfer - Sideways distance a ship travels when turning 90° from its course.

transom - Flat plane of plating formed at the aft end of the hull.

transverse - At right angles to the fore and aft centreline.

trim - Difference between the draught forward and the draught aft.

trim, bow down - see **trim by the head**.

trim by the head - If the draught forward is greater than the draught aft, the vessel is said to 'trim by the head'.

'tween deck height - Vertical height measured between the plating surfaces of two adjacent decks.

upper deck - Deck which forms the upper boundary of the hull of a ship. Otherwise termed the main or weather deck.

uptakes/downtakes - Ducts through which air is drawn in to or exhausted from the ship.

voluntary speed loss in waves - Reduction in speed made, as a matter of good seamanship, to avoid undue risk of heavy weather damage.

wake - Term used to describe the motion imparted to the water by the passage of a ship's hull.

waterline - Intersection line of any selected plane, parallel to the baseline, with the moulded hull surface.

waterplane - Longitudinal plan section of a ship coincident with the still water surface.

waterplane entrance angle - see **angle of entry**.

wave energy spectrum - The energy in a seaway as a function of frequency.

wave energy spreading - The distribution of wave energy about a predominant direction.

wave height - Distance between successive peaks and troughs in a seaway.

wave height, significant - Mean of the highest one-third wave heights in a seaway.

waves, irregular - A series of waves of different heights and periods.

waves, regular - A sinusoidal waveform with fixed period.

weather deck - see **upper deck**.

weight, group - Sub-divisions of the total weight into named groups.

weight growth - Assumed growth in a ship's displacement during its service life, generally taken as a percentage of the deep displacement.

wetted surface area (S) - Surface area of the underwater body of a ship.

yaw - Oscillatory rotation of a ship about a vertical line through a point on the ship, usually the centre of gravity, caused by the action of waves.

APPENDIX 10

SYMBOLS AND ABBREVIATIONS

ABMTM	Associated British Machine Tool Manufacturers
ASW	anti-submarine warfare
BHC	British Hovercraft Corporation (now EEL)
BHP	brake horsepower
BMT	British Maritime Technology (amalgam of NMI and BSRA)
BSHL	British Shipbuilders Hydrodynamics Ltd
BSRA	British Ship Research Association (now part of BMT)
BTTP	British Towing Tank Panel
C_A	supplementary resistance coefficient
CODLAG	Combined Diesel-Electric And Gas Turbine propulsion system
DSAC	Defence Scientific Advisory Council
EAF paint	erodable anti-fouling paint
EEL	Experimental and Electronic Laboratories
EMI	electro-magnetic interference
FHV	Frederikshavn Vaerft A/S (now Danyard A/S)
F_n	Froude Number
g	acceleration due to gravity
GM	metacentric height
GM (fluid)	transverse metacentric height (GM) corrected for the effect of liquid free surface
GODDESS	Government Defence Design System for Ships (computer aided ship design system)
ITTC	International Towing Tank Conference
k_1	the ratio between ship quasi-propulsive coefficient (QPC_s) and model quasi-propulsive coefficient (QPC_m)
k_2	the ratio between the actual ship propeller speed (N_a) to deliver P_{Da} and predicted propeller speed (N_p) to deliver P_{Dm}
KM	height of metacentre above baseline or keel
K_x	radius of gyration in roll
K_y	radius of gyration in pitch
L/B	length to beam ratio (usually related to the length and beam values of the deep waterplane)
LCG	longitudinal centre of gravity
L	length, general
L_{pp}	length between perpendiculars
LR	Lloyd's Register
lub oil	lubricating oil
MARIN	Maritime Research Institute of the Netherlands
mcr	maximum continuous rating
MoD	Ministry of Defence

MTBQP	mean time between quiescent periods
N	propeller rotational speed
NBCD	Nuclear, Biological, Chemical and Damage (control)
NES	Naval Engineering Standard
NMI	National Maritime Institute (now part of BMT)
NSR	Naval Staff Requirement
NST	Naval Staff Target
NUPC	net unit production cost
PC	propulsive coefficient $= \eta_H . \eta_R . \eta_o . \eta_S$
P_D	delivered power
P_E	effective power (resistance $\times$ speed)
P_S	shaft power
QPC	quasi-propulsive coefficient $= \eta_H . \eta_R . \eta_o$ (relates effective power to delivered power)
R & P	resistance and propulsion
RADHAZ	radiation hazard
RAS	replenishment at sea
REA	radar echoing area
RFA	Royal Fleet Auxiliary
RN	Royal Navy
rpm	revolutions per minute
SHP	shaft horsepower
SMM	subjective motion magnitude
SWATH	small waterplane area, twin hull
TAS	towed array sonar
TGA	Thornycroft, Giles & Associates Ltd
t	thrust deduction
UPC	unit production cost
VCG	vertical centre of gravity
V	ship speed
WG	weight growth
w_T	Taylor wake fraction
$(1+k)$	form factor
$(1+x)$	ship performance prediction factor
η_H	hull efficiency
η_o	open water efficiency of the propeller
η_R	relative rotative efficiency
η_S	efficiency of the mechanical transmission system between the gearbox output shaft and the propeller
δC_t	supplementary resistance coefficient
ΔGM_T	GM loss due to free liquid surfaces

Printed in the United Kingdom for Her Majesty's Stationery Office

Dd 290916   C25   5/88